THE
SURVIVAL
HANDBOOK

BY RAYMOND MEARS

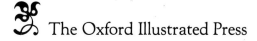 The Oxford Illustrated Press

© 1990 Raymond Mears

ISBN 0 946609 88 8

Published by:
The Oxford Illustrated Press, Haynes
Publishing Group, Sparkford, Nr Yeovil,
Somerset BA22 7JJ, England.

Haynes Publications Inc, 861 Lawrence
Drive, Newbury Park, California 91320,
USA.

Printed in England by:
J.H. Haynes & Co Limited, Sparkford, Nr
Yeovil, Somerset.

**British Library Cataloguing in
Publication Data:**
  The survival handbook: a practical guide
  to woodcraft and woodlore.
  1. Backpacking. Camping.
  Backpacking & camping
  I. Title
  796.54

  ISBN 0-946609-88-8

**Library of Congress Catalog Card
Number:** 89-82495

Contents

This book is dedicated to the memory of
Kingsley Royce Hopkins my guide and mentor
for nearly sixteen years, who passed away
during the production of the manuscript. His
will be a tough act to follow.

Acknowledgements

I would like to thank all those people who have encouraged
and supported me during the writing of this book, and the
fellow outdoors enthusiasts with whom I have shared campfire and trail. In particular, I would like to mention the
following in no specific order: my patient and long-suffering
parents, Nick Crane the instigator, Philip Wells and Sally
Collings, James and Brenda Locke, Roger Hopkins for some
twentieth-century wizardry, Vivien Drake, Roy Belanger,
Charles 'Badger' Taylor, Richard Kluckhohn, Scott Kuipers,
Mike Clinchy, Robert Craigie, Kurt Folsom, Richard and
Ruth Bennett and the seventh Purley Scout Group.

Introduction

'My son, you know no one will help you in this world . . .
You must run to that mountain and come back. That will
make you strong. My son, you know no one is your friend,
not even your sister, your father, your mother. Your legs are
your friends; your brain is your friend; your hands are your
friends; you must do something with them.'

(The words of an Apache father, *An Apache Life* by Morris
Opler.)

Do you like clean air, fresh water and the wonders of the natural world? If so read on for this book is written for you.

The skills contained within this book are not new, experts have been writing about them for nearly a hundred years, grouping them together under the well-suited title of 'woodcraft'. In more recent years they have somehow acquired a macho image and been renamed survival skills. There is no real harm in this but for the fact that in the process, many of the techniques have been inaccurately described. To those of us who grew up with, and still use the original skills of woodcraft, these errors are alarming if sometimes funny. But more importantly they represent the watering down and gradual disappearance of knowledge and experience which was formerly passed from father to son, mother to daughter. Were these skills to disappear altogether it would be a tragedy, for they are our birthright, a living link with our palaeolithic ancestors, that allows us to see nature with native eyes and understanding.

Today the skills are less easily acquired; many of the old masters are gone, and without the reality of living and having to survive in the wilderness, few have time to serve the long apprenticeship in the wild.

However if you are in no hurry to master them the techniques which follow can be gradually learned and perfected. They are the skills of the native which, once learned, can enable you to be totally self sufficient in a natural environment. In studying them you will certainly learn much about yourself. But this is not the only value of the skills, for even in our age of space exploration the awareness, understanding and attunement to nature which is a natural by-product of their study will boost your confidence, enhance your appreciation of the fragile world we inhabit and enable you to enjoy your outdoor pursuits more fully. Like suddenly taking off a blindfold you will be dazzled by the view; the plants and animals around you will become more familiar, useful and meaningful.

All of the skills covered in the following pages are described from practical experience. In choosing which skills to include I have described those techniques which can be most easily self taught, and wherever possible have included alternatives. Whilst this means inevitably that I have described the techniques I most often employ myself, I must stress that these are not the only ways to do things; hopefully you will gradually evolve your own techniques.

5

The aim is to describe the methods by which you can find natural alternatives to modern outdoors equipment, and by so doing enhance your perception of nature. Since I began my own study of these techniques my view of the natural world has radically altered: the grass is like a carpet and the sky a ceiling; many fears have evaporated allowing deeper enjoyment, and on those few occasions each year when I 'go walk about' and rely solely upon my woodcraft abilities and nature's gifts, the feeling of refreshed wholeness and connection with wild things is indescribable. Even when climbing or backpacking, woodcraft skills cannot be turned off and you will find yourself watching woodpeckers and magnificent birds of prey from crag tops or, supplementing your pre-packaged 'trail mix' with fresh wild delights. Recently a youngster I was teaching said, 'you would be alright if you lost your rucksack and all your gear wouldn't you?' He had hit the nail on the head. When you understand nature and know how to procure your needs from her gifts there is little to fear and everything to enjoy.

For my own part, the study of woodcraft has taken me to many beautiful areas of wilderness, and introduced me to experts, craftsmen and fine people, many of whom are interested in wildlife and the future of our own species. Undoubtedly these experiences have influenced my own attitudes to nature although perhaps the strongest influence has been my study of Native American survival techniques. Many of their ways coincide with Native Australian attitudes to the land and if you search hard enough the same attitudes can be found in Europe. Of course, whenever one speaks of the native peoples of a continent there are bound to be generalisations. So allowing for this fact, and the truth that even nature-based cultures sometimes are guilty of damaging their environment, the following is a generalised perception of life common to many hunter-gatherer communities around the world both past and present.

* * *

The native American lived in a world of meaning. Every tree, plant, animal, rock, type of soil had its use. Through careful observation of wildlife and weather patterns, the natural cycle of a year might be divided into as many as twelve or fourteen distinct seasons. A closeness to the Earth and a detailed understanding of the environment were the real secrets of survival. To them the Earth was their mother; people were born from her and returned to her at death. Home was the 'wilderness', and life was a gift to be enjoyed and made full use of, man's role in nature being to 'look after the land'. The workings of nature were a constant source of wonder and fascination.

Tempered by the reality of their hunter-gatherer existence they did not cloud their vision of life with romantic notions, they accepted that to live they must take the life of a plant or an animal. This showed no lack of reverence for the living, in fact many native hunters would say prayers and leave offerings to their prey who they believed allowed itself to be caught because it recognised the hunter's need for food or clothing.

Without the equipment to see viruses and bacteria, diseases were attributed to bad spirits, and were eloquently explained in folklore. Compared to our sophisticated modern view of the world these beliefs seem comically primitive, but in reality they provided a detailed working guide to survival in an untamed wilderness. Today we can understand and explain many of the phenomenon that so puzzled these hunters; we are able to avoid the bad spirits at a water hole from making us ill by purifying our water. But this can make us complacent for when faced with a river to cross we have no more control over the torrent than our forefathers or the Indian brave – although they stopped to leave an offering of food or sacred tobacco in recognition of the danger of the crossing. Recognising danger is the first step to avoiding it. For this reason let us absorb the native folklore that is of use and fill in the gaps with our own wisdom. And like the native hunter or warrior, let us pay heed to the teachings of the animals, masters of stealth, camouflage and awareness. This is the study of 'Woodlore'.

Days spent in the wilds or on the trail are challenging and exciting—full of life—there is the campfire, rain, sun and wind; the sweet comforting scents of the differing seasons; the sounds of lizards scuttling under stones or mice daring to cross your trail; these are the things you will remember. Yet there is risk, danger and intoxicating adventure in which you can drown if you are careless. So, before you set out there are certain things which you should be familiar with. I call them the Twelve Woodlores. Born out of experience and observation they will keep you safe and preserve the wilds for other adventurers.

The Twelve Woodlores

1. Don't challenge Nature, challenge yourself: Occasionally you will hear people talking about beating the elements by conquering a mountain or crossing an ice cap or some such brave deed. The truth is that the challenge is internal. Have you the skill? Can you overcome your fear? No one can beat the elements; all those who fail to heed the warning signs or have the stupidity to press ahead regardless, die. Instead of taking unnecessary risks challenge yourself to know when to turn back; learn to be more skilful; above all challenge yourself to better understand the way nature works.

2. If you're roughing it, you're doing something wrong: Any fool can be uncomfortable, you gain no points for carrying a heavy backpack, or for any deeds of self-imposed endurance. While you may train for an expedition by roughing it, if there is a way of making yourself more comfortable, without the effort becoming a disadvantage, do so. In emergency situations in particular, just a small amount of hardship can prove to be fatal once your level of morale has dropped.

3. Always give 100% effort the first time: Whether shelter building, firelighting, or whatever, if you don't set about it in the right way the first time you are wasting your energy and will simply have to start from scratch again.

4. Aim to achieve maximum efficiency for the minimum effort: To work you need energy; for energy you need food. In the outdoors finding food is work. When you gather your firewood for your fire do you carry large armfuls to the log pile or do you only fill your hands?

5. Never pass by an opportunity: This is very important. As you travel along, should you find suitable water, food or firelighting materials, gather them as you pass since you may not have the opportunity later when they are needed. This is particularly true of fire building materials where by the end of a day's travel it may be raining or have rained earlier soaking the available tinder. Many of my old shirts and jackets have birch bark pieces in the pockets that I gathered some years ago now.

6. As far as you can, adapt your expectations to a level which you can meet given the circumstances: If you cannot build a large comfortable shelter, be satisfied with a small shelter. If there is not a wide variety of wild foods available to you, be grateful for the one type you can eat. Make your psychology work for you. Be realistic— make yourself comfortable but do not over-work yourself to achieve this: it's no use building a palatial shelter if you then collapse with exhaustion inside it. But also do not underestimate what you can achieve.

7. Only eat that which you have positively identified as edible: Do not trust taste tests or in any way experiment with unfamiliar plants or other materials for use as food. The only real way to eat in safety and confidence is to learn what can be eaten and just how to prepare the food before you set out. If this seems like hard work you should not be eating wild foods.

8. Suspect all water as being infected: Even the cleanest, coolest most alluring water may well be contaminated; you cannot tell at a glance. Boil or purify all water—check in particular for signs of chemical pollution, this may be concentrated by boiling!

9. The state of your fire is directly proportionate to your level of morale: Whatever your level of morale, if you can light a fire it will be raised, but if you fail it will plummet like a stone. If you are not confident of your ability to light a fire in the rain it may well be better to wait until the rain stops before trying.

10. Whenever gathering your resources use natural selection as your guide, this is the 'way' of nature: Leave the strong, harvest the weak; when gathering food you should always leave a proportion of healthy plants, shellfish or whatever to continue the line. By this lore stronger healthy creatures will have the best chances for survival and thereby proliferate in the future.

11. Take only memories leave only footprints: Wherever possible minimise your impact upon the natural environment, and always aim to leave a campsite in a better state than you found it.

12. Be fit, able to swim and do not give

in: Every single skill or technique which follows is easier to learn and master if you are fit. The outdoors is filled with risks and the danger of unpredictable circumstances. Your fitness may well be your last line of defence in such circumstances.

* * *

These lores are the guide to successful backwoodsmanship, but in writing them I have assumed that you are able to carry out basic first aid. If you cannot you should attend a course run by an organised body such as the Red Cross. Almost invariably every outdoors man or woman will have recourse to such knowledge at some time or another. One aspect of first aid of particular relevance in the outdoors is an understanding of how hot and cold environments affect your body, these are problems you will face on a regular basis.

Exposure

Exposure, or as it is more correctly called 'mountain hypothermia', is the greatest enemy of the outdoors enthusiast. Gaining a working knowledge of what it is and how to prevent it is the single most important first step to enjoying outdoors pursuits in safety. So before we study any other skills let us lay a sound foundation.

Mountain hypothermia is a profound cooling of the human body in the mountain or outdoors environment, such that the temperature of the body's vital core falls to a level at which mental and physical abilities are impaired. If allowed to worsen it can lead to death. It is a problem which is particularly associated with adverse weather conditions, or people who are exhausted.

While anyone can become exposed those most at risk are: the young, people from warm climates especially those with dark skin, people who are slim with little insulating subcutaneous fat, the unfit, anyone who is injured or in a state of shock, and people who have low morale or are experiencing stress such as in the case of becoming lost. The risk from exposure is greatly reduced by the use of outdoors clothing appropriate to the prevalent conditions.

The external factors: Cold, wet, and wind are the three external factors which are responsible for exposure. A combination of any two of these will bring about exposure, but the worst possible situation is when all three are present. Of the three external factors the most dangerous is wind. Even on a warm dry day the wind can cause you to feel cold; this is known as wind chill. The stronger the wind the colder you will feel; also wind acting upon exposed flesh increases your rate of dehydration. Wind chill can have dramatic effects upon your body temperature, and must never by underestimated. Excepting really unusual circumstances, cold on its own can be countered with insulative clothing. Wet on its own such as a summer shower is of little danger.

The internal catalysts: When any two, or all three of the above factors are encountered you can reduce heat loss from your body by donning protective clothing or finding shelter. To maintain a constant temperature you must keep your internal boiler stoked by eating food. Carbohydrates are the foodstuff most readily converted into energy by your body, particularly sugars. If you fail to eat food containing sufficient calories you will hasten the onset of exposure. Lack of food is an internal catalyst to exposure. There are two more internal catalysts to defend against: dehydration and exhaustion. Dehydration impairs your ability to convert food into energy and also impairs your ability to distribute heat effectively throughout your body. It can also adversely affect your powers of reasoning and decision making. Especially in cold weather, thirst is less obvious and easily neglected.

By far the most dangerous internal catalyst to exposure is exhaustion. This can be prevented in three ways: firstly by maintaining a level of personal fitness above that ordinarily required of your usual outdoor activity, secondly by reducing dehydration and eating sufficient calories. But thirdly and most importantly of all by avoiding overstretching yourself and your energy reserves. When walking in the hills try to maintain an even rate of heart beat despite the terrain. This will mean shortening your stride as you move uphill which will seem slow but in the long run you will be able to walk for longer and further in this way. If you are faced with appalling conditions do not rule out stopping in shelter and waiting for better conditions while you are still fit and able, many people have collapsed and died in the British hills while making a last dash for safety. The best example to follow is the Canadian Eskimo, who, if caught out in severe weather would find the best shelter he could and sleep the storm out, conserving his valuable reserves of energy.

Symptoms of exposure: The symptoms of exposure are anything but obvious. In fact one of the greatest problems in diagnosing it, is that those developing exposure are often quiet and go unnoticed. They may also fail to recognise any changes in themselves and claim that they are fine, so if you are in a leadership position it is important to watch closely for signs of exposure. If you suspect a member of your party is developing the problem you might shorten your route or make an impromptu stop in the lee of some rocks for a warming brew and sugar snack. This is always more preferable than confronting a party member with the suggestion he is suffering from exposure.

Once exposure sets in, deterioration can be very rapid and if untreated can lead to death. After a period of worsening lethargy and further loss of sensory faculties, shivering stops and the body begins to close down in a last effort to maintain life, the casualty slipping from unconsciousness into a coma, which may precede death. Even though these stages are extremely dangerous, death is not the inevitable outcome. With the advantages of modern medicine and first class rescue services there is every reason not to give in. Should the casualty's respiration stop, treat them for exposure and carry out artificial respiration for as long as you can, making certain that you do not exhaust yourself and become a second casualty.

Signs to watch for are complaints or signs of coldness, tiring and lethargy, dragging feet, slurred speech, bursts of energy, lack of physical co-ordination, slipping and tripping, failing vision and involuntary shivering. The last two are serious warning signs which must not go unheeded. If you walk with a regular circle of friends it is a good idea to try and adopt a steady calm walking pace by habit, in this way any unusual behaviour signs will show up more easily. A couple of years ago while walking in the Peak district I came across one of the most flagrant examples of inadequate attention to exposure I have ever seen. While ascending a ridge with some friends I noticed some unusual tracks. The

weather was not good, with heavy driving rain, strong winds and visibility down to only a few yards. Just as I was about to stop to figure out what exactly was odd about the tracks we caught up with the person leaving them. She was a lady of about middle age and average build who was dragging her feet and quite obviously developing exposure. She was part of a rambling party a quarter of a mile ahead. When we caught up with the rest of the party we discovered the leader was totally unaware that she had been left behind.

Treating exposure on the trail: Treating exposure in the wilds is much more difficult than taking steps to avoid it in the first place. The treatment must firstly prevent any further cooling of the vital core and then gradually effect a rewarming. Place the casualty out of the reach of the external factors which have contributed to the exposure, perhaps in a tent well insulated from the ground. Then place him into a sleeping bag. If the casualty is wearing wet clothing it is better to place a waterproof layer such as a poly bag between him and the dry insulation of the sleeping bag. The classic rewarming process is to place a fit and well person in the sleeping bag with the casualty as a heating element; this is best effected through skin to skin contact. If you are able to warm the tent or shelter with a stove do so but make sure that you allow adequate ventilation. If the patient is capable of taking them, warm sweet drinks can be administered.

The most important aspect of treating exposure is that the rewarming must be gradual, if you try to rewarm the patient too quickly he can go into shock or become more exposed. This happens because as your body becomes cool the blood vessels which carry warm blood to the extremities contract to reduce heat loss from these areas, so that the bulk of body warmth is retained in the vital core. If these extremities are suddenly heated by the use of hot water bottles or a fire, the vessels expand allowing the blood flow to resume normally. This sudden turning on of the radiators drains the vital core of heat, thereby worsening the problem.

A classic, more minor problem particularly associated with backwoodsmanship in winter conditions, is that while building a shelter the backwoodsman may frequently stop to rewarm his hands by a fire and once they feel warm again resume work. He is of course increasing heat loss for the above reasons. The best way to rewarm hands is to place them under your armpits or in your crotch where they will warm and regain sensation but not to the excessive degree of fire warming. With all of your rewarming efforts direct them at the body core, chest and abdomen, leaving the extremities till later.

While mentioning exposure we should also look at frostbite. As mentioned above, when extremities become chilled, the body reduces heat loss from them by reducing the supply of blood to these regions. Frostbite is the freezing of tissue and is greatly hastened if you are dehydrated, because your blood is more viscous and cannot reach the extremities such as finger tips and toes when the vessels contract. Were you to be fully hydrated the warm blood would reach these areas more easily.

Heat Exhaustion

Heat exhaustion is caused by over exertion in conditions where the body's heat cannot be lost quickly enough, particularly hot and humid conditions. In simple terms your body becomes overheated and dehydrated. this is frequently encountered in expeditions where the members are working at altitudes above those of their normal environment, especially when insufficient time has been allowed for acclimatisation.

Heat exhaustion can easily be avoided by wearing sensible light airy clothing and reducing pack loads. Before starting the day's activities drink as much water as you can, and make full use of the cooler temperature of the early morning and late afternoon, stopping at midday for a siesta.

The symptoms of heat exhaustion are general discomfort in the head, headache and nausea, a ruddy complexion, cramp and even some disorientation. If allowed to worsen the patient may develop heat stroke, stop sweating and eventually collapse. This is very serious.

To treat heat exhaustion rest the patient in some cooling shade, loosen his or her clothing, apply wet towels to the limbs, and gradually administer clean water to rehydrate them. Under no circumstances give the patient salt.

* * *

So having equipped yourself with a firm foundation for outdoors safety and a skeleton of lores on which to hang the details of the following skills, you can begin to develop your expertise. The most important thing to remember is that you will only learn the following techniques by practise; practise and experience is what counts. I cannot stress this enough; the only way to learn is to have a go yourself. Simply reading, watching or listening is not enough. To help you in your endeavours I have included as many clear illustrations or photographs of the techniques as space will allow.

Possibles

'Although I had lost my rifle and all my plunder, I felt quite
rich when I found my knife, flint and steel in my shot pouch.
These little fixin's make a man feel right peart when he is
three or four hundred miles from anybody or any place.'

(Hugh Glass according to Hall)

Equipment, kit, duffle, tackle, gear—
whatever you call it—has always been a
major topic of conversation between outdoors
folk. During the hey day of the fur traders,
rifles and other items which exchanged
between Indians and mountain men earned
powerful reputations and some such as
Hawken rifles and Hudson Bay point blankets
are still sought after today. So respected was
the judgement of these pioneers that every
aspiring mountain man would try to emulate
them.

Today things are somewhat different; reputations are not earned in the field so much as
in the media where the hype and publicity
surrounding the launch of new outdoors gear
matches that of any other product. A side
effect of this is that fewer and fewer manufacturing firms put practicality and durability
before a fashionable colour and styling. While
such clothing and equipment is suitable for
day hikers, the more adventurous outdoors
person who aims to explore the wilder regions
of the world often has to fall back on the
soldier-proof khaki and camouflage clothing
of the military. In most cases an unpopular
choice.

For the emerging outdoors enthusiast no
path has more hidden pitfalls and hurdles
than the one which leads to the outdoor
outfitters. Walk into any outdoor pursuits
shop and you are met with a sophisticated
sales pitch on the latest revolutionary materials, and a range of clothing supplied in
every colour of the spectrum and sporting the
price tag to match. Fortunately though, the
backwoodsman's needs are simple, and the
equipment he or she carries will form the
foundation of a kit that is suitable for most
other more specialist outdoor pursuits.

Before discussing clothing and equipment
though, I would point out that the most
important items any outdoors person can
carry are know-how and training. These are
much harder to lose than a knife or cagoule,
and will never be left behind. Train yourself
to be self reliant and able to improvise an
alternative for every piece of equipment or
clothing you carry. Use your knowledge
instead of high-tech gadgetry. So often I see
folks burdened down with all manner of
knick-knacks which are unnecessary ballast in
the backcountry. On one particular occasion
I met a backpacker who carried a survival kit
which weighed as much as his tent and
sleeping bag combined! He did not seem to
realise that his tent, sleeping bag, knife and
other conventional gear was the only survival
kit he needed. By simplifying your needs you
will lighten your load as well as your budget.

Like many people, when I first started
camping I couldn't afford either a sleeping
bag or a tent, and I was forced to improvise
cooking pots out of old biscuit tins and a tent
from polythene. I can clearly remember an
early hike made with a school friend who was

also adept at improvisation. Without sleeping bags we spent the night around the campfire warmed by the flames and above all enjoying the sense of adventure and new-found freedom we had discovered. The advantage of a sleeping bag was not obvious even then and it was several years and many trips later that I bought my first sleeping bag—a two-season bag which on its first outing was pressed into service in a winter bivouac with temperatures as low as −27 degrees. Now I can look back at my tenderfoot years and laugh at the first time I sat on a sleeping mat and realised its obvious advantage, or the snowy night I sited my bivouac in the wrong place and was kept awake by repeated facefuls of snow from the swaying trees. But that is the essence of the great outdoors: the excitement and wildness of it all which make the hardships seem unimportant. Today when I work with youth groups where the youngsters are fully equipped from the start, I realise that it was in those green novice days that I was tempered to the trail and I wonder if they aren't missing something.

The equipment list which follows is not essential, it simply represents the gear you might eventually gather. Of the students I have taught it is often those who cannot afford the fancy gear who learn bushcraft the quickest and most thoroughly—and in doing so gain in experience and confidence.

Clothing

Your outdoors clothing is your first defence against the elements; many disasters could be averted if everyone who ventured into wild places wore the correct clothing. So what is the 'correct' clothing? In Britain this has become rather stereotyped into cagoule, breeches, walking boots and a day-sack containing the obligatory cheese and pickle sandwich. The answer to the question is clothing which suits the prevailing conditions while allowing full and free movement of the whole body. Comfort is your instinctive guide to correct clothing. Then it should be easily adaptable to the widest range of situations you will face. In hot conditions your clothing should be light and airy, preferably with long sleeves and trousers which will prevent sunburn and reduce moisture loss. In cold climates your clothing should enable you to maintain an even body temperature. This may mean extra layers for use when standing or sitting still and clothing which can be easily vented to prevent you over heating when working hard. As a general rule stick to clothing which is uncomplicated with the minimum fittings to go wrong. Always it is best to work on the layer principle so that you have maximum flexibility; three or four layers of t-shirt, shirt, then woollen jumper jacket will cater for many more situations than just a heavy jumper and waterproof.

Underwear: As the layer of clothing closest to your skin, it is most important that your underwear is chosen carefully and fits well; it can otherwise be the cause of some nasty problems. Any clothing that is too tight will not provide adequate insulation in cold weather, but underwear in particular can cause painful chafing; especially when damp from perspiration. Comfortable underwear is a priority when dressing for the outdoors, so, choose carefully and if in doubt buy on the large side. If you expect to be wading through rivers you might substitute a swimming costume, but this is generally too tight for normal use.

In really cold weather you will need underwear which covers as much of your skin as possible with long sleeves and legs. Thermal underwear though a little more expensive should seriously be considered, otherwise those made from synthetic materials, are cheap, long lasting and effective. More expensive still are silk garments—but they are more comfortable and some would say warmer. Cotton can be worn in dry, cold environments, but it loses its warmth when wet, as it has the unfortunate habit of absorbing moisture like blotting paper and being reluctant to give it up; it is better to avoid cotton underwear.

Do not wear warm underwear simply because the weather is cold; consider whether or not you really need to. Consider your metabolism, your amount of body fat, and how much strenuous activity you will be doing. Make your choice of clothing to suit the conditions you are to encounter.

Shirts and sweaters: Usually the second layer of your clothing, the choice of material falls between cotton, synthetics and wool. Cotton shirts are best suited to hot climates, although brushed cotton is an acceptable second layer in cold dry conditions. Wool shirts are an excellent choice for winter or as a warm night garment on the summer trail.

Wool has long been a favourite material amongst hunters and trappers, because of its ability to remain warm when wet. In really cold weather I prefer a roll neck sweater to a shirt. Increasingly there are synthetic alternatives to wool which should be considered as they are often as warm yet absorb less moisture than wool, making them lighter when wet and enabling them to dry far quicker.

Jersey and thermal jacket: While the oiled wool Jersey or Arran pullovers are still a common sight in the hills of Britain they are no longer the most popular. Now they must compete with a host of synthetic alternatives, most notably the fibre piles. The great advantage of fibre pile is its ability to cope with wet conditions. It is also very hard wearing; I have a Helly Hansen pile pullover which is now seven years old and still in constant use. Very often this pullover is the outer layer of my clothing; had it been wool, it would long ago have been pulled to pieces by snagging branches and thorns. However wool still remains a favourite material which is functional and aesthetically pleasing; it is also less costly to the environment to produce.

Thermal jackets are best suited to extreme cold and situations where you may be standing around for long periods. For the outdoorsman or woman the weight of such a garment would be more usually better spent on several independent layers of insulative clothing. In this way you can tailor the insulation of your clothing far more closely to your actual needs.

Trousers: Trousers are a most essential article of clothing for many reasons. They give protection from the ravages of coarse foliage and biting insects as well as providing essential warmth in cold weather and shade in hot. They take a constant pounding from being in constant movement as well as from sitting down on the ground, and unlike other layers of clothing which come off and on with the changing weather, trousers are expected to do their job regardless. Yet for all this they remain the article of clothing that is least well served by most clothing manufacturers.

What is needed are trousers that are lightweight, which dry fast when wet, while remaining strong, are resistant to abrasion and do not melt with the merest spark from a campfire. They should also provide adequate resistance to wind. As yet I have only found a few varieties of polycotton trousers to meet these demands, the best of which are the lightweight trousers used by the British Army.

Windproof jackets: To stay warm you must prevent the loss of body heat. This is best achieved by using layers of insulative clothing to trap layers of insulative air. To take full advantage of such layers you must prevent them moving or being replaced by cold air. This is where a windproof shell to your clothing is essential. This can either be a specific garment such as a ventile or buckskin jacket or can be a waterproof cagoule.

Socks and gloves: The hardest parts of your body to keep warm are the extremities which are farthest from your heart—especially your feet. Always make certain you have plenty of spare pairs of socks. 80% wool, 20% nylon mixes are the best. To avoid blisters check the socks for any fluff balls or loose threads which may rub sore spots. Change your socks when they become damp from perspiration. You should always have dry socks to wear at the end of the day. Some people prefer two pairs of thinner socks to one thicker pair.

Because you can warm your hands under your armpits or between your thighs, gloves are slightly less essential. However they should be of either wool or pile and preferably a mitten design. Some excellent versions are currently available which have waterproof outers with changeable inners. In cold, damp conditions carry two pairs.

Footwear: This has been a point of contention for many years. In general I would advise you to choose a quality pair of walking boots with a sole that allows the fitting of a waterproof gaiter. In this way you are equipped for the mountains and bad weather conditions. Make certain you choose the type of boot which has a flexible sole. It will take some time to wear the boot in so never buy boots just prior to an expedition.

My own preference in footwear is for good quality fell running shoes. These are light and comfortable, less tiring to use than boots and enable me to remain nimble. They are the closest approximation to moccasins that I can find, but with the added advantage of a good gripping sole. In damp weather they are not as waterproof as boots, though they do dry quicker; and I can carry two pairs with several changes of socks and still they weigh less than boots. However in really damp conditions or winter mountain conditions I resort to good boots. You must make your own decision, though if in doubt, don't choose expensive boots until you have the experience to decide for yourself.

Head gear: You will be surprised at just how much warmth your body loses from your head. Always carry a hat in cold weather; the most versatile of these is a woollen balaclava which can be worn either rolled up as a normal hat or rolled down to give almost total cover to your head if the weather really turns cold. In hot humid conditions a bush hat will provide protection from sun and biting insects.

Waterproofs: It is in the field of waterproof clothing that modern materials really strike gold. In recent years there has been the development of breathable fabrics which are totally waterproof yet which allow perspiration to escape, meaning you stay drier inside. Most notable of these is Gore-tex which despite its high price is invaluable. To help the consumer this fabric is only available to manufacturing firms that meet the Gore-tex manufacturing standards such as Berghaus.

* * *

Cutting tools

There is no tool more useful in the backcountry than a knife; it will enable you to construct and improvise from local materials with swift and efficient ease. At a pinch any knife will do, but the seasoned woodsman learns to be very particular about his choice of knife. The size, weight and design of a knife are the vital factors, always assuming that it is made of suitable material. For the full range of jobs it will be put to, no one knife is perfect for everything. For this reason you should ideally carry two or more knives; usually a small whittling knife and a larger camp knife. I use a range of knives for different purposes: if I am backpacking I am most likely to take a small home-made carbon steel sheath knife, whereas if I am travelling further afield I will carry my large knife plus a small folding knife.

Knives do not come cheaply these days and there is much controversy surrounding their use. In general, people underestimate the size and strength of knife they need. Your choice of knife will almost certainly be a matter of personal preference and if you are unused to

using a knife for long periods you will probably buy several before you finally find that which suits you best. If you are in doubt ask a friend or expert to explain their choice and show you the knives they prefer to use; their advice and experience will be invaluable.

My own search for a practical knife led me to many different makes of knife, even to making and designing my own. There are many different factors to consider when choosing your knife, all of which will have a bearing on its field performance. The following are the key criteria of choice.

Stainless or carbon steel: The difference between carbon and stainless steel knives is more than just that stainless does not rust whereas carbon steel does. Carbon steel is softer than stainless which means that it is easier to sharpen but will not hold its edge as long (although there are now some high carbon steels which are hard and virtually rust proof). In general you are more likely to buy a good knife made of carbon steel than stainless; the knife market is flooded with cheap stainless steels which do not take a sharp edge. Stainless is however a more hygienic steel which will resist corrosion under the worst conditions; if you can find a suitable knife made from a high quality surgical or cutlery steel you have the most perfect compromise. These steels, while not cheap, will take a razor edge and hold it through thick and thin. With experience you should be able to look at a knife blade and judge the properties by the colour of the steel; a good stainless steel tends to be a blue grey while cheap steel such as that used in many diving knives is more a yellow grey.

Temper: When a blade is manufactured it is hardened by heat and then tempered which is a lowering of the hardness to prevent brittleness. If a blade is soft tempered it will not hold an edge but will resist chipping. A blade which is hard tempered will take a very sharp edge and hold it but will become brittle and prone to chipping.

For a woodsman's knife you need a blade which is tempered with the best of both qualities—soft enough to resist chipping and shattering yet hard enough to take and hold an edge. The hardness of the steel is a part of the manufacture process of modern knives which can be precisely controlled and is quantified in either a Rockwell or Vickers

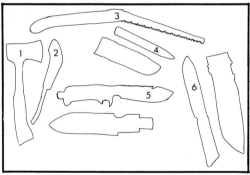

A good cutting tool is essential for any outdoors person, the wilder the country you explore the more important it becomes. The rule is always to buy well the first time.
1 Light tomahawk made by Estwing. 2 Crooked knife, made by the author to a native American design; a combination draw knife and gouge. 3 Folding bush saw for cutting logs or even snow blocks, by Sandvic. 4 A small general purpose knife made by the author. 5 The Wilkinson Sword survival knife, designed by the author to combine the ideals of a woodsman's knife with the requirements of an expeditioner. 6 The Wilkinson Sword Type 'D' knife adapted by the author, an alternative for those who prefer carbon steel to stainless.

hardness rating. A reputable manufacturer should be able to give you the specifications of their blades on request; although every steel has its own properties, a hardness rating between 55 and 58 Rockwell is about the average for a good woodsman's knife, although 55 or below (i.e. softer) might also be acceptable. Unfortunately many manufacturers over-temper their blades to gain good edge retention; these are actually dangerous as they can shatter or break suddenly when under leverage.

If, as I do, you carry a small and a large knife, have the small knife of a higher temper and use your larger knife for prising and levering.

Design: Your large knife should be of a size you can easily carry. Machette and two-foot blades are common features on survival courses but are seldom found in genuine use outside of tropical climates; your aim is to carry a complementary system of cutting tools. A survival knife is a general-purpose knife which should be equally at home either hammering in tent pegs or doing fine carving. It needs therefore to span a range of tools in function, giving you maximum mechanical advantage for slashing and chopping, while remaining strong enough to be used as a frue for splitting. Yet it must also be of a size convenient to carry on a belt or in a daysack. The size I prefer for this style of knife is overall about 310mm in length with a blade 6mm thick and varying in width according to a shape which is efficient for cutting. The blade and handle should be all of one piece of metal, the handle remaining strong throughout, not narrowing at the guard as many fine skinning knives do. A guard is not essential but is a good idea if you are not used to using a knife extensively. The guard needs only to prevent your fingers slipping onto the edge itself. Saw backs, hollow handles and other gizmos are not essential but provided they do not weaken or hamper the knife I would rather have them than not; they often can prove very useful in unusual situations.

The grip should not be metal but made of a user-friendly material and oval shaped to accommodate your grasp. It is sometimes necessary to build up or carve down a grip to fit your hand. I prefer not to wear a lanyard with a knife of the above dimensions; it should not be so heavy as to pull loose from your hand, and if it does you are either not using it correctly or it does not fit your hand properly. If you decide though that you prefer to use a lanyard, fit it so that the blade will not swing towards you if you lose your grasp.

Small folding knives should have a blade about three inches long, my own favourite for many years being the Opinel No7 which can be used to produce sparks for firelighting (see Chapter Four). Choose a rugged knife which will take rough use (not a gadget knife); one good blade is all that you need. If you choose a knife with too long a blade you will be tempted to lever with it; this is not good for any hinged blade.

Maintenance and sharpening: A good knife becomes a part of your hand enabling you to produce the finest wood carvings. It deserves the best care and attention you can give it. Stainless steel blades are sterile, mechanical and efficient requiring only sharpening but were it not for their practical use I would never tolerate their presence in my rucksack. A carbon steel blade on the otherhand sings as it cuts; it tarnishes in response to sap and weather, always changing its appearance, demanding attention to be lavished upon it. In time such blades acquire a stain or patina which gives them some protection from the elements but care must always be taken to clean the blade and hone the edge.

Once your knife is sharp, keep it so by regular honing. I carry a set of two ceramic sharpening rods (coarse and smooth) in a hand-made holder.

Two things are needed to sharpen your knives: a large Arkansas or Washita sharpening stone for serious base camp sharpening and a set of coarse and fine ceramic rods for use in the field. If you keep your edge constantly honed—which may mean stopping to re-hone it in mid job—you will have few problems maintaining the edge over long periods away from a sharpening stone. In the worst circumstances you can use a smooth boulder from a river bed as a hone.

The sharpening stone should be used to maintain the correct angle of edge. To be used most efficiently they must be lubricated to prevent metal particles clogging the pores. Any stone you expect or intend to carry on the trail should only be lubricated with spittle or water. But stones which you know will remain in the work shop, can be used with oil—my preference is to use a fifty-fifty mixture of motor oil and methylated spirits. Worked together into an emulsion on the stone this keeps the stone clean and yet allows it to bite into the steel.

The possibles bag: Sometimes called a ditty bag, the possibles bag contains those vital bits and pieces of equipment which make life possible! You might call this the backwoodsman's survival kit. There are no hard and fast rules about what this should contain; the contents will probably change from season to season and trip to trip. But the following are the items which seem to live permanently in my possibles bag, in addition to the small

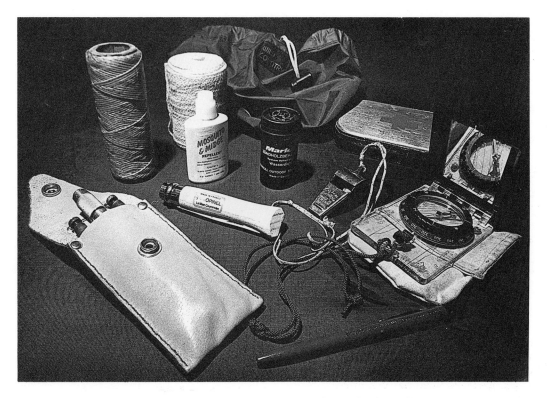

The items most often found in my possibles bag are: compass, loud whistle, waterproof match safe, insect repellent, folding knife, personal medical kit, three-inch crepe bandage, strong twine, honing rods, chinagraph pencil.

folding knife and set of ceramic sharpening rods.

Compass with a whistle attached: A compass is an essential piece of navigational equipment which will give you the freedom needed to strike safely off trail in the backcountry without losing your way. An important part of your outdoors know-how is almost totally intangible; it is the store of experiences you gain by moving about confidently off trail, amongst the shier animals. The whistle is the simplest way to attract attention and has saved the lives of many outdoors people. The international emergency signal is six blasts in quick succession with a minute gap. Along with these navigational aids I often carry a chinagraph pencil so that I can make notes and annotations to my route on a covered map or map case.

Matches: Take strike-anywhere friction (red) matches. To keep them safe and dry from the elements I use a match safe. This is a small box with screw lid which is waterproof. The design I prefer is made of alloy and has a smaller box inside which actually holds the

matches—the idea being that you can lift the matches out and strike them inside the protection of the outer case which is lined with a striker paper. I find this rather fussy and have modified my match safe by fixing a piece of coarse wet-and-dry paper to the underside of the inner case; this is a more reliable striker but will only work with strike-anywhere matches. Contain the matches in your match safe so that the heads are down and you will not impart moisture to the heads when you remove a match for use. It is also a good idea to carry an artificial flint bar in your match safe as a back up. This can be used on the tinders described in chapter four. On a major trip I will carry a backup supply of matches in another match safe and in another part of my duffle.

Insect repellent: Usually only a small bottle of very strong repellent. In general I try to avoid using this if at all possible but there comes a time in every outdoorsman's experience when the mosquitos become too much and begin to interfere with the enjoyment of a canoe trip or camp-out. Choose repellent which contains

95% Diuethylmetatoluamide and keep it well away from your compass or any perspex or plastic as it is a solvent and will make these materials opaque if it comes into contact with them.

Emergency medical kit: Designed to fit into the back pocket of a pair of jeans, this is more than a first-aid kit and contains prescription drugs tailored to my specific backcountry needs. This kit has grown from experience. For years I carried a comprehensive first aid kit in my rucksack but on one occasion I had left base camp and hiked deep into a forest following a deer trail taking as was usual, only my knife, waterbottle and metal cup. Having come to a suitable site I stopped to brew a herbal tea and set about shaping a bow drill to light the fire. It was a hot day and there were a lot of horse flies buzzing around. Just as I was making some hefty chops to shape the hearth, my eye was momentarily distracted by a fly and the knife cut flesh instead of wood. That was as close as I have ever come to removing a digit. Somehow my reflexes stopped the blade at the bone which could be clearly seen in the cut which began to well with blood. Wrapping the cut tightly with my bandana I remembered that I had some powdered yarrow in the bottom of my day-sack which helped staunch the bleeding and prevent infection (see Chapter Six). The journey back to camp was much longer than the journey out, and gave me plenty of time to consider the stupidity of carrying my knife and no first aid kit. In some of the regions I have travelled alone, this relatively minor wound could well have proven fatal. The kit I now carry is deliberately small enough to not be a burden and yet is sophisticated enough to provide practical aid for serious injuries assuming that bandages can be improvised.

Make certain you learn from my mistake and carry a small-cuts kit at the very least whenever you carry your knife, for it is a certainty that if you use a knife, no matter how careful you are, you will eventually cut yourself. As your experience grows you will come to know your medical needs very well and might then consider consulting your doctor about upgrading your first-aid kit, to cope with those situations when you are three or four days away from assistance. Along with the medical kit there should be room in your possibles bag for a three-inch crepe bandage.

Twine: Another item which commonly travels in my possibles bag is a reel of strong twine which is an essential part of any outfit. I prefer to carry a twine made from natural fibres as this will decay swiftly if accidently left behind in the 'bush'. But if you would rather carry the strongest, use Dacron sea-fishing line.

Torch: A mini maglite torch with fresh batteries is the last perennial traveller in my outfit. These torches are one of the few pieces of modern equipment which are earning a reputation the old way by being simply the favourite amongst professionals.

Other items: If I am travelling in the mountains I will usually augment this equipment with a large survival bag, some strong nylon cord, a slow-burning candle and a head torch with spare batteries.

Other items you might consider carrying are a fishing kit, emergency flares or smoke distress signals.

Water Bottle

Without water you cannot live for more than a few days; while water is heavy to carry you should always carry some with you. There are many good designs of water bottle available. Military waterbottles are excellent for woodcraft purposes. It is better to opt for a large rather than a small bottle, my own preference being for a water bag, or best of all a U.S. Army 2-quart canteen.

If your canteeen comes in a cover, include a Millbank bag for filtering sediment out of muddy water. Purification tablets can also be carried in the cover, some of which are equipped with a special pocket for this purpose.

Sleeping Bag and Blanket

This is one of the most important items of outdoors equipment you will ever buy. Your sleeping bag should give you countless nights of silent slumber on the trail. But buying a sleeping bag today can be a complicated business. Each year sees the announcement of a new design, or super-warm synthetic filling. Without going into too great detail, here are some practical tips to guide you in your choice. When it actually comes to making your decision ask around amongst dealers and manufacturers outlining to them the sort of use your bag will be put to. Don't skimp on this item of equipment; a good night's sleep is worth its weight in gold. Sleeping bags come in a variety of fillings but very basically they can be broken down into three categories

Down-filled bags: These are the warmest bags weight for weight and have captured the hearts of many mountaineers. They are best suited to dry cold conditions or to campers who always use a tent with a sewn-in ground sheet. If they become damp they lose their loft (the ability of the filling to trap air) and with it their insulative properties. Even in the driest, coldest conditions this can happen if the user does not air his bag thoroughly each day to dry out the moisture given off by the human body. Used for what they are intended, these bags are excellent, and can be used for general purpose use as well—so long as you keep them dry. Their greatest drawback is their price tag which in the case of the finest bags can reach four figures.

Bags with synthetic fillings: These are heavier warmth for warmth than the natural filling bags. But in recent years they have swamped the market because they are a comparatively low price and have the marketing advantage of not losing as much loft when wet so should provide better insulation in damp conditions. This does not however mean that it does not matter if the bags become wet. Any sleeping bag which becomes damp will lose much of its insulative properties. These fillings in my experience do not last as well as natural filled bags.

Fibre-pile bags: These are excellent in damp conditions and for mountain rescue use as they conform well to the user's body, trapping air efficiently. They are also very comfortable to use, as well as being hard wearing, but their drawback is that they are heavy and bulky. Fibre pile liners designed to upgrade a sleeping bag are very useful.

Most manufacturers specify what temperatures their bags are designed to be used in. This is most usually in the form of a season rating: 1 season being designed for summer use and 4 or 5 seasons being designed for the coldest conditions. For most practical situations a 3 to 4 season bag is the best. If it has a full length zip fitted even better, as you can then vent it to cool off in warmer conditions.

The shape of the bag and the way it is constructed also have a large bearing on performance. Although most modern manufacturers of quality sleeping bags use good construction techniques, what you end up with will depend more or less upon what you have paid.

For woodcraft use you will need a versatile bag. Choose one which has a 3–4 season rating and a full length zip. A synthetic filling is the most suitable for bivouac use and very importantly make sure your bag is mummy shaped with a cowl hood and boxed foot. When you have searched through the brochures and found a selection of bags go and try them out in the shop. Make absolutely certain that the bag is big enough for you, allowing adequate shoulder and knee room. Lastly try to choose a bag with a comfortable lining. My favourite bag which should have been replaced ages ago, survives because it has a red polycotton liner which is really inviting and comfy. The previous bag had a white nylon lining which wore better, but was not so inviting or comfortable against the skin. Remember at the end of the day you are buying a good night's sleep. (See Chapter Three for natural beds.)

Sleeping Mats

Despite having the warmest sleeping bag, you will be cold without insulation between you and the ground. A sleeping bag works by trapping an insulative layer of air but where you lay, it is compressed and cannot provide insulation. For this reason a sleeping mat of some sort is even more important than a sleeping bag. Several times I have slept in relative comfort with only a thermarest beneath me and a cagoule for a blanket.

Any sleeping mat will do although some are better than others. Closed-cell mats are warm but somewhat uncomfortable. They are very strong and long lasting but difficult to pack. Their chief advantage is that they are very cheap. Air beds are comfort personified but need a jersey or some similar garment placed on top of them to prevent your heat being carried away down the channels between the segments. They are also heavy and prone to puncture.

But without any doubt the best bed is the thermarest which combines the warmth of a foam mattress with the comfort of an air bed. These beds are not cheap but more than any other item, will contribute to your beauty sleep, I have used a standard three-quarter length version for many years, camping on rock, forest floors littered with thorns, and in cactus-filled deserts without ever developing a puncture. After ten minutes on the mat it warms you like an electric underblanket and best of all, when packed up, will easily fit inside your rucksack. (See Chapter Three for natural sleeping mats.)

Shelter

For a light shelter the tarp or army poncho is the most versatile. These can be easily erected as fly sheets in a variety of ways using improvised pegs and some nylon cordage. They are strong and cheap. In recent years Gore-tex bivvi bags have become popular as they simply fit over your sleeping bag but they are very expensive for what they are.

Tents are more specialised shelters which like sleeping bags must be carefully chosen to meet your needs. Take specialist and detailed advice before investing in such a long-term shelter. (See Chapter Three for natural shelters.)

Cookware

It is in the camp kitchen that stainless steel really wins out over all of the rest. While you can improvise billy cans from catering-sized tin cans nothing really equals the convenience of well-designed cooking pots. Round are best for they are easily cleaned, cook food evenly and fit well over both fires and hike stoves alike. Choose your pans to have lids and all-metal fittings if they are to be used on the campfire. If you intend to carry only one pan carry a large one rather than a small one as this is more practical—especially in regions where you have to boil all of your drinking and washing water.

For most of your needs one large pan and a cup will suffice adding an extra pan for up to three people. With your cookset (which should be contained in a stuff sack) carry a stainless steel spoon and fork, and any condiments you prefer to use (see Chapter Ten).

Rucksacks

To carry all of this gear you will need a rucksack of a suitable design. Here again modern technology has revolutionised matters and made the choice a matter of complication. Whatever rucksack you buy and whatever the manufacturers claim, it is not going to make your burden any lighter.

But a well-chosen rucksack will enable you to carry the load further and for longer by allowing you to maintain a good body posture. In general you should be looking for a reputable make of rucksack which is designed to carry the majority of your load at or slightly above shoulder height. Avoid the old-fashioned rucksack which is wider at the bottom than top.

Make certain that the rucksack is fitted with a padded waistbelt which is designed to transmit some of the load to your hips. Women must choose their rucksacks particularly carefully as most sacks on the market are designed around male anatomy. Despite manufacturers' claims, depending on the shape of your back, one make of rucksack may fit you better than another. Try them on and if possible ask shop assistants to load them with genuine gear for weight rather than featherweight padding for bulk. The best way to find a sack which suits you though is to try or borrow a friend's to gain some idea of fit and how design features work. Some of the better-known manufacturers produce sacks in different back lengths. Check with them how to measure your back to discover what size you need. Be very wary of over enthusiastic shop assistants; a wrongly fitting rucksack could very easily damage your back.

Choose a large capacity sack which has compression straps that allow you to reduce the sack's volume when you are carrying average loads. The large size is not intended for weight but to accommodate the bulk of winter insulative clothing. Choose a sack which has an internal frame which will conform to the shape of your back; this is more comfortable and convenient than an external frame. Lastly, more by personal preference than practical import, choose a simple sack without too many straps and buckles.

In General

While good outdoors equipment will enhance your enjoyment of the outdoors it is all too easy to become preoccupied with it. Equipment does not make you a better outdoorsman or woman; that comes from skill, patience, enthusiasm and practise. For that reason I have deliberately curbed my discussion with regards to gear.

Shelter and Protection

'When your days of travelling are over, and it is your turn to
remember the adventures and excitements of the past, it is by
your former campsites that your memories will take their
bearings. So take my advice and choose your campsite well
when setting up for the night, for in truth you are setting a
stage for your memories.'

(Unknown traveller)

Occasionally people are lured far from their campsite by the hypnotic meander of a brook or the glimpse of a spire-like peak waiting to be climbed; the halfway point of the day's travel is passed unnoticed, and a return to camp before nightfall impossible. For the tenderfoot such a moment can be frightening; in the silence of the forest the shadows lengthen and the obscuring trees can seem to crowd threateningly, causing him to panic. For the experienced outdoorsman, however, such a moment is the perfect excuse for a memorable wilderness adventure, perhaps a moonlit hike back to camp or an impromptu campout.

Secure in the knowledge of his practised skills, the experienced backwoodsman will select his building needs from the natural materials which surround him and will calmly construct his home for the night. By the time the dark blanket of night has fallen, he will have settled down by the warmth of his campfire and be listening to the nightshift going about their dark business, until with a hearty yawn he falls victim to the sweet aroma of his leaf bed.

The ability to find or provide yourself with shelter is a fundamental step towards being at home in the outdoors. In most situations this is not a difficult task to achieve, but it nearly always requires the investment of physical labour. For this reason it is essential that you know how to go about the task in as efficient a way as possible. The key to a good shelter is practical planning and organisation. Any shelter must provide two things; firstly protection from the prevailing elements and secondly the comfort of a good night's sleep. At the same time it must not be so ambitious as to drain you of precious energy reserves. Strive to achieve maximum efficiency for minimum effort.

Having been a witness to shelter building by widely varying individuals and groups of individuals I have come to realise that there are essentially four 'internal' factors which will determine how successful your shelter building efforts will be:

1. *Attitude:* In a wilderness situation you will find life less stressful if you are able to adapt your attitude and aspirations to your immediate physical needs. In this way comfort becomes a relative consideration. The most successful backwoods men and women are those who make the most of their circumstances and optimistically anticipate an improvement.

2. *Brains:* Your greatest asset in life is your ability to conceive an idea before you set to work. Yet all too often shelters show little or no planning in their construction. When I set about building a shelter, at least 80% of the process is planning: choosing the shelter location, carefully scrutinizing the lie of the land, searching for a site which might provide a beneficial feature to include in the shelter design and visualising the shelter in situ at every stage of construction so that by the time I start to gather the building materials I know precisely what I am looking for. As the shelter is erected I remain flexible and will make alterations to my original plan as I gain a better understanding of the building materials I am employing.

3. Confidence: Without any doubt, anyone who has been taught and practised shelter building begins with a great advantage. Experienced people, even when faced with a totally alien environment will set about the task of building a shelter with a self assurance which not only totally removes the fear of failure but reduces it to a series of practical problems. The advantage of practise cannot be overstressed in shelter building.

4. Determination: All too often the inexperienced will spend too long building the structure, leaving little or no time before nightfall to insulate it or gather wood for a fire. The wise woodsman or woman works hard to finish their shelter early so that he enjoys a warm night, insulated from the cold. While as a general rule you should work at a leisurely pace in the outdoors this does not hold true for shelter building. If you do not achieve a warm, comfortable night's sleep your morale is greatly reduced and the next morning, instead of getting on with other important tasks you must spend valuable foraging time improving your shelter. The quicker you complete and refine your shelter the quicker you are going to adapt to your new environment.

What Type of Shelter?

There is an unlimited number of shelter designs at your disposal for a wide variety of situations and environments. So how do you choose which suits you best? The answer is usually decided for you by the circumstances. Is your shelter for an emergency? Are you injured? Are you alone? Is your shelter an overnight shelter or a long-term shelter? What building materials do you have at your disposal? How much daylight do you have left? What useful materials do you have with you that could be incorporated in the construction? What must the shelter protect

you from? Can you light a fire? Do you have a sleeping bag?

The above questions will help you establish your aim, identify your resources and highlight any difficulties. Shelters fall into two categories: those that have to be built and natural shelters you can 'borrow'. Each type of shelter has its use so never rule one out without careful evaluation of its potential. Whilst most people might, given a choice, opt for a natural shelter, in my experience they often require as much effort to make habitable as a tailor-made shelter built from scratch. A middle course is to look for an easily adapted natural feature.

If you find yourself caught without shelter make every effort to find terrain which will provide you with plenty of shelter-building materials; ideally woodland. This cannot be overstressed. While it may take you an hour to walk back to where you last saw a suitable site, that time will soon be regained in the time you will save building your shelter.

Natural Shelters

Caves: Theses are the most obvious form of natural shelter; after all they provided early man with shelter from weather and wild animals for many thousands of years. But not all caves are suitable for habitation—they are frequently damp and drafty and are always dark. If you were able to travel back in time to observe Stone Age cave communities you would find the scene a smelly and smoky one with animal bones and fat being burned to provide light and warmth. Caves in many regions of the world are associated with evil and bad luck and this in some cases can be linked to the large populations of bats which inhabit some caves: a fungus on the guano of bats, if breathed in, can lead to a very serious illness called Histoplasmosis which has often proved fatal. There is also evidence of the disease occuring in association with large bird populations. Some caves of course will provide excellent shelter but they are in my experience few and far between.

Cliff overhangs: These are the next best thing to a cave and in many parts of the world are still in use as homes. Very often walls are built under the overhang to reduce drafts and give a sense of cosiness. Nearly always these shelters are found on south-facing cliffs which make best advantage of the sunlight and local winds. In New Mexico the cliff faces were so soft that the Anasazi inhabitants were able to carve homes out of the rock itself, almost invariably on the sunny side of the Mesas. If you find a cliff overhang which you think will make a good home for the night feel the ground at its base for dampness. This will tell you whether or not the overhang is a good rain shelter. You will be able to reduce chilly drafts by constructing low walls at ninety degress to the cliff at either end of your sleeping area. For insulation and further comfort you can build a sleeping mattress and blanket (see Beds).

Arbors: These will usually provide cool shade from the bright sun but can also on occasion provide a waterproof canopy. Many's the time I have taken refuge from a heavy downpour inside the dry shade of an old holly tree and enjoyed the bonus of finding in the fallen leaves and branches at the tree base, the fixings of a small fire, enough to warm a drink with. Usually evergreen trees such as yew provide the best rain cover. While arbors provide excellent short-term shelter they are not suited to longer stays, although you might construct a more permanent structure under the protection of an arbor. In this way you will find that even in quite heavy downpours your general living space will be spared from the discomfort of mud and you will be able to go about your chores without the effort of enlarging your shelter or building a porch.

Siting: The siting of your shelter will be crucial to its success and to the amount of labour it will require to construct. Until you develop an experienced eye for just the right location take your time to select it carefully. You are looking for a compromise: a site which is not too far from water yet not so close as to bring you within striking distance of biting insects. Also check that you are not too near to wasp or hornet nests. The site should provide you with plenty of easily available materials and fuel for your fire.

Check that it is not on the runs of any dangerous animals and that it is not overhung by any dead branches. Consider whether you are building in an area full of poison ivy or whether you risk a flash flood for example in the base of a canyon. A few minutes spent in this way can save you many hours of discomfort.

Man-Made Shelters
Lean-tos: Fallen trees, are often quoted as being the ideal foundation for a bivouac,

Lean-tos are the simplest of the survival shelters and in many cases are the most practical to build. Most, however, require a fire to keep the occupant warm. A tip: if you are relying upon a primitive firelighting technique, light your fire before you expend precious energy building your shelter.

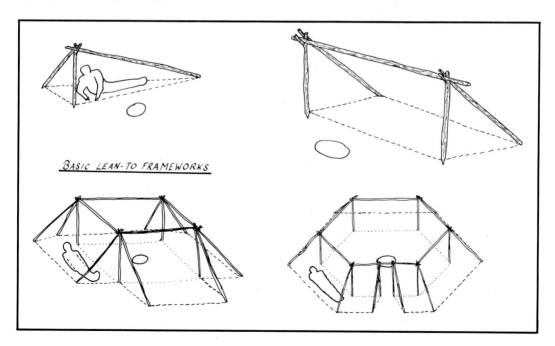

BASIC LEAN-TO FRAMEWORKS

A classic shelter design, the fallen tree lean-to is very strong, weather proof and requires no cordage in its manufacture. It is one of the few lean-tos not specifically designed to incorporate a fire.

although they are used in this way far less than is suggested. This is because they pose several problems. To construct a weather-proof lean-to against a fallen tree, the roof in most cases needs to extend beyond the apex of the bole's camber to prevent rain from running off into the living space. Looked at another way this means that part of your living space is taken up by the tree! However there are occasions when such a shelter is the obvious option—especially when cordage is unavailable and you are short of daylight.

Choose your tree as carefully as you can, it needs to be high enough to provide your roof with an adequate run off angle but not too steep. If you choose a high apex you will have considerable difficulty draft proofing the ends of the lean-to which is a very important factor in the success of this shelter. Fallen trees tend to create channels for wind and drafts to follow. If you do not block off these drafts you will not only experience a considerable loss in insulation but of sleep as well. The construction technique you employ will depend upon the building materials you have available, the easiest method is to construct your roof from

tightly spaced struts leaning against the tree or suitably shaped rock. This way you need not employ any cordage. To weather-proof the roof use either leafmould piled thick, or overlapping birch bark, cedar bark, paper bark, or basswood bark slabs or strips. Only backcountry areas can provide suitable bark, and in fact I find the more widely available leafmould is a much better insulator anyway. In the deep coniferous forests you can use evergreen boughs although they work better if hooked onto a grid type roof frame.

Once you have finished your roof put in your bedding (see Beds). With a roof over your head and a cosy nest to curl up in you can make your refinements. Block off all the drafts you can find, I usually erect close-fitting walls at either end of the shelter filling any gaps with leafmould, moss, or adobe (mud or clay mixed with grass or a similar fibrous material). If you are going to use this shelter for several days (especially in cold weather) you can even consider fitting an adobe fireplace with a hollow log for a chimney. Fit this at one end of the lean-to. An alternative roofing material which works well

The open-fronted lean-to is quickly and easily constructed and can be used in cold weather although it relies for its warmth on a reflecting fire at the entrance and walls at both ends to exclude draughts.

for this type of shelter is turf. It can either be laboriously cut from the ground or more easily pulled from rocks or boulders where it will often be found growing. If you want to encourage turf to grow and become a living roof, lay a covering of earth on the rafters before you apply the turf.

Open-fronted lean-tos are commonly employed in survival situations—especially in cold dry climates. However, they rely upon a fire for their warmth so do not build this type of shelter if you are unable to light a fire. For the uprights choose sturdy poles preferably with branches forking off at their tops which can be used to lodge the ridge and support poles, saving you the task of making cordage. The frame must be sturdily constructed to take the weight of the roof, which can be built in the same way as for the fallen tree lean-to. Again construct end walls to reduce cold drafts. The beauty of this shelter is that you can build a fire in front of the open side with a reflector behind it to bounce heat back into the shelter; this makes a considerable difference (see Fires). If you are short of daylight construct the shelter with only one end of the

ridge pole raised. In this way you will halve the amount of roofing materials needed as well as improving the warmth.

If you are not alone it is better to build one of these shelters for each person so that the fire is contained between them. In this way each person receives warmth from their fire along the whole length of their body, the opposing shelter acting as the reflector for the fire. The logical extension of this process is to construct a completely circular shelter for a group.

The group lean-to is the five-star-hotel of shelters. The secret is to keep it small with a maximum of seven occupants, any more than this and the fire must be enlarged to uneconomic proportions. With careful construction you should not need to use any cordage in its construction as every upright and ridge pole supports every other. I once used this shelter with a mixed group of able bodied and handicapped youngsters some of whom were wheelchair bound and would have had difficulty keeping warm. They tended the fire while the others built the lean-to around them and that night they sat round the campfire watching the trees above

The optimum size for a group shelter is 7 people. Any more and one fire is not sufficient to heat everyone. Note the doors which both exclude draughts and turn the shelter into a chimney, making the smoke rise straight up.

Because this lean-to is circular, the supporting posts support each other and with care no cordage is needed. Well-constructed survival shelters are usually warmer than tents as they can often be centrally heated and have good insulative walls.

dancing to the rhythm of a November gale which could not penetrate their sanctuary. Another advantage of this shelter is that once a door is fitted the fire is completely hidden and the smoke is drawn straight upwards. Even if there is a frost, despite being open to the elements, this shelter remains welcoming; the warmth strikes you as you walk in.

Tripod Structures

The tipis: The classic native shelter built around a tripod is the tipi, and that used by the plains tribes of North America was at the peak of its development. While some nations favoured a four-pole foundation the majority favoured a tripod against which the additional poles were leant and eventually lashed. Today these tents still find favour with youth groups since they make a romantic as well as a practical addition to any camp. I have been asked by friends who use the latest hi-tech mountain tents how tipis fare in high winds, their being so tall. In the answer to this question lies one of the tipi's design features which is not obvious. The tripod structure of the tipi does not stand perpendicularly; the pole which faces away from the wind is extended further than the other two poles. This stabilizes the structure as well as streamlining it. The tripod is then anchored

Wigwams: Of course other nations employed tripod structures; in the woodland regions wigwams were covered with different barks such as birch, cedar, and basswood. These are however quite elaborate shelters best suited to long-term occupation.

The Wikiup: This is a large tripod shelter which *is* of short-term use and which is covered with brush and general natural debris to a depth suitable for the prevailing weather: a light covering for instance provides shade from the harsh desert sun and the chill, night breezes, while heavier coverings will give protection from snow. A wickiup can be built can be built to quite large proportions though a five-person version is about the largest I would advise. It is possible to use a fire inside this shelter though you will need to be very careful to avoid sparks which might set the roof alight.

One or two-person tripod structures: For the majority of your backcountry travels you are most likely to be travelling either alone or with one other companion. For these situations smaller tripod-based shelters are better suited to your needs. There are two basic designs you can employ, the first of these is arranged so that the tripod is formed from two short poles with one long pole forming a

Tripods are one of the strongest shelter structures. By shortening one or two of the tripod legs two other variations are possible.

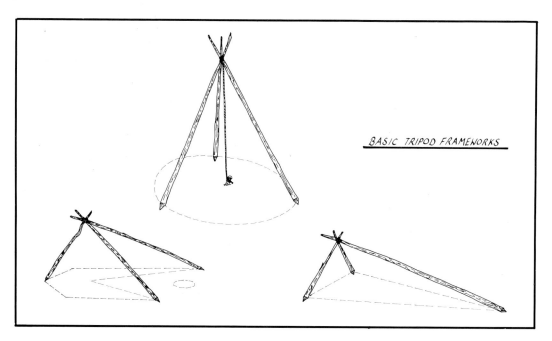

BASIC TRIPOD FRAMEWORKS

Large tipi-shaped shelters can be difficult to thatch adequately. By shortening two of the poles a one- or two-person shelter can be constructed. Because they are small they are strong and warm.

ridge. The shelter opening lies between the two short poles, the roof being constructed along the ridge which sweeps to the ground. A design error in many shelters which incorporate a ridge pole is a tendency to choose a ridge pole which is too short. Test your structure before you roof it, if the pole is too short you will not have room for your feet, also remember that the pole will settle under the weight of the thatching material. This shelter design is well suited to wet weather providing as it does, all-round roofing. Its shortcomings are that it does not allow you to make good use of a fire for heating. If you are without sleeping bags build this shelter small so that you save your body heat. At least double your bedding materials and most importantly construct a doorway which will exclude as many drafts as possible.

My favourite tripod shelter is almost the complete opposite to this structure, having two long poles and only one short. The opening is between the two long poles where a reflecting fire can also be located. In effect the shelter is two quick lean-tos facing each other

except that by sharing the same upright there is more storage space at the head end. When you are laying on the roof supports allow them to overhang the ridge poles; at the head end you can allow them to overhang enough for the two sides to meet at an apex for a few feet. The best use of this shelter is as an overnight stop for two people. Its great advantage over other shelters is how quickly it can be built; it can easily be done inside an hour if you work hard and the materials are to hand. For your beds build the high-walled cot design described later, this will prevent you and your bedding from shifting out of the lee of the roof. As with all shelters which incorporate a fire, keep a stock of firewood and kindling inside in case of bad weather.

Four-Pole Structures
The Trapper's Shelter: Along the lines of the wickiup but incorporating four poles instead of three as its base is the trappers' shelter. This is one of the best one-man survival shelters, being well suited to both medium and long-term occupation yet

The beauty of this overnight tripod shelter is that it can be built very quickly. Designed for two occupants it requires only the same amount of thatching as a one-person shelter. It can be constructed in under half an hour by an experienced team.

Once the roof is thatched, two small sleeping areas are created, leaving the space between the long legs open. To heat the shelter a small fire with reflector is placed on an imaginary line between the ends of the long poles.

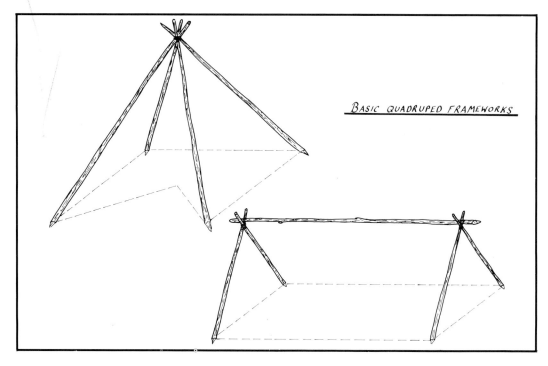

Quadruped shelters are chosen when a rectangular floorplan is desired. They comprise two 'A' frames which either meet at their apex or are spaced apart with a ridge pole. They tend to be substantial and used more long-term.

The wickiup is my favourite quadruped shelter that is especially versatile. Firstly it is a good long-term shelter which allows the use of a fire, provides good working space, and food can be smoked in the eaves. Secondly it is especially useful in arid windy lands, and thirdly in winter or subarctic forest conditions a tight fitting door, a ventilation port and extra insulation of snow on top can be added.

quickly built. The quadruped base should be set up to form a rectangular base, with the long side as long as you are tall plus an arm length, and the width two thirds the length. Only three sides of this shelter are roofed—one long and two short sides—the remaining long side becoming the entrance with a reflecting fire in front of it. At the apex the shelter should be about chest to shoulder height. The advantage of this shelter is that it provides a good living space which is heated as well as offering ample storage space and room to work in when the weather is bad.

It should not be underestimated how important living and working space is when you are billeted in a shelter for more than a few days. Cramped conditions lower morale very quickly, especially if you are knocking yourself on protruding branches in the roof. Whatever the design always spend a few moments tidying the shelter up as you build, the more it looks like a home the better you will feel about it. If at the end of your stay in a backwoods shelter you feel sorry to leave it you have succeeded.

The Brush Hut: This is one of the most often described backwoods shelters. It is constructed around a skeleton which comprises two A frames linked by a ridge pole. As a shelter it is fine and has found favour among a number of native tribes. But it is slow to build, cold, drafty and difficult to heat. I rate this as greatly inferior to the other shelters described, unless it is tightly thatched and much effort is spent on draft-proofing it. In hot conditions however, it is acceptable as a shelter to provide shade.

Bent Sapling Shelters
In some cases you may find young saplings more abundant than dead branches for building materials. This being the case you will need to adapt your construction technique to suit.

The hoop kennel: The easiest sapling shelter that can be built is the hoop kennel. To construct this shelter you bend wands (saplings about finger thickness) into hoops which are pressed into the ground, the hoops should be 60–80cm high with the ends 80cm apart. Place the hoops parallel to each other and at about 30cm intervals so that they form a tunnel shape. If you cannot find saplings supple enough to form hoops use two shorter saplings pushed into the ground so that they face away from each other then bend them together and intertwine them to form a hoop. Once this tunnel is complete weave longer saplings along the tunnel walls to add structural strength. With this done it is usually easier to fill the shelter with your bedding material before you thatch the shelter. At the feet end of this shelter weave saplings to close it off in a bullet shape. To

Dome and tunnel-shaped shelters can be exceptionally strong and are easily constructed. They are less tiring to build but generally more difficult to thatch.

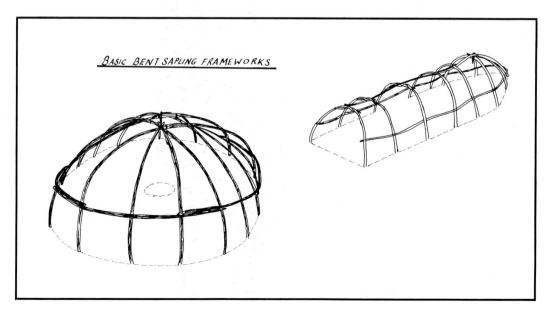

BASIC BENT SAPLING FRAMEWORKS

The hoop kennel is the quick overnight bent-sapling shelter. It can be built for one or two persons and makes an excellent framework for a large shelter sheet. Thatching requires careful interweaving of the framework with withes, fibrous barks or grass before covering with leaf litter, turfs or slab-like barks.

roof the shelter you can use leaf litter, bracken, long grass, bark, reeds or a combination of these things. Start thatching at the ground on both sides of the kennel and work to the apex where your last layers of thatching should overlap. This is an excellent overnight shelter which is quickly built, requires no fire or sleeping bag for warmth, is weather proof and cosy. The most common mistake made in the construction of this shelter is to skimp on the bedding. Make absolutely certain that you create a springy mattress that will keep you well off the ground.

Domed shelters: For a larger sapling-built shelter you should consider a dome structure. In North America people built waginoogans, wigwams or domed-shaped homes covered in bark. In the African Congo pygmies construct dome-shaped shelters which are ingeniously tiled using large (Mongongo) leaves, whilst on the North American plains sweat lodges (backwoods saunas) were also created from saplings. Dome-shaped shelters are extremely strong, as was proven to me one summer in the

British Lake District where I was involved with a camp. Not untypically for that region the rain had not stopped for a week and when a gale blew up we were forced to abandon the sweat lodge we had begun to build and retreat to our tents. But that night a full-blown gale struck, causing the collapse of any worn-out or badly-pitched tents. The sweat lodge was pressed into emergency service for half the camp and when they emerged in the morning to the scene of ripped canvas and vanished tents all commented how secure, sturdy and cheery the sweat lodge had been compared to their tents.

For group activities large dome shelters can make an excellent focal point, especially in the cold winter months. Unless you are in an area which is blessed with an ample supply of bark, the traditional covering is out of the question. If you are planning to build this sort of shelter then a practical solution is to use ground sheets or polythene sheeting—although a woodcraft solution would be to tile your shelter with grass blankets or similar woven mats (see Basketry).

To build a large dome shelter the technique is essentially the same as for the hoop kennel except that the hoops are much larger and the ground plan is an oval.

Shelters made of Snow

Despite popular belief emergency snow shelters are not toastingly warm. They are last-resort shelters which are used when other materials are frozen up. They work by providing a warmer environment inside than outside, by blocking off the chilling wind, and by trapping body heat. Ground warmth is also significant but you will need to provide this in the form of pine boughs, skins or sleeping mats. The choice of shelter you decide to build will depend upon the conditions you are faced with, terrain and most importantly the type of snow. Snow is not a static material; it is always changing and as it changes so do its properties and usefulness. For this reason no one type of snow shelter will always be usable.

The most useful type of snow you will encounter is névé which is porous ice that has not yet compacted to form solid ice. Because of this it is full of air and acts as a good insulator. This type of snow can be carved and even quarried into blocks from which igloos and snow walls can be built. Its handling qualities are very similar to large blocks of polystyrene. When used for more than a couple of days the snow will gradually become compacted into ice and will therefore lose its insulative qualities, making it necessary to build a new shelter. This compacting process is greatly speeded up when a stove is used inside the shelter.

The Quinze: With powdery snow it is a complete waste of time trying to construct igloos or snow trenches as the snow has no structural strength. To overcome this or for use in areas with only a light covering of snow, the hunters of the north devised the 'quinze' or snow-heap igloo. This will only work though if the temperature is below twenty degrees. To build this type of shelter select a suitable location and stir the surface thoroughly in a circle about eight to nine feet in diameter. Having done this begin piling surrounding snow into the circle if possible allowing it to settle gently by falling from a height of several feet. Keep piling the snow on until you have a mound about six to seven feet tall. Now you must leave the heap for

between one to three hours until the snow is firm enough to carve. What actually happens during this time is that the snow recrystalises and binds together.

A labour-saving dodge explained to me by a friend who is an Alpine guide is to pile the snow over a cairn of rucksacks, which are excavated when the snow hardens. In this way you need to pile less snow to the volume of space occupied by your rucksacks.

Once you are able to carve the snow, shape the mound into a dome. This will provide better structural support than the cone which tends to be top heavy with the risk of the roof caving in. Hollowing out the dome is relatively easy. Simply tunnel in at ground level. I usually tunnel in three to four feet and then excavate the sides of the initial tunnel starting from the entrance where I can accurately judge the wall thickness. This should be about 30cm thick at the base and taper to 15cm at the apex. Be careful and avoid tunnelling too fast or you may tunnel out of the side. To help judge the wall thickness you can use a thin piece of wood similar to a knitting needle, it is a good idea to stop regularly to check your bearings. Some people advocate placing an upright pole in the centre of the heap and another leading along the ground to the upright. These are to act as way markers as you tunnel, though I have not found them to be necessary.

As soon as you can, cut an 8-cm vent hole near the top of the shelter. This will help to prevent carbon monoxide poisoning from your stove, but as with all such vents make certain that you can keep it clear of snow. The finishing touches to your shelter are to clear the snow to earth level if that is possible: the Native American will tell you that Mother Earth will warm your shelter and they are right, for under these conditions the ground is warmer than the snow. Also smooth the walls of the shelter to avoid annoying drips from melting snow. Apart from laying in pine boughs or some such bedding you are finished.

Snow caves: Deep snow drifts, especially on sloping ground or against a bank of earth or a boulder, can provide the basis of an easily-built shelter. The snow however must be either wind packed or have been lying a couple of days so that it is firm enough to excavate. Start your excavation by tunneling straight in to the snow drift. Avoid overheating and sweating by removing some clothing as your temperature rises; if you do not do this your sweat will reduce the insulative properties of your clothing.

As you tunnel, throw the excavated snow behind you where it can be further shifted by a colleague. Stop frequently and surface for air. When you have tunneled in for about a metre begin to excavate a chamber, this should be longer than it is tall with a raised sleeping platform. The raised platform is necessary because the warmer air inside the shelter is always near the roof and the colder near the floor. Just as you did with the quinze, cut an air hole. This is vitally important if you do not want to risk poisoning yourself with carbon monoxide, a risk increased by the use of a stove inside the cave. Even a slight lack of air can cause problems, for without sufficient air your body cannot burn food efficiently and you will be cold. In fact it has been known for men to become frozen solid during their sleep waking to find themselves unable to move!

Once the excavation of the cave is complete the procedure is the same as for the quinze: smooth the walls and create an insulated floor with whatever you can. A final refinement you can make is to create a draught-proof entrance by building a wall outside the tunnel entrance. By burning a candle inside the snow cave you can considerably raise the morale of the occupants by increasing the temperature and creating a cheery light. As the shelter is used however, combination of heat from your body, stove and candle will cause some melting and therefore a reduction in insulation. Depending on local conditions you will need to build a snow shelter every few days.

Snow trenches: The quickest and easiest of all snow shelters to build is the snow trench, it also has the advantage of not being enclosed so reducing the risk of suffocation. Its disadvantage is that it is generally colder than the more draught-proof snow shelters.

The simplest snow trench which can be built is a grave-sized trench with a roof made from branches laid across and covered with

When snow is hard and packed it can be cut into blocks and all manner of wall-like constructions can be built. The ultimate of these shelters is the igloo which is a wall that spirals around up and over into a dome. The most important factor is cutting the blocks so that they lock tight with their neighbours. This is not a shelter to build for the first time in an emergency.

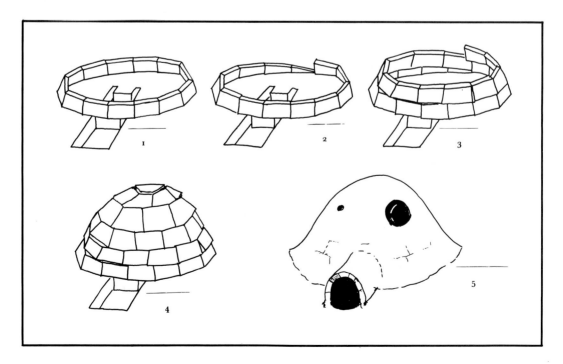

The secret to building an igloo is to use the force of gravity to lock the blocks together.

snow (snow is an excellent insulator). If you are a skier a similar shelter can be improvised using your skis and ski poles as roof supports and a poncho or ground sheet as the thatching material.

If none of these materials are available you can always use the snow itself by constructing an arched roof of snow blocks.

The igloo: This is the snow shelter which rightly earns its reputation as a classic. Essentially it is a shelter for two or more people and given the right conditions and team work, Native Canadians have been known to build an igloo in under forty-five minutes.

To build an igloo you must begin with good wind-packed snow. This should be quarried into blocks which are roughly a metre long by half a metre wide and fifteen centimetres thick. If the snow is of a poorer quality than usual you may be forced to use smaller blocks; these will work but are much harder to use. To cut the snow use a long bladed knife or improvise a snow knife from whatever you can; the natives used to use snow knives made from wood or bone. The snow blocks are

heavier than you might imagine so work steadily. The best method is for one person to construct the igloo while the other members of the party cut and transport the snow blocks to the building site.

Choose a level area to build on and start by constructing a ring of snow blocks each of which tilts inwards and contacts with its neighbour. This low wall is the foundation of the igloo so make sure it is stable and solidly built. The secret of building an igloo is to use the force of gravity to lock the snow blocks together. This is achieved by laying the blocks in an upward spiral so that as each block is laid it rests against the layer below it and the block laid previously. The spiral starts at the foundation wall where the wall is cut to produce a slope from the base of one block to the top of its fourth or fifth neighbouring block.

Start laying the blocks making sure they make contact in three places; this is essential if they are to hold together. As you progress increase the angle at which the blocks lean inwards, if incorrectly built the wall will begin to take on an alarmingly unstable appearance. If you do not tilt the blocks in enough you will end up with a more conical than hemispherical igloo, which is an inefficient shape for warmth retention as the warm air near the ceiling is allowed to rise above the sleeping platforms. As the blocks spiral in to enclose the roof you will need to cut them to a suitable shape, so that the king block (the last block which locks the structure into a stable shape) is fitted wedge like with bevelled edges.

Built correctly, the builder should be entombed in the doorless igloo. The next task is to cut a ventilation hole in the roof and a doorway at ground level. To wind proof the tunnel you can either dig it as a trench which has a right-angle turn up into the igloo, or you can construct a walled tunnel into the interior. The finishing touches to an igloo are to caulk any cracks in the walls with loose snow and to pile snow against the wall base to prevent the foundation from being eroded by wind. If you have access to a slab of ice you can even fit a window.

As with all snow shelters you should arrange a sleeping platform to raise you off the floor and away from the cold air. Heating can be provided from a candle or hike stove (ventilate well). Traditionally the *koodlik*, a lamp which burns crushed seal fat by means of a plant fibre or moss wick, was used for this purpose.

Beds in the Backcountry

No matter what type of shelter you are building it will not provide you with a proper night's sleep unless you arrange a bed of some sort. This has to be the most under-rated survival chore. The choice of bed you choose to make will depend upon the conditions, materials and time available to you.

Cot wall bed: The simplest bed which provides adequate insulation for general use is the cot wall bed. This has for its base a layer of wood designed to raise your body off the warmth-sapping earth, which is then further insulated and sprung with bracken or dry leaves in quantity. The best wood for this is dead dry branches with an average diameter of three finger widths. Lay these so that they are horizontal to the length of your body and then construct a wall of two long logs, one on

The cot wall acts as a restraining barrier to prevent your insulative bedding from shifting in the night. Seen here in a tripod shelter it has the added task of keeping the occupants snugly in the lee of the shelter.

top of the other, either side of the log bed. If possible use the back of your shelter as a substitute for one side of the cot. The purpose of the walls is to contain the insulating layer of leaves and prevent it from shifting under your weight. I find that it is unnecessary to wall in the head and feet ends. Do not underestimate the amount of leaves you need when you have filled the cot. A good guide is to treble the amount you have included to allow for compression. Just as with a sleeping bag, air the leaves each day.

Saplings and branches: This is the woodsman's spring mattress. Gather springy young branches from a recently fallen tree (ideally an ash tree). Bundle these springy branches together and lay them as a mattress, testing it to ensure that there are no cold spots. If you do the job correctly you will be suspended at least three inches off the ground. The comfort of this bed is improved by adding a further layer of leaves or better still a blanket which can be woven from plant materials if you haven't got a woollen one with you.

Spruce bough bed: If you step into a hunting lodge of the woodland people of the far north you will find the floor carpeted with a thick layer of spruce boughs which send their sweet aroma to the rafters. The spruce bough bed is made from the tips of spruce branches which are nipped off by hand at about fifteen centimetres. They are then laid upright so that the broken woody stem is touching the ground, each bough being supported by its neighbour. It helps with a small bed to construct a frame to enclose these boughs. Costly on branch tips, this technique must be reserved for those wilderness areas where the spruce and balsam trees grow thick and close. An alternative to spruce bough is heather; this works equally well and once provided me with a slumber akin to hibernation.

Hot coal bed: In the far north the temperature can drop so low that your hands exposed from gloves for more than a few minutes begin to bleed from the cold. To survive the night in these conditions the native inhabitants learned to make a bed which gives out heat. By clearing the ground to bare earth and lighting a large fire on it for several hours, depending on the fuel used, the ground becomes dry and hot. To make the bed clear away the embers with an improvised rake and brush away all of the ash ready to take your bedding. The ground if heated long enough (and with adequate insulation underneath yourself) should warm you through the night. The biggest problem with this bed is that the ground may be too hot.

A variation on this theme which gives heat of more even temperature is the hot coal bed. The technique is the same except that fist-sized rocks are added to the fire (these must be dry and non glassy as such rocks may explode when heated). When you are ready to turn in for the night you can dig the embers and rocks into the ground and give them a generous covering of earth to prevent an unpleasant awakening! Allow any moisture which may steam from the ground to cease before laying down your bedding.

Fire

'Oh, the magic of the campfire! No unkind feeling long
withstands its glow. For men to meet at the same campfire is
to come closer, to have better understanding of each other,
and to lay the foundations of lasting friendship.'

(Ernest Thompson Seton, *Two Little Savages*)

The Indian knew that, 'Grandmother Fire,'
the bringer of warmth and light was a force to
be respected. Without the convenience of
modern materials and firestarting equipment,
he had to know in which trees she slept and
how to coax her from slumber to his aid.
Today she still sleeps in those same woods and
the competent backwoodsman need never be
without fire once he has learned to call her.

Fire by Friction

Of all the ancient survival skills, friction
firelighting is the hardest to master, requiring
perseverance and determination coupled with
technique and physical fitness. From a techni-
cal point of view it is theoretically very simple
and once mastered, is practically very simple.
The difficulty lies in adopting the correct
mental approach. Time and again I have seen
students with the correct technique fail
because they gave up on the verge of success
or did not attack the problem with success in
mind. Determination counts for a great deal,
as was borne out when I demonstrated the
bow drill to a friend who had been wanting to
learn this technique for years. Once he had
the correct apparatus in his hand there was no
stopping him and despite an inefficient
technique which was painfully less effective
than the ideal, when he was on the verge of
collapse he produced fire. Do not expect to
emulate quite such success on your first

attempt as you have to master making the
apparatus as well as the technique. But make
sure you put in one hundred per cent effort at
every stage. Success comes from the right
combination of wood, the correct apparatus,
the correct technique and a determination to
succeed.

Fire Drills

There are two main fire drills—the bow drill
and the hand drill—and as their names
suggest, the technique of using them involves
drilling one piece of wood into another at
ninety degrees to the grain. The difference
between the two is the method by which the
drill is spun ranging from using a count-
erweighted flywheel to simply spinning the
drill between your palms. The secret is to
achieve the correct ratio of drill rotations to
downward pressure, this is something you will
get a feel for as your experience grows, and
will vary from wood to wood and technique to
technique.

The bow drill: This is the most popular
friction firelighting technique. It earns its
popularity from its success in damp conditions, and was commonly employed by the
native peoples of the central Canadian Arctic.
For survival purposes it would be ideal except
for the fact that it requires a piece of strong
cordage which is not always to hand.

With any friction firelighting technique
you are wasting your time and hard-earned

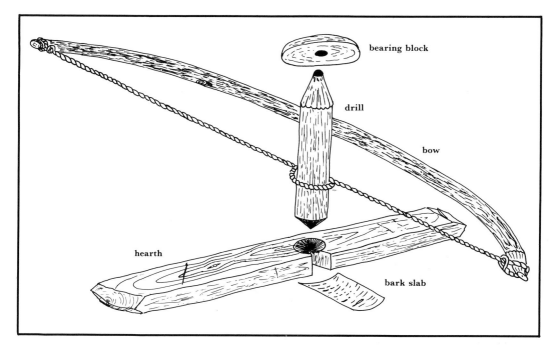

Used as far north as the Canadian Arctic, the bow drill fire set is the most practical primitive firelighting technique in emergency situations. To succeed though, every part must be precisely manufactured.

energy if you try to conjure fire from the wrong woods. Listed below are some of the most suitable woods for the bow drill technique, the list is not inclusive of all woods which can be used as it would take a lifetime to try every possible combination. Instead it covers those woods you are most likely to encounter or succeed with. You would be wise however to experiment when and wherever you can.

Bow Drill Woods

Aspen	Hazel*
Red Cedar	Oak*
Cottonwood	Poplar*
Elder*	Sotol
Balsam Fir	Yew*
Field Maple*	Birch*
White Pine	Cherry Root*
Saguaro Rib	Cypress
Willow*	Slippery Elm
Basswood and Lime*	Juniper*
White Cedar	Lodgepole Pine
Cottonwood Root	Wild Rose*
American Elm	Sycamore*
Yucca	

* = *European woods; others are American*

The condition of the wood you select for making your fire drill is important. Green wood is far too damp to produce fire and

rotten wood will simply crumble when used. Ideally you must look for dead wood which has not quite begun to decay. While you can occasionally find such wood on the ground the best source is often those branches which have broken off yet have remained suspended or snagged in the tree and have therefore remained comparatively dry. An alternative source can be found in a copse where saplings have been damaged by animals or affected by drought.

If the wood is suitable you will not need a knife to break it free since it should snap sharply, although not too easily. Check that the wood is not rotten at its core by inspecting the break; it should be firm rather than either too hard or soft and in a condition fit to carve.

If you have found the right piece of wood, which may take several tries, you now need to study the wood. A good woodsman can see what he is trying to carve in the wood as though it is trying to jump out, his task being to merely free it. Using your stone tools or knife carve the wood to the design of the apparatus. If you have chosen your wood wisely it should need little work and be nearly of the correct dimensions already. The drill is about 20–25mm thick and about 20cm long (whenever carving allow at least an extra

41

finger thickness at each end). It is important that the drill is perfectly cylindrical and straight. The end which rotates in the 'hearth' must be blunt pointed to create maximum friction while the opposite end should be sharp to reduce friction at the bearing block. The hearth should be produced from the same type of wood as the drill. To make the hearth, square off three sides of this limb so that you have a board about 40mm wide, 5mm thick and at least 30cm long. The hearth and drill are the only parts of the bow drill set which need to be carved of the correct wood.

As long as it serves the purpose intended any wood can be used for the remaining parts. The bearing block is best carved in hard wood and can even be green; it should be from 8 to 12cm long and carved to fit the hand comfortably, with a small depression carved in it to locate with the pointed end of the drill. Your aim with this piece of the apparatus is to apply downward pressure to increase friction at the hearth. If however too much friction is

created at the bearing block you will not succeed, and then to help reduce the friction you can lubricate the bearing block depression with pine resin, fat or waxy leaves such as holly or laurel.

To provide the rotation to the drill you will need a piece of strong cordage; this is usually the hardest part of the set to make. The problem is that the string needs to be both strong and resistant to abrasion. Very few plant fibres are suitable for this purpose, stinging nettle stems are one of the best sources but require laborious preparation and doubling twice (see Cordage). In arid country yucca and similar plants will provide suitably strong cordage quickly. For the most part I take- cord with me and prefer it made of rawhide or gut (see Hideworking). The cord should be a little over a metre long and fitted to a bowed piece of wood; it is a common misconception that this 'bow' must be springy like an archery bow. On the contrary this bow should have little or no spring in it. Choose a light strong wood with as near perfect a shape

If your bow drill technique is correct and you are using the correct woods, you should be able to produce fire easily within a minute.

as possible. String it with the cordage so that when the drill is twisted once in the cordage it is gripped firmly.

Working In: If you have followed the instructions carefully you should be ready to fine tune your fire-starting kit. Take a sharp implement (stone or knife) and gouge a shallow depression in the hearth board. The depression should be located in the centre of the board and about 40mm from one end. Now, holding the equipment as shown in the photo, begin to drill into the hearth. If you are using the correct technique you should find the drill beginning to smoke at the hearth. Stop after a couple of seconds and inspect the depression; it should now be a charred circular depression the same diameter as your drill. If you have difficulty with the drill spinning out, either the initial depression you made was not deep enough or you are not keeping the bow parallel to the ground as you drill.

Having burned in the hearth depression there only remains the notch to cut. This is critical to the success of the apparatus. As you drill, some parts of both hearth and drill are consumed, becoming a fine hot black dust. By cutting a notch you enable the dust to collect in one place as a 'coal'. When enough of this hot dust or coal has gathered, it will begin to coalesce just like cigarette ash and it is from this that you will generate fire. The notch is a straight forward 'V' cut extending from the edge to the centre of the hearth depression. In size it is just over one eighth of the depression. Try to copy the illustration exactly. Assuming you have built your fire and have prepared your tinder you are now ready to light your fire.

Place a small slab of bark under the notch to prevent the coal falling onto the damp ground. Once you have produced the coal you will be able to use this slab to transport it to your prepared tinder. Some people prefer to compress their tinder and place this under the notch. This works just as well although there is a risk that your tinder will become dampened.

Using the Bow Drill: Do not be surprised if it takes you several attempts to succeed; this is normal. In fact you will probably need to make several depressions and notches. Use the accompanying photographs as a guide to how to make it work. If you are left handed read left for right and vice versa.

Place your left foot on the hearth just left of the depression, with the hearth under the arch of your foot. Place your right knee on the ground about a thigh length behind your left heel, with your right foot extended behind you. Now take the drill and twist it into the cord as shown. Place the friction end of the drill into the depression and place the bearing block on top, making sure you have taken steps to lubricate it.

With less suitable wood types, damp conditions or when you are tired, what is otherwise a simple task can become very difficult. Working with a friend can help.

Hold the bearing block with your left hand and reinforce this hold to prevent wobble by resting your left wrist against your left shin. This is very important. Grasp the bow in such a fashion that your fingers are wrapped around both bow and string so that by tightening your grip you tension the string. Now, being sure to keep the bow parallel to the ground begin to drill. Your aim is to develop a rhythm and then to increase pressure and speed until a coal is produced. This will take some practise but as a guide, watch the amount of smoke you are producing and as soon as the hearth begins to give off smoke increase both your downward pressure and speed to the point where the smoke is so thick you cannot see the hearth; this can be rather acrid. Once you reach this point make long powerful strokes of the bow being sure to maintain the same level of smoke. With practise you will be able to judge when to stop, but while learning count twenty long strokes before stopping.

Now, if all is well you should have a pile of black powder smouldering in the notch. Do not panic or rush things—sit back and relax—many a coal has been lost through over haste. If you fan gently with your hand or blow gently on the coal it should smoulder more hotly and begin to glow, as well as holding together better. Next take a small twig or pine needle and carefully place it on top of the coal and roll the hearth away. You should now be able to lift the coal by the piece of bark and drop it into the tinder bundle you have previously prepared. Make sure that the coal is tightly surrounded by finely teased tinder and blow on the bundle so that the coal can grow. Once the bundle is glowing brightly it normally only takes a final puff to set it aflame.

Troubleshooting: If you have not produced enough powder to fill the notch despite athletic attempts to do so, there could be several things wrong. One of the most likely is that the wood of the drill and hearth are of a different hardness therefore one is simply consuming the other instead of producing a coal. Another is that you may not be drilling hard or fast enough; an indication of this is if the coal is more brown than black. If you are pushing down harder than you are drilling fast you will find that the powder is more fibrous and less powdery. If the notch is filled with powder but is not smouldering you are not putting enough effort into the process and must push and drill harder.

Alternative methods: There are several other methods of firestarting that are very closely related to the bow drill method. A technique employed in arctic regions where wood long enough to produce a decent bow can rarely be found, was to use a thong with a toggle at each end. This works for one or more people. If you are using it by yourself then you hold a toggle in each hand and bear down on the drill top with a bearing block which is carved so that it can be held between the teeth. An easier way is if there are two or three of you and then one can hold the bearing block and the other one or two can draw the thong backwards and forwards. When working as a team you will be able to produce fire from a far wider range of woods than when working solo.

Another method of fire lighting often quoted is one using a set-up similar to the pump drill the notion being that you can produce fire with less effort. Such a device was used by the Iroquois to make ceremonial fires using a shaft over a metre long. I find this method to be impractical despite all its advocates: the apparatus involves considerably more effort to produce than a bow drill and in operation it is slower. A practised fire-lighter can usually summon fire from a bow drill considerably quicker than with a pump drill.

* * *

The Hand Drill: The easiest fire drill to make is the hand drill. As its name suggests this technique involves generating fire by spinning a drill between your hands. Its great advantages are that it is easy to make and that it does not require any cordage. It is also light and easy to transport. Its drawbacks are that it is less effective in damp conditions than a bow drill and that the wood it is made from must be perfectly dry. It is also a difficult technique to perfect to the point where you can rely implicitly upon it. However this should not put you off. Even in damp England I use the hand drill to light my fire at least twice as often as the bow drill. After all if you fail you can always fall back on the bow drill.

Compared to the bow drill the hand drill requires great finesse since you are generating heat with less mechanical advantage. For this reason the drill must be of a smaller diameter. Because the process is less violent you can make the drill from wood which has a soft pithy centre (many of which would be unsuitable for the bow drill). The secret to success lies in achieving the perfect balance of speed to pressure, but because this method attains little mechanical advantage the timing and execution of your technique must be absolutely perfect or you will exhaust yourself long before you produce a coal.

Your choice of wood is directly related to the technique you must use to drill. For example if you are using a drill of elder or a Field Maple hearth you will need to drill fast with as much downward pressure as you can generate, while if you are using a drill of Cattail (Greater Reedmace) which is very papery you would need to use a very fast drilling action with little or no downward

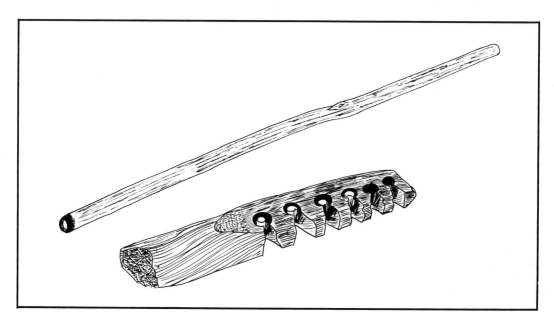

The hand drill does not require the use of any cordage but does require an absolutely perfect technique. Many pithy-centered woods can be used for the drill.

pressure. You will also find that the drill tips need to be prepared in slightly different ways. This knowledge will come with practise but to begin with you just need to be aware that differences exist between woods and combinations of woods.

Hand Drill Woods

Drill Woods	Hearth Woods
Aspen	Aspen
Buckeye*	Burdock*
Burdock	Cedar
Cattail*	Clematis*
Cottonwood	Cottonwood
Elder*	Elder*
Juniper*	Juniper*
Lodgepole Pine	Lodgepole Pine
Mullein*	Field Maple*
Sage Brush	Mullein*
Saguaro Rib	Pinon Pine
Sotol	Red Swamp Maple
Sycamore*	Saguaro Rib
Willow*	Sotol
Pussy Willow*	Sycamore*
	Pussy Willow*
	Willow*

* = European woods; others are American

Choose your woods carefully making absolutely certain that they are as dry as you can find. In most cases the drill should be as long

The hand drill is spun between your palms while exerting a downward pressure. Watch the hearth to see when you have produced a 'coal'.

45

and straight as possible (with practise you will find you can use shorter drills). With a long drill you can apply downward pressure more easily and can drill for longer without stopping. The diameter of the drill will vary from wood to wood, but to give you some indication, I found some of my drills to have the following dimensions: elder drills were between 13 and 11mm in diameter and between 500 and 630mm long. Mullein drills were between 8 and 10mm (though more often 10) in diameter and somewhat shorter—between 375 and 460mm. Cattail drills which are very fragile averaged 9mm in diameter and 480mm in length. I only measured what I consider to be the average drills; quite a few in my collection are considerably shorter, but most of these started out at an average length and have become shorter through use. For your initial attempts do not use a drill shorter than 700mm.

The hearth is made in the same way as you make the hearth for the bow drill except that it is scaled down in size to match the drill, do not make this too thick—15mm is thick enough. As you will see from the list the hearth wood is often a different wood to the drill, it is not necessarily the case that the drill must be harder than the hearth as some have suggested. The relative hardness of drill to hearth will vary from combination to combination; experimentation is the only way you can tell what will or will not work.

Using the Hand Drill: When you first come to use this technique solo, it will feel very awkward to be holding the hearth still while you are trying to spin the drill fast. All these techniques benefit from practise and I would suggest you try it with a friend first who can hold the hearth for you until you learn to produce fire. Once you can do this you can then develop your own method for holding the hearth as you drill. To perfect the drilling technique you need to learn to drill continuously by spinning the drill between your palms and applying considerable downward pressure. In doing so you will find your hands will gradually move down the drill. To spin the drill continuously, you must learn to move them back up the top again by stopping drilling and holding the drill in the hearth with one hand as you reposition the other at the top of the drill. This action must be smooth and swift as the longer you stop the colder the coal will become.

Begin drilling slowly and gently (keeping the wear and tear of your hands to a minimum) and as you see smoke beginning to rise from the hearth gradually increase your speed and downward pressure to your maximum. This is the art of the technique; with the bow drill you can drill longer and harder because of the mechanical advantage the bow gives you, but with this technique it is down to your own stamina. If you can learn to judge when to apply full power, you will find this technique much easier, and will avoid developing blisters so quickly. The coal which you eventually produce though is much smaller than with the bow drill so must be treated with a little more care.

Alternative method: To apply downward pressure on the drill an alternative technique is to use a bearing block held between your teeth. This can be useful in so far as you can produce fire from harder woods than would be possible with the hand drill, but the drill must be perfectly straight to reduce the sensation of the vibrations scrambling your brains!

A variation on the hand drill is to apply downward pressure with a mouth-held bearing block.

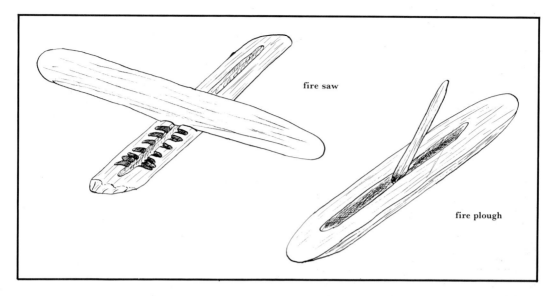

fire saw

fire plough

The fire saw and fire plough are two less commonly found fire lighting techniques which are very simple to operate. I have found that they work best when employed by a team of two.

Fire Saws

Exactly as its name implies, this technique involves sawing one piece of wood into another, and just as with the drill techniques, if you saw the pieces of wood hard and fast enough, you will produce a powder which eventually becomes a coal. You use the same woods as you would use for the bow drill. The saw should be no smaller than 500 to 750mm wide, 60 to 90cm long and 120mm thick in its middle, tapering like a blade to the edges. The hearth has the same dimensions but has a groove carved down its centre parallel to the edges. This groove serves the same purpose as the notch in the drilling techniques, it should be about 80mm wide and the same deep.

Take the saw and begin sawing across the hearth at right angles. This will produce a furrow and when this is apparent but not yet established, stop sawing and rest in preparation to produce fire. The secret to success with this technique is a short fast sawing action combined with as much downward pressure as possible. It is absolutely essential that the hearth is securely anchored to the ground. Even if you are working as a team of two, peg the hearth to the ground to help prevent sideways movement.

Begin sawing at a medium pace but accelerate quite rapidly, for as the saw cuts its way into the hearth the friction increases,

slowing your sawing action (thus it is important to make full use of the extra speed possible at the start of sawing). Exactly in the same way as for the bow drill, use the amount of smoke produced as your guide to when to stop. The tendency with this technique is to stop sawing too soon or to slacken off the downward pressure as it becomes more difficult to saw. Compared to the above techniques this method is extremely labour intensive but it is simple and easily manufactured. If you can work as part of a team of two this technique is much easier, but you will need to make the equipment large enough for you both to handle comfortably.

Fire Ploughs

Fire ploughs are similar to fire saws in that they involve rubbing one stick against another but in this case they are rubbed in line with the grain. Of the principal friction firelighting techniques this is my least favourite, as it is a difficult technique to impart to students as the coal does not collect in such a definite and obvious manner as the other techniques. For the hearth you will need to carve a board about 60cm long, 25mm thick and 50 to 75mm wide. Establish a groove down the centre of this board parallel to the edges, this only need be deep and wide enough to keep the plough stick

Above: The principle is simple. One piece of wood, when sawn against the other at ninety degrees, produces a coal which forms in a groove down the middle of the hearth piece.

Below: Modern firelighting equipment.

from slipping off the board while starting to plough. The plough stick should be from 30 to 60cm long and from 12 to 20mm in diameter. Here again the bow drill woods list can be used as your guide to woods.

To use the fire plough place the hearth on a slight incline, I prefer 45 degrees, away from you. At the foot place your tinder, then plough the groove with a stick scraping off the powder which will be clearly seen falling down the groove towards the tinder. It is important to plough hard and fast; if you have someone with you, ask them to steady the hearth and with a small stick help to gather the powder together into a coal. To obtain the maximum downward pressure kneel on both knees and use your whole body in the ploughing action. Unlike the previous techniques you will be able to see the coal as it is produced and so can easily judge when the right moment to stop has been reached.

Fire from Sparks

The tinder box with flint and steel were the common firelighting tools until very recently.

Today, outfitters of survival equipment sell synthetic flint substitutes which shower sparks on tinder. But producing sparks naturally is more difficult and the quantity produced is far smaller requiring more thoroughly prepared tinder and a more precise technique.

Basically there are two ways of producing sparks effectively in the backwoods. The first of these involves the use of flint or quartz against iron pyrites. The second method involves striking flint against steel such as a strike-a-light steel or a suitable knife blade. Both techniques require the same sort of tinder which must be dry and well prepared.

Glistening gold on the stream bed, small particles of iron pyrites have many times seduced the greedy eye of would-be gold prospectors, earning this ore the backcountry name of 'fools gold'. But the native knew that when the winds blew cold and the trees popped from the expansion of their frozen saps, fools gold could be a truly priceless gift from nature.

Iron pyrites can be used to produce sparks for firelighting by striking them, with a flint. Flint tends to be brittle and unwilling to give

Flint and steel strike alights. Simple and effective, sparks struck from steel or iron pyrites can be used to set tinder smouldering.

sparks, but if struck a sort of sawing blow with the edge of a hand axe (see Chapter Fourteen) small amounts of yellow-orange sparks are produced which will set carefully prepared tinder a glow.

The strike-a-light steel is a far more willing provider of sparks. These specially-prepared firelighting tools were the standard method by which the earliest white pioneers secured fire. They were also quickly adopted by local natives. The European steel tended to be U-shaped and was held steady while struck a planing blow with the edge of a flint shard or gun flint, which showered the red-orange sparks in quantity downwards on to the tinder, which was usually carried in a tinder box or tin. Natives including the nations of the Far North preferred to hold the flint still and strike it a scraping blow with the steel. This showers the sparks upwards into the tinder which could be held on top of the flint. With this method the tinder and flint were usually carried in small buckskin strike-a-light pouches worn around the neck. These are well suited to situations where the ground is often damp.

It is unlikely that you will have one of these special tools but you may be able to improvise using the back of your knife. Although not all knives will produce sparks (stainless steel will not work nor will many good carbon steel knives of a relatively low temper), if the knife has a folding blade, wedge it slightly open so that you do not skin your knuckles with the flint, and use it in the manner described for the U-shaped steel.

With strike-a-light techniques the most important aspect is the tinder. This must be bone dry and carefully prepared. In their heyday these lighters were used with special tinders impregnated with salt petre. But this is not available to you in the backcountry, so here you will need to search for plant downs (see Tinder List) which late in their season can make excellent tinder. Alternatively the dusty particles of decaying wood, called 'punk' can be used. With the exception of some plant downs these tinders will smoulder rather than burst into flame; nurture these glowing coals to life just as you would the friction coal. Once you have your fire alight you can produce a more reliable tinder from cotton clothing. Cut this into strips set it well alight and then quickly smother it with sand or step on it. The result should be a strip of cotton charred black which will take sparks very easily.

Constructing a Fire

Some things in nature seem timeless. Take for instance the novice learning to construct a fire. Having once seen an expert kindle a fire with deft speed he tries to emulate the skill as he perceives it rushing to ignite a poorly chosen heap of leaves and twigs, and finding it difficult to emulate the expert's success. Such failures can be discouraging, but in my experience are the vital steps to developing real expertise. The next time that novice has the chance to watch an expert laying a fire, every step will be scrutinised and committed to memory. The student with real promise will apply the lesson he or she has learned, to any skill which is taught by demonstration.

Fire lighting depends upon three factors, the availability of suitable materials, the ability to produce a flame, and the ability to use that flame to start a fire. To be really proficient you should practise lighting a fire by natural means in many different terrains and under the most adverse weather conditions. However in realistic terms this is only feasible for the really dedicated or professional. Should you find yourself caught out in bad weather it is certainly true that a fire can be a cheery morale booster. On the other hand if you fail to light the fire it can have the opposite effect on your morale and in the process of trying you may unnecessarily expose yourself to the elements thereby worsening your condition. In such circumstances it should not be an automatic response to light a fire. Consider these factors first: are you capable of lighting a fire in the present conditions? Could you find nearby shelter and wait for more favourable fire lighting weather?

Remain adaptable. If you decide to try and start a fire but find that you are having difficulties don't be too proud to stop and start again from scratch or simply to wait for better conditions. Many times I have seen scouts and campers feeding match after match to a sodden bundle of twigs and sticks, despite having been taught better.

The expert outdoorsman or woman should always be one step ahead so that when it is decided to stop for a hot drink or pitch camp a site is chosen which will provide the materials necessary. This is especially true of firecraft where the expert will choose a site which will provide a safe bed for the fire and plenty of fuel, even selecting a variety of fuel in preference to a neighbouring alternative. This may seem a great deal to think about but in time and with practise it becomes an almost subconscious thought process. The fire is planned well before it is lit whether it is needed for warmth, light or cooking, or a combination of uses. In a party of experienced outdoors folk, one person will set about gathering fuel in a pile while another sets about gathering the tinder and kindling and another produces the fire-starting equipment. With the fire kindled and the kettle on, the other camp chores can be settled.

The first fire you should learn to construct is the tipi fire, this is the fundamental emergency fire especially useful if it is either raining or you wish to avoid detection. It gains its name for several reasons: firstly it is shaped like a tipi but more importantly because it was the way a fire was started inside a tipi because it acts like its own chimney forcing the smoke to rise straight upwards. Because of its shape all of the heat is used to consume the wood which drives off the smoke-producing moisture in the wood so once started, the smoke soon ceases. As a general rule this lay is only used to start a fire which can then be tailored to use.

Assuming you are located near to a source of suitable fuel, the first consideration in fire construction is the site you choose. This must be away from any vegetation which might catch light from wayward embers or sparks. Ideally the ground should be level, if not you may be able to level the ground yourself. Avoid building your fire on peat as it is possible for this to become ignited from your fire and burn underground eventually re-emerging to start a forest or heath fire. This is also true of fires built on roots. Consider also access to the fire: is it a comfortable site to work around? Is there plenty of room? Will it turn into a quagmire if it rains? With these considerations taken care of, you can begin to lay your fire.

Start by clearing a patch of ground to bare earth—this should be on average about a

Once you have your tinder bundle alight you must not waste it. Make certain that you have already prepared your fire, and have plenty of kindling ready. The tipi fire is good in these circumstances as it catches quickly, burning to embers very fast.

metre in diameter. This will be the fire site, if you are laying a pit-type fire this should be dug now. If the ground is damp lay a platform of dead wood about 30cm square and comprising wood of about thumb thickness. This is a good firelighting habit to adopt but only really essential in damp conditions. The next step logically is to lay the tinder but if you do this the chances are that it will be damp before you come to light it so gather it and place it in a pocket or under a jersey where it can stay dry.

For tinder use any convenient dry fibrous material or plant downs. Those listed below are better suited to strike-a-light techniques when mixed in with other tinders. The most commonly available and best known of these tinders is birch bark, which burns long and hot even when wet because it contains oil. Unfortunately you can visit few campsites which have birch trees without seeing the scars where the unskilled have cut this bark loose. This causes unnecessary damage for birch bark peels naturally from the tree as though made for our convenience. Only take what is being shed naturally or from trees which have fallen. Cherry bark can be used in the same way. The best tinder I have yet encountered is 'fat lighter'—this is wood from the stump of a decayed fat pine. Being saturated with pine resin it only takes a small flame to set a large piece of wood ablaze. I first saw the remarkable properties of this fabled wood in the State of Georgia where I was camping with some friends, many of whom are survival experts in their own rights. As two local men lit the campfire, something did not seem right. Then it dawned on us the fire had been started from wood as thick as a finger and straight to wood which was wrist thick just in one stage. As the light of the fire revealed my look of amazement, one of the fire-lighters said with a slow Georgia chuckle: 'Our fire light'n skills are reeeel poor 'cos of the fat light'r' and we all laughed. The wonders of nature never seem to cease. I have since tried other woods from decayed evergreen stumps and found them to work well though not as well as the fat lighter. Look for decayed evergreen stumps and cut the wood into chips, that's all there is to it.

Another excellent tinder is the crampball; a small black/brown bracket fungus which grows on horse chestnut and ash trees. These are usually brittle and dry, but broken loose from the tree and set alight, they make an aromatic alternative to charcoal briquets.

Pine cones make excellent tinder as do pine needles; these need to be of the dry brown variety. Set a large bundle alight and then fan them to life.

Tinders

Birch bark	Dry grass
Birds nests (empty)	Old holly leaves
Cattail down	Honeysuckle bark
(Greater Reedmace)	Oak bark (inner)
Cedar bark	Thistle down and
Cherry bark	dry heads
Clematis bark and	Willowherb down
down	Fat lighter
Cotton grass down	Dead bracken
Pine cones and	Crampballs
needles	

As a general rule, with the larger less fibrous varieties of tinder, try to wrap them into a fibrous mass to help their ignition.

Kindling is the next stage in the construction. This is the intermediate stage between tinder and fuel. For this you can use any variety of very dry twigs. They need to be at least brittle dry and the best source is those snagged in branches off the ground. Gather a tight bundle of these twigs which should be at least 30cm long—the tendency here is to break the twigs too short thus making them difficult to handle in construction. With the kindling gathered, split it into two handfuls and arrange these on the ground or fire platform so that their tops overlap and interleave, leaving a gap for the tinder in their midst. In practice I usually place half of the tinder under these twigs to lend support. With this base constructed, lean other dry twigs against the kindling starting with those pencil thick and working in logical stages to those thumb thick. With this done you are ready to light the fire by igniting the tinder you have saved and placing this under the tinder contained in the fire.

With the fire burning you can add wood but with this design it is best not to build the fire too large as it is unstable and will eventually collapse. When this happens rearrange it to your needs by using one of the designs listed below.

The indian's fire: This is the fire of the trail, it comprises a tipi fire collapsed so that the major pieces of fuel wood (no thicker than

The indian's fire is ideal for overnight campouts or quick-stop snacks. It comprises several pieces of medium-size wood being fed into the embers.

your arm) meet in the centre of the embers; as the fuel woods burn they are gradually fed into the centre. Especially when used with a fire pit, this type of fire is excellent being both economical and practical. When you are busy elsewhere simply push the logs together, heap some ash over the centre and it will smoulder slowly until you are ready to once again fan it into life. It is a common fault of the greenhorn to think that unless a fire has flames it is not doing its duty. To keep a fire in flames is a costly business requiring constant collection of firewood; flames are only a small part of the gift of fire—they provide light to work by and will fry and boil but that is about all.

Often confused with the indian's fire, the star fire comprises four or five much more substantial logs. A fire for a fixed campsite, it works best with a firepit.

The star fire: Often confused with the Indian fire, the star fire is fuelled with four or five logs 15cm thick or more. Their ends rest in the embers close together, maintaining a slow steady heat, and they are fed into the fire just as with the Indian fire. But being thicker they can be used to support a kettle or billy with small cooking sticks being fed in between them and fanned for extra heat. More a fire for the fixed camp, this is an economical fire which will burn for long periods with little or no attention.

The hunter's fire: This is the fire of the white man and is of more use in the fixed camp than out on the trail. The native has learned from centuries of practical backcountry experience that it is wasteful to use any more effort than is required to achieve his aim. This fire requires a higher degree of organisation than previously mentioned fires, but for those who like to see things neatly arranged it remains a perennial favourite. Its greatest strength is that it can be adapted to many special cooking situations, especially baking and grilling, and is easy to arrange and control for groups cooking for large numbers of people. Its disadvantage is that unless carefully used and correctly vented, it will not allow adequate combustion of the fuel—causing much eyewatering smoke. A familiar sight on many youth camp grounds!

The simplest arrangement is to build the fire between two logs or rocks which have been placed so that cooking utensils can span the gap. If no rocks or suitable green logs are available, a trench will serve the same purpose, making a more economical fire for areas short of fuel. In length the fire needs to be about a metre long and as wide as the utensils used on it. Arrange the fire so that the prevailing breeze enters one end of the trench at a slight angle.

Because large green logs are used for this fire it is not an uncommon sight to find the half consumed remains of these fireplaces slung into the undergrowth around a camping place. While it can be argued that they will decay and return to the forest they are a sign of sloppy camping by people with little regard for the natural beauty of the wilderness. If you cannot burn the fireplace you are intending to build before you depart, use a trench or another type of fire altogether.

Fires with rock surrounds: Surrounding fires with stones is often said to be a good way to prevent the fire from spreading. But in truth a correctly sited fire will not spread beyond itself. Rocks can be placed around a fire to heat them for rock boiling (see Chapter

Three) or drying woollen socks or such uses, but care must be used. Never heat damp or glassy rocks such as flint as these contain moisture and air pockets which when heated cause the rocks to pop open. At most, this usually only scatters some embers, but there is always the danger that the rocks will explode more violently.

If you can avoid it, it is better not to build a fire place of rocks at all as they become blackened and look unsightly when you leave them behind.

The criss-cross fire: Some winters ago, while working for Operation Raleigh, I was involved in the selection of some youngsters for a TV adventure expedition. For part of the selection process they were taken to a remote outdoors location and given various cunning initiative tests to complete, and were filmed in the process. On the second day we awoke to find a heavy blanket of snow on the ground, so by lunch time everyone was pretty cold and the producer asked me if I could provide a campfire for everyone to eat their lunch around. In all there were I suppose about thirty people which posed a problem. How could I provide sufficient heat to warm so many people from a comparatively small supply of wood?

The criss-cross fire is best used for cooking and burns quickly and evenly.

The solution was to build more than one fire and with a colleague I elected to build three fires in a triangle large enough to accommodate thirty people in the centre. Several small fires are always warmer than one big fire. We chose the criss-cross fire for the job because it burns fast and hot to give a good even bed of embers, and because it is stable unlike the tipi fire. Each fire was about 60cm square and 90cm tall. They were lit five minutes before lunch was served, and by the time the first of the crew arrived, it was already too hot to stand comfortably in the middle of the triangle! We were all astonished at just how effective the fires had proven, testifying the fact that several small fires are warmer than one larger fire.

Despite the fact that the criss-cross is probably the finest fire lay for producing cooking embers, I also use it when I need a very warm fire very fast even in bad weather. It has several times won me bets in such conditions and I think this is because it remains tightly packed as it burns down and it settles on top of itself; the tipi fire for example usually needs the addition of fuel and attention once it has collapsed.

Reflector fires: By building a reflector on one side of your fire you will greatly increase your warmth. It can also be used for cooking when baking bread or biscuits (see Cooking). To make a really effective reflector partly enclose the fire with a reflecting wall and then place another reflector behind you to give all round heat; you will be surprised at just what a difference this makes. Reflectors can be made of wood or you could simply place a rucksack or an emergency foil blanket (if carried) by the fire.

Fuel

So far we have looked at how to light a fire and what shape of fire to build, but these techniques are all dependent upon your burning the correct fuel. I doubt there is any other aspect of backwoods knowhow that will save you as much effort as knowing which woods burn best. Amongst other things, which woods a backwoodsman gathers reveals how skilled he is. In unfamiliar terrain the expert will either make enquiries of the locals or carry out quick experiments by gathering different local woods in each load.

As a general rule, woods which are physically soft tend to burn fast and give few embers but a lot of light, whilst hard woods burn slowly and very hot giving good embers for cooking, though some may need soft wood to help them to burn. Green hard woods burn slowly, and moderately hot and are ideal for overnight logs. Biologists term hard woods as flowering trees and soft woods as cone-bearing trees but since this makes balsa a hard wood and teak a soft wood, you should use this definition as a guide line only.

It would be easily possible to fill a whole chapter on the different burning qualities of a variety of woods, but in woodcraft we do not gain from memorising comprehensive lists. Learning comes best from practical experience and experimentation. So the list of woods I have included is deliberately short, you should be able to find one or more of the listed woods in your region, but by burning it and then referring to the list you will gain a reference from which to make your own judgements. There is however one way to remember the best fuel woods if you are in doubt: BOAC the old British Overseas Air Couriers translates well into beech, oak, ash, chestnut—the best burning woods you will find most commonly.

Fuel List

Soft woods: Balsam, Spruce, Pines, Alder, Basswood, Cedar.
Best fuels: Apple, Ash, Beech, Holly, Hawthorn, Hornbeam, Oak, Chestnut.
Green overnight: Ash, Beech, Birch, Oak, Maple.

Other fuels than wood: In some regions wood may not be the most available source of fuel; on the prairies for instance you may be better off gathering the droppings of herbivores which, if dry, make excellent fuel. Fat-soaked bones can also be burned effectively as our Stone-Age ancestors would attest, although they do not make the most aromatic fuel. In the far north fat has been burned for centuries in oil lamps.

Cooking fires

For cooking you need embers, although if equipped with modern cooking utensils you can use flames to boil and fry. For elaborate meals you can lay a criss-cross fire for this purpose but for most of your on-trail-needs the Indian fire can easily be adapted by widening a gap between two of the major logs and scraping forward some embers. In this way you can use the rest of the fire to provide light, heat and more embers. Particularly if you are broiling meat on such a fire, an excellent method is to cut the meat into many small segments which can be skewered on small green sticks and barbecued. Many of these backwoods saté sticks can be cooked at once by arranging a simple support for the spits—perhaps two small logs, one to raise the sticks and one to anchor the other end. If you need more heat you can either rake more embers forward or as I usually do, lay some dry wood which is about pencil to finger thick on the cooking space and then fan this with a bark slab. In this way you can achieve far more precise control of the heat. This is an excellent way to cook snake, snails, slugs, lizards and grubs (more cooking fires are covered in the Cooking chapter).

Wet and Windy Weather: Having already said that if you are not certain of your abilities at firelighting in bad weather you should consider waiting for clear skies, I must also say that it is whether or not you can light a fire in bad weather that separates the men from the boys. If you have ever spent time in the British mountains you will know that there are times when the rain may not stop for several days. Just such a situation arose when I was running a course for the army in the Elan valley in Wales. Soon after we arrived at the bivouac site the heavens opened and stayed that way until just before we departed three days later. The course having been designed to be a testing experience, it became even more so in those conditions. Even with instruction and the advantage of modern firelighting equipment, it took all of the groups several hours to light their fires. The reasons for their difficulties are the classic reasons why those with less determination fail altogether.

Firstly they rushed into the task of firelighting with little thought or planning. I have noticed that in rain and other inclement conditions people tend to look down at the ground too much instead of looking around. This is precisely what happened in this instance and many of the fires were poorly sited as became evident later on. But the classic mistake they made was that the kindling they gathered came from no more than a few yards from their fire sites, and was damp. In the backwoods you will not always find all of your resources near to hand; it is often the case that you will need to hunt around over some distance to find what you need. In this case it would have been sensible to have spent one hour gathering kindling which was dry rather than three hours trying to ignite soaking wood.

In bad weather you need to prepare your fire very carefully, doubling up on the tinder and kindling you would normally use. Take full advantage of any of the barks and especially useful tinders already mentioned. In windy weather I triple the kindling, staking the extra wood on the side that the flames will point to. It can even be necessary to erect a canopy or roof over your fire while you build and light it. It can be a good policy to build your fire a little at a time once you have lit it, only adding more wood when you see flames coming through the layer you previously laid.

One answer suggested to help you light a fire in bad weather is to carve feather sticks. These are finger-thick pieces of wood which have been shaved, leaving the curls of wood attached at one end. They are best made of split wood which usually remains dry in the centre. A few of these sticks piled together will do the trick, although if you can find wood dry enough to make these you should be able to find tinder and kindling. Poke around under logs and evergreen trees which might provide dry shelter for kindling. If you practise your firelighting technique in bad weather you should have few difficulties in a real emergency. This is an absolutely fundamental skill for self preservation.

The Travelling Fire

In a real emergency, once you have struggled to light your fire do not let it go out. At night pile on plenty of fuel and cover the embers with ashes and soil to slow down the combustion. Take some tinder and kindling to bed with you so that you have dry material the next day. A good way to prepare this is to wrap a bundle of kindling twigs with a dry fibrous bark or grasses. A couple of these 'faggots' will guarantee you a fire. When travelling, adopt the habit of stopping to make such faggots when you pass the correct materials; it will save you much time at the end of your day, especially if it has decided to rain.

If you intend to move around or travel any distance you can carry your fire with you

quite easily. Make some larger cigar-like bundles of dry fibrous bark moss or other suitable material. Form the cigar (which should be about two feet long and two inches in diameter), around a finger-sized stick, packing the fibrous material together quite tightly, enclosing it with bark strips on the outside all bound up with improvised cordage. Remove the stick and the cigar has a draft channel. Simply light the cigar and let it smoulder at its own pace, and as you travel ensure that it is receiving a draught of air. If you find that the match is nearly exhausted kindle a fire and make another. There are still a number of tribes in remote parts of the world that carry their fire; some even claim to have forgotten how to light a fire.

Leaving No Trace

When I take students on survival treks they are often surprised at the lengths I go to in removing any trace of our campfire. But it is an essential act. If we do not disguise our passing, the land would be covered in old campfires. In fact in many wilderness areas this is already the case, with sometimes as many as six stone-encircled fires within spitting distance of each other. Very often these fireplaces are littered with old tin cans and broken bottles making the unsightly mess even worse. The real sadness for me is that these fires are usually sited in special places which drew the campers to their natural beauty. Such desecration is the sign of an amateur outdoorsman. My preference is to leave no trace of a fire but in those sites where there will always be a fire, it is often worth removing any lesser fireplaces so that one good firesite remains. This should be tidied up before you leave in such a way that it is obvious that you have made an effort, with any spare firewood stacked neatly to one side or placed where it will remain dry. The best way to educate the less skilled woodsman is to teach by example, the silent way.

When you build your fire where there was no previous fire your aim is to leave the site as it was when you found it with no sign of your ever having been there. Avoid building your fire on turf at all costs, if this is unavoidable lift the turfs and excavate a bowl-shaped depression forming a rim around this with the turned turfs. Adding some water to the hole, mix the earth like plaster and smear the bowl smooth and cover the rim turfs so that all the grass is protected from the flames. This plaster will harden in the heat, forming a neat fire place. When you have finished, extinguish the fire and scoop out the cold embers and ashes which should be widely scattered some distance from the fire site. Break the hardened bowl, fill in the earth packing it tightly, add some animal droppings for manure and replace the turfs combing up the grass with a branch, there should be no signs of scorched grass. No turf lifting is ever fully effective but in carrying out the above you minimise the damage, create an excellent fireplace and are more likely to replace the turfs carefully. This is perfectly suited to youth and scout groups.

When you are in woodland with your fire on bare earth try before extinguishing the fire to burn all the fuel wood so that you are left with a neat pile of white ashes. Let this go out naturally or extinguish it with water, before lifting and wide scattering some distance away, then rake the area clean and redisperse any leaf litter you may have gathered.

Embers must be extinguished fully before lifting and scattering. You should be able to handle them by hand if they are fully out. NEVER bury embers; they can smoulder for many days underground and in dry conditions possibly cause a forest fire.

Water

'Visit any modern shopping mall and you will find a
fountain of crystal clear water, and in the bottom of that
fountain pool coins cast in by passers by, who would
perchance a dream come true. For as the light shimmers
from these offerings it illuminates, deep within our subconscious minds, visions of the life-controlling water spirits who
alone, by Arthurian legend have puissance enough to hold in
stillness Excaliber.'

All around the globe people have revered
water and in some parts of Britain ancient
ceremonies linked to holy wells and springs
are still enacted. If you are lucky to be
walking in the Peak District in the spring you
might find a well adorned with flowers by
people who carry on the tradition of well
dressing. But there is nothing surprising in
this for water is life and as every backwoodsman knows, it is his most important daily task
to find it.

Water is an elemental part of outdoors life
and an understanding of it, and respect for it,
are essential to safety and well-being on any
outdoors trek. Just as fire can be both a
beneficial and harmful force of nature so too
can water; there is much to learn about
harnessing it to your benefit and avoiding its
hazards. Moreover in recent years we have
become complacent about our water supply,
losing our respect for it and casting into it our
effluents and poisons which pollute and kill.
Rare now is the sight of otters playing in
rivers, even in wild and remote country. It is
hard to imagine that these mischievous
creatures—whose appearance now symbolises
healthy water habitats—were once a common
sight. Pollution by chemicals is now a
problem which outdoors men and women
must learn to watch for, even though it is one
of the hardest of all problems to detect.

Why Water?

Within your body, water acts as a regulator,
helping you to stay warm in cold environments and cool in hot environments. It also
plays an important role in distributing food
and removing waste products. Without water
your body cannot function and if you cannot
replace the water your body loses naturally,
your health will deteriorate to the point
where you are no longer physically able to
collect or search for water. If you find yourself
cut off from a source of water the length of
time you can expect to stay alive will vary
according to a variety of factors: how much
water your body already contains, what the
temperature is, how fit you are, whether or
not you are eating or smoking, what clothes
you are wearing, whether you are calm or
nervous and how hard you are working. But
as a general rule four to six days would be an
average maximum.

As you travel through wilderness areas try
to plan your routes to take in regular
watering halts, and make certain you have
enquired about the availability and safety of
water from locals; they may be able to warn
you of seasonal flash floods or poison waterholes. If you are unable to make such
enquiries or you are without a map, as you
travel make full use of high ground to scan the
valleys below for indications of water. Above

all take steps to reduce the rate at which you are dehydrating, in fact this is a policy you should employ whenever you are travelling in remote areas unfamiliar to you.

Dehydration and How To Reduce It

Tireless warriors of the desert, the Apache trained their braves from childhood to endure hardships and to be self reliant. Schooling in survival techniques was of paramount importance, for a warrior was expected to raid on foot and make his escape alone. With the location of the water holes known to the enemy no survival skill was of more importance than being able to find water where others could not. Trained also to avoid resting in the shade, an obvious place for an enemy to search, the first lesson the aspiring brave learned was to avoid losing the water his body already contained.

On long training runs the boy was forced to retain a mouthful of water, in this way he learned to breathe through his nose to avoid breathing out his water reserves. Sucking a stone achieved the same effect, and was a technique employed by more seasoned warriors (if you breathe onto a piece of glass or mirror you will soon see how much water can easily be lost from your mouth). The clothing worn by these desert wolves was also chosen to reduce water loss; light and airy it covered most of their exposed skin. In this way they prevented excessive evaporation of sweat to the surrounding air. The temptation in hot arid conditions is to strip off because you feel cooler that way. The reason you feel cooler is that your sweat is evaporating giving a cooling effect. This is fine when you have plenty of water but has often proved lethal in desert survival situations, where many bodies found are completely naked. In really serious conditions you may even have to cover up completely, including head and face. Although less comfortable you will at least live longer. To further reduce water loss the young warrior was taught to make full use of the coolness of the morning and evening and to stop in the heat of midday for a siesta.

When a war party came to a water hole they would suck down the water in great volume. One observer's account actually describes the thirst of the party being so great that they almost sucked a water hole dry. Water is always of more use inside your body than inside your canteen. Never ration your water; drink as much as you can whenever you can, but make certain it is safe to drink first.

Pilots who operated in desert regions during the Second World War would tank up with water before a sortie by drinking as much as their bodies could stand. This policy saved the lives of many airmen who survived being shot down, some of whom walked back to their own lines across the desert. Frequently their journeys lasted several days and they had to make do with only the water they carried inside themselves. A problem often encountered by doctors working with expeditions in arid regions is that of progressive dehydration, where the expedition members are drinking only enough water to slake their thirst. This is not enough water to prevent a build up of body salts, which over a prolonged period of time can lead to nasty problems such as kidney stones. Fortunately we are all able to ascertain whether we are drinking enough water or not by studying the colour of our urine. As we become dehydrated the colour of our urine will darken from its normal light straw yellow colour. Remember, when it comes to water, if it is safe to drink you cannot drink too much; your body functions will rid you of any excess.

If you are short of water do not eat, you can live many days without food but only a few without water. To digest food your body needs water which it will draw from your reserves.

Salt

Under no circumstances should you take salt when short of water though some confusion has arisen over the value of salt in hot climates. If you are working in a hot environment and perspiring above average, slightly extra salt should be included in your food to replace what you have lost. But if you are short of water, taking salt will only make matters worse. This is because the salt within your body must remain in solution at a more or less constant level. If you take extra salt your body will try to dilute it to the required level of salinity—and if you are unable to drink, the water thus needed will be drawn from other parts of your body.

In cold climates the problem of dehydration is slightly different. Then you tend not to drink because you are not obviously thirsty. In fact it is highly unlikely that you will die from dehydration in a cold climate. But this is little comfort, for if you become dehydrated your body loses efficiency for keeping you warm thereby accelerating the likelihood of hypothermia and frostbitten extremities. The traditional remedy for cold problems, a tot of brandy or some such, while livening some sensations will only further dehydrate and chill you, making matters worse.

Finding Water

Every backcountry traveller will tell you that water is an everyday necessity of outdoors life, and that when on the trail a nearby source of water is often the deciding factor in their choice of campsite. Most will also have tales of a time or a journey when water was scarce or in short supply, even when in apparently green and lush surroundings. It is at such times that backcountry know-how is at its most useful, turning an uncomfortable experience into a rewarding if novel demonstration of the wisdom of having practised your training. For all its cunning elusiveness water can be found in more cases than not, but this does not mean that it will always be obvious. Just as a good hunter knows the habits of his prey so you must know the habits of water:

1. Water seeps in to porous ground, but runs across rock and clay. Because of this you will be more likely to find water in rock or clay conditions. If you find an area of porous ground which is saturated with water it is possible to extract it.

2. Water runs downhill along the path of least resistance. For this reason it is nearly always best to start your search at the foot of steep slopes or cliffs and in the bottom of valleys and canyons. Narrow canyons are often a good bet as there is more shade and less chance for moisture to evaporate.

3. Where there is water there is nearly always an abundance of lush vegetation, particularly water-loving species such as ferns and mosses, willows alder, rushes, cattails, elder and marestail. In some circumstances you will be able to spot these trees and plants from a distance. Make the best use of high ground to scout ahead for obvious signs of water. This is a habit to adopt regardless of the abundance of water; you should always be gathering information concerning your surrounding topography.

4. The activity of local wildlife can be an excellent guide to your proximity to water.

Grain and seed-eating birds must have water as must frogs and similar amphibians who may lead you to water by the sound of their croaking. The trails of larger mammals will eventually lead you to a source of water and their very presence is a good indicator that you are searching in the right area.

While these guidelines may seem obvious written down here on paper they are more difficult to apply in practice. To reach water may involve pushing through thick tangles of thorny vegetation on your hands and knees. Under such circumstances it is very easy to pass by a small brook or stream which is obscured by undergrowth that superficially does not seem promising. When you do eventually find a source of water it may not be in a form you are used to dealing with.

Sources of Water

In the Kalahari desert the bushmen live with virtually no water at all. To supplement their meagre supply of water they have learned to search for substitutes; water found in roots for example is extracted by grating the root and then squeezing the gratings. The stomach contents of recently-killed game can be drunk for moisture and when the rains come, excess water is collected and stored in ostrich eggs. To a bushman every drop of water is precious, when he wrings moisture out of a root every drop is carefully directed along his thumb into his mouth. It is highly unlikely that you will ever know a thirst as great as his, but if you do run short of water you can learn from his adaptability. There are many sources of water available to you if you are familiar with them.

Dew: Dew is probably the most reliable of all water sources, in fact many small creatures rely upon it completely, even in some of the most arid regions of the world. It begins to condense on foliage and rocks just after sunset and can be gathered until sunrise. To collect it you need to improvise an absorbent mop, this could be a T-shirt or bandana or a large bundle of finely teased bark (not poisonous) similar to that which you use for tinder. Generally speaking, the larger the mop the better; you will find that fitting a long broom-like handle helps alleviate backache. The best areas to gather dew are low lying areas of grass or similar vegetation. Once the mop is saturated, wring it out into a container for purification. While dew itself is a pure form of water, in the process of mopping it up you will also be mopping up bacteria and possibly parasites from the ground, so make sure you boil it before drinking. This is an underestimated source of water; with suitable containers and good conditions a determined person can gather several gallons quite easily. Even under less favourable circumstances sufficient quantities can be collected to greatly increase your morale. If you have a shelter sheet or large plastic bag with you leave this out for the dew to collect on, if both your mop and sheeting are clean you can drink this water straight away.

Rain: Rain is usually the safest natural source of water which can be collected by the opportunistic backwoodsman. It can be collected straight into a suitable container by arranging a suitable collecting funnel—basically any wide flat surface that the rain can run off into a container. During World War II the whole of Gibraltar was thus supplied from two enormous rain traps. You might use a suitably angled rock slab or large broad leaves or a shelter sheet. Of course you can also create rain reservoirs of water by deepening existing puddles and damming small streams (see Puddles). Whatever your method of collection remember that your rain water is only as pure as its container and your gathering apparatus.

Snow: Snow is an interesting substance in that you can be surrounded by it and yet be struggling to provide yourself with water. The problem is that it contains ten times as much air as it does water, so for every pint of water you will need to melt ten or so pints of snow. Without a container which can be heated over a fire this can pose a difficult problem. However, clean white snow is a pure source of water, which should not need boiling.

Eating snow does not make you go blind or dehydrate you as some have suggested, but it can take quite a lot of body heat to collect a quantity of snow which will yield only a futile amount of water. Avoid packing your container too tightly with snow when melting it over a fire; it is an excellent insulator and it has been known for aluminium mess tins to burn through before the snow has melted. Probably the best way to melt snow is to use the eskimo method of creating a hot plate which is angled slightly to allow melt water to run into a carefully placed container. Another eskimo method of obtaining water from snow

Because snow is mostly composed of air it can take much energy to obtain sufficient quantities of water. If you melt it down, do it slowly, and never pack the billy can tightly, otherwise the snow will act as an insulator and you can burn through the bottom of the can. Alternatively pack a T-shirt with snow and allow it to melt slowly or use a slanting hot plate.

was to fill a seal skin with snow which was then suspended inside the shelter (where there is plenty of warm air) and as the snow melted it would drip through the skin into a container. I have used this method several times, substituting a T-shirt for the skin—although the water does need purification!

Ice: Unlike snow, ice is not a pure source of water; freezing is no guarantee that the bacteria and other micro-organisms are dead. Always boil ice water before consumption. But unlike snow, ice consists solely of frozen water so what you melt is what you get. There is also virtually no risk of burning through the bottom of your container. Ice can frequently be found in the form of icicles hanging from trees, if these are dark brown avoid them as they will contain tannin which has leached out of the bark. If on the other hand they are only slightly stained, so long as you boil the melt water you will be fine. In arctic conditions, snow is generally more pure than otherwise, but always collect new ice. Glacier ice is another story altogether as are streams of glacial meltwaters. As a glacier moves across rock it gouges and grinds the rock, becoming filled with minute particles of rock dust. If drunk this sediment must be filtered out or your stomach and intestine can be damaged by the abrasive action of these particles passing through the gut.

Puddles and hidden water: Muddy puddles may not be the most beautiful wells but they can provide you with your needs. Very often they are the only reliable water source that is easily accessible to the local large mammals, drying up for only a short period each year if at all. The water in these is fine so long as it is purified.

In Britain the early farmers of chalk downland devised ingenious dew ponds for their upland herds. These were made by digging large depressions out of the chalk which were lined with straw and then clay, so that they trapped and collected the dew. Some of these dew traps are still functioning today. The water from both these sources will need to be filtered until the water is as clear as possible before thoroughly boiling.

Stagnant water also comes into this category of drinkable water that may not look good. Even after careful purification you may not have removed the bad smell though, and then there is only one thing to do—hold your nose, close your eyes and swallow!

Rain water can also be found trapped in rock depressions, often referred to as kettles. If fresh (recently trapped) clear and cool, this water is probably safe to drink, although it is of course safer to boil it first. You may find such rock kettles partially filled with decaying plant matter but by clearing this out you can easily produce a first-class rain reservoir. If you travel frequently through an area of backcountry which is sparsely supplied with water or where the water takes considerable effort to collect, consider creating natural reservoirs. So long as you only enhance existing natural features and leave no obvious sign of your labour you can create a chain of water holes along your route which may save you long treks to a spring or stream.

Trees which are hollow or have hollows in the folds of their branches and roots can provide another source of trapped water. To extract this you may need to improvise a straw from a stalk of elder with the pith removed. Very often however this water is too contaminated with tannin to really be considered potable. This contamination shows as a dark translucent brown stain in the water. Tannin water such as this should not be discarded though as it can be used as a first rate antiseptic once it has been sterilised by boiling. Slightly diluted and taken as a tea it is also an effective remedy for diarrhoea. If you find trapped water which is not badly polluted by tannin purify it before consumption.

Note: Only gather water trapped by non-poisonous trees. Common poisonous trees which trap water are yew and holly.

Saps: During the early spring, the sap from some trees can be tapped to obtain a thirst-quenching drink. This sap is not a long-term substitute for water as it has too high a sugar content, however, it will help to raise your morale and keep you alive until you can find a more reliable source of water. The fact that the sap is rising in the trees is a good indicator that there is water available so redouble your efforts to find it.

Of the trees that can be tapped for their sap, the maple is the best, particularly the sugar maple whose sap runs fast and long. In the same family the sycamore can also be tapped though I have found this to give much less sap. For emergency purposes though you can always fall back on the remarkable tree which provides so much to outdoors folk, the birch tree. This tree can be tapped like the others during the early spring (the end of March and the beginning of April are best), especially after recent rain or thunder storms. Choose only mature trees for tapping.

To tap a tree, make two diagonal slashes in the bark about eighty centimetres above the ground. Cut to form a 'V' shape, with each slash being about ten centimetres long, two centimetres wide and deep enough to cut into the sap wood layer (the cambium). Below this, cut a vertical channel about ten centimetres long to feed the sap onto a ten centimetre peg driven into a cut below the channel. This peg should be angled downwards at about a forty-five degree angle, and grooved to allow the sap to run accurately into a container placed below it. Without this peg the sap will run away down the bole uselessly. It is possible to put two taps in one tree, but if you do this you must make certain that the bark is not cut all the way around the trunk as this will kill the tree. An easy way to avoid this problem is to stagger the taps at different heights.

The Chippewa people of the Great Lakes region of North America have for centuries tapped maple and birch trees for their sap which they then boiled down to produce maple syrup and sugar, if you have the time, the sap and the utensils you might also try producing this delicacy.

Springs and seepages: If I only had a pound for every time I have heard outdoors folk refer to springs as guaranteed sources of clean water, I would be a rich man. It seems that because the water springs from the earth it must be inherently blessed with purity. Of course this is nonsense, whatever the water source you must treat it as you find it and if uncertain, purify it before consumption.

While most springs run with cold clear water (coldness and clarity are not indicators of water purity), some run with warm or even hot water; the ideal breeding place for waterborne bacteria. Warm water must always be purified before consumption.

Not all springs which you find bubble forth from rock; many are no more than saturated patches of ground. This does not pose too great a problem though, as water can be easily extracted from such ground by digging an Indian well.

To make an Indian well, choose a patch of saturated or damp ground and dig a round hole about sixty centimetres in diameter and the same depth; if you dig this hole at the lowest point of the ground you have chosen, the water can more easily drain into the well. Soon you will find that the hole begins to fill with murky water. Wait for it to fill nearly completely and then bale this water out (if you are desperate you can filter and purify this water). The next filling of the well should be less murky. Bail this out and allow it to fill again. The well will fill less quickly with each bailing but if you are careful not to disturb the sides of the well as you bail out the water should run clear after two or three emptyings. The bottom layer of water will always be murky but the top water can be carefully ladled out and should be nearly as clear as tap water.

Streams, rivers and lakes: Rain falls on the land, it seeps into gullies and gathers pace as it grows from brook to stream to river to lake, or estuary and ocean. As it makes its long weary journey it becomes more and more dirty. In our age of weedkillers and chemical fertilisers we must regard all sources of water from rivers upwards as polluted, and avoid using them as sources of water for even boiling does not purify chemically contaminated water; indeed in some cases it can concentrate the chemicals.

Sea water and the sea shore: Salt water is not a substitute for pure water. Because of its high salt content, drinking it can actually cause you to further dehydrate just as with salt tablets. Along the sea shore you should be able to find fresh water. Search for rockpools after the tide has gone out and taste the surface layer of water for its saltiness. Because salt water is heavier than fresh water the top few inches may be salt free or at least not so salty as to do you any harm. Where there are no rockpools and only a sandy shore you should search above the high tide mark for trapped water or saturated ground suitable for the site of an Indian well, skim off the surface water in these cases and taste it the same as you would at a rockpool.

Poison water holes: Fortunately these are extremely rare, but may be encountered in some remote regions. Today you are far more likely to find a water hole which has been contaminated by industrial or agricultural pollution. Look for obvious signs such as the remains of dead animals, a lack of healthy water-loving vegetation. Rather more vague, but every bit as valid, you may just have a bad feeling about the place.

Purifying Water

In the world of woodlore every skill is linked to every other; it is impossible to learn one skill without recourse to another, and so it is with water. THE ONLY SAFE WAY TO PURIFY WATER IS TO BOIL IT THOROUGHLY. To boil water you are going to need fire, and more likely than not a suitable container. For those who have studied survival techniques and practised them, this should not provide too great a problem, although it will take some time. But for those who have not perfected these skills, pure water may seem out of your reach tempting you to risk drinking unpurified water; unfortunately there are no short cuts in nature.

Our health is something we tend to take for granted when we have skilled doctors and powerful, quick-acting synthetic drugs at our disposal. But in the bush, removed from these advantages, the simplest of infections can prove fatal. Consider the full implications of developing a simple case of diarrhoea. This infection causes a rapid and unpleasant dehydration of your system; it makes you feel uncomfortable, lowers your morale and generally makes a safe standard of personal hygiene difficult to maintain. To counteract the effects you will need to drink plenty of pure water; if you were short of this to start with you are in trouble. Under such circumstances maintaining the will to get yourself out of the situation, or in extreme cases to live, can be very difficult.

There are a number of different waterborne infections, and some of them can cause problems far more debilitating than diarrhoea. Some of them do not respond to the effects of chemical purifying agents. For this reason, to purify your water, boil it for at least five minutes. The general rule is to boil water furiously for five minutes plus an extra minute for every thousand feet you are above sea level.

Containers for water are described in Chapter Eleven. When it comes to purifying water there are basically two types of container:

1. Kettles which are used directly over the heat source. These can be manufactured from flammable materials so long as the flames cannot reach beyond the level of the water which prevents their consumption.

2. Cauldrons which will hold hot water but cannot be used over a fire. In the case of these vessels the water is heated by dropping heated stones into the water. This is an effective and easy way to cook, but you must choose your stones carefully. They must be of an easily manageable size and weight and collected from dry ground (stones which are damp or have been sitting on a riverbed contain moisture which when heated expands causing the stone to explode. Also avoid glass-like rocks such as flint or obsidian as these also explode). Heat the rocks until they are hot, brush off any ash (or quickly rinse this off in some other water) and then transfer them to the cauldron using suitably improvised tongs. The ash is rinsed off to prevent the water you are boiling becoming too alkaline.

Apart from the cauldrons already men-

tioned you can also use hollows in trees as cauldrons or even make a gypsy cauldron: a bowl dug out of clay and lined with broad non-poisonous leaves. The water from this cauldron is less safe than the other methods and tastes awful but is a simple emergency technique.

Filtering water If the water you have gathered contains sediment it will need filtering before boiling. This is a relatively simple operation; the easiest filter to improvise is that using your trousers. Turn one trouser leg inside of the other so you have a double thickness of cloth and tie a knot in the end. Arrange this filter on a frame suspended over your container and soak the cloth before use. Fill the trouser filter with dirty water, leave the first part of the filtrate to run through before collecting. If, despite several times through the filter, the water has still not cleared, fill the trouser filter with cold charcoal NOT ASH.

Should you find yourself without trousers a filter can be made from a large cone of birch bark filled with charcoal and finely teased non-poisonous plant material. Perforate the outside of the cone with tiny holes.

Rehydrating

Once you have found and purified your water, do not drink it down too fast or you may make yourself sick. This is especially true of very cold water which can be a shock to your system. It is very dangerous to gulp down icy water if you are still hot from hard physical exertion, sip your water until your body has had time to adjust to the cold or better still brew a warming mug of tea.

* * *

There are many times I must admit when I have not bothered to purify my water, and to date I have not been struck down by any bugs my stomach could not handle. But there are also times when for no good reason I can give, other than perhaps an instinct, I have insisted on purifying my water. Above all trust your instincts—but if in doubt boil. On one backcountry hike with two very experienced outdoors friends one of them came down with a case of Giardia, a particularly nasty micro-organism (resistant to chemical purification agents, but killed by boiling). We were all drinking from the same water source and didn't boil the water; he was just unlucky. However, we all paid the price as we walked along behind him, as severe flatulence is one of the symptoms of this unpleasant and potentially very serious illness.

As a general rule though, always gather water from the purest source available to you, always purify it and don't be lulled into a false sense of security by crystal clear water.

Skimming off clean water from an Indian well.

Using heated rocks to boil water in an animal hide.

Using a millbank bag to filter sediment from water.

Tannin water found in tree hollows.

The correct way to tap the sap from a birch tree, with a watertight bark container.

Plants

'With the Indians generally, medicinal barks, roots, and
herbs are thought essentials in their household contents. Even
in their journeys, such are most likely to be wanted as part of
their necessary outfits.'

(From *Memoirs of a Captivity among The Indians of North America*
by John Dunn Hunter)

Already in the skills of fire lighting, shelter building and water procurement, it has become evident that the ability to recognise trees and plants is important. But more than this, they can provide you with food containers, cordage, tools, medicine and even clothing; the more plants you can recognise and know the value of, the better equipped you will be to travel. To begin a study of plants is to set foot on an endless path of growth and learning. Whether you study plants of utility or those of beauty you will enhance your vision of the natural world by their study. If you watch a party of ramblers, you will easily spot those who have befriended the plant world, for where other members of the party have passed straight by, they pause to acknowledge the presence of friends. You may think that I am anthropomorphising weeds, but every spring as the snows recede and the green of grass shows again I look forward to meeting plants of long acquaintance as they re-emerge for the growing season, precisely as I might look forward to seeing again a friend who has been away travelling for many months. This is not so strange: after all, a plant is a living organism—like you or I—so in a way they are brothers.

I first became seriously interested in plants in my early teens. I can well remember my first encounter with wild edible plants. After several months of reading about the various wild foods available in my locality, I found a pocket-sized field guide in the local library which contained photographs rather than drawings. Having been brought up, like most people, to fear wild plants as poisonous, I wasn't taking any chances. Armed with suitable books for cross reference, and with the photographic field guide I set out on my first plant hunt, excited by the preparations.

I did not need to go far before I found plants which I suspected were edible. There was a lacy white-flowered plant which I thought was probably cow parsley but was put off by my guide telling me that it could easily be confused with the deadly hemlock. The day was warm and bright and the sounds and smells of the season drew me into the dappled shade of the woodland. As I moved along the trail I was careful not to make any careless sounds or movements, hoping to catch a glimpse of the local fox sunbathing on her favourite fallen tree. Ahead of me I noticed something blue moving—it was a fledgling jay that had not quite mastered the fundamentals of flight. I watched absorbed as after great effort it took off, and managed a wobbly flight to a low oak branch. After a few minutes and a few perilous flights it was safe in the higher branches and the parent birds returned to feed the wayward youngster. Hoping to find some interesting tracks, I stopped to scrutinise the spot I had first seen the young bird, but there was nothing except a downy feather. And then I noticed it. A small clump of emerald green, clover-like leaves, still clad in droplets of dew. It did not take long to find the plate in the field guide that matched: *Oxalis Acetosela* (wood sorrel), contains oxalic acid but is edible in small quantities. With great trepidation I carefully selected a couple of the tenderest young leaves and ate them. To my surprise and pleasure the leaves tasted just like apple peel and from that moment on I have been hooked on wild plants for food—even though not all taste as pleasant as wood sorrel! As I walked home that day I felt different as though I had just been accepted into an exclusive club and even now, when I discover a new plant I feel as though the plant has revealed itself to me rather than I have sought it out.

Learning to Recognise Plants

In the modern age, science has greatly simplified the process of identifying plant species using standardised terminology to describe their form and labelling. Each species with a scientific name and classification. Absolutely essential to your study of plant species will be suitable scientific field guides. All of these books should explain how their identification key works. Make sure you thoroughly familiarise yourself with this. As you study plants, use the scientific name for reference purposes; in most cases this is the standard name for a plant species throughout the world. This is not a fanciful notion but a very practical and important part of your learning. Local names are often an excellent way to learn a plant's characteristics or where it grows, but they can sometimes be very confusing. For example 'Jack by the hedge' which is the country name for *Alliaria petiolata* derives from the fact that this edible species frequently grows by hedges and smells of garlic as in folklore did the devil, or 'Jack's breath'. Another country name is 'Old man's beard' which usually refers to the seed down produced by *Clematis vitalba* a poisonous plant, however I have come across the same country name 'Old man's beard' being used

to describe *Epilobium augustifolia* which is an edible and useful species, more usually known as 'Fireweed' or 'Rosebay Willowherb'. As you can see, even within the same country, local names can vary widely even between edible and poisonous plants, so always double check your research using the scientific name.

However learning to recognise plant species is not as simple as just looking them up in a field guide. Even the best guides with clear photographs or botanical drawings suffer from being two dimensional, and the text—no matter how carefully crafted—is woefully inadequate for describing a plant's subtler characteristics such as scent, taste, texture or even the sound the leaves make as you brush past them. The best way to learn about plants is to accompany an expert in the field learning a few at a time. For survival purposes you must be able to identify the plant at all stages of its development; not just when it is in flower. Pay extra careful attention to the fine details. When I introduce a group of students to plants there are those who from the start examine the species in detail and those who give them only a fleeting glimpse. When later in the day I compare the details of a poisonous plant to one of the plants covered earlier there is an obvious look of panic in the eyes of those who did not pay adequate attention. Fortunately I am able to recap what was seen earlier, but when you are in the company of an old herbalist or tree expert such luxuries are rare. Train yourself to absorb all that is said and to look more closely at the fine detail. There are a number of occasions I have been fortunate enough to have spent a few hours in the company of real plant experts—old country folk who grew up surrounded by traditional herbal remedies and woodcraft the source of which must stretch back many centuries. On such forays I found that I would start thinking of the implications of what they had said and in so doing not absorb fully what they were saying. I could kick myself when I cannot remember the fine details of remedies to ills which they used. With rural families dispersed to the urban jungle the old ways are struggling to stay alive. If you have the opportunity to listen to the reminiscences of a member of the older generation take a tape recorder with you!

Poisonous Plants

Clematis vitalba

Alder buckthorn *(Frangula alnus)**
Anemones *(Anemone spp)**
Arnica *(Arnica spp)*
Arums *(Arum spp)**
Baneberries *(Actaea spp)**
Black locust *(Robinia pseudo-acacia)*
Bryony's, bittersweet *(Bryonia spp)**
Canadian moonseed *(Menispermum canadensis)*
Castor bean *(Ricinus communis)*
Clematis *(clematis vitalba)*
Columbine *(Aquilegia vulgaris)**
Darnel rye grass *(lolium temulentum)**
Deadly nightshade *(Atropa belladonna)**
Dogs mercury *(Mercurialis perennis)**
Enchanter's nightshade *(circaea luteviana)*
Ergot *(Claviceps purpurea)*. Although a fungus this is associated with grasses.
Fools parsley *(Aethusa cynapium)**
Foxglove *(Digitalis purpurea)**
Fritillary *(Fritillaria meleagris)**
Giant Hogweed *(Cheraclenm mantegazzianum)*
Hellebores *(Hellebore spp)*
Hemlock—see poison hemlock
Henbane *(Hyoscyamus niger)**
Horse chestnut, buckeyes *(Aesculus spp)**
Ivy *(Hedera helix)*
Jimsonweed, thorn apple *(Datura stramonium)**
Lantana *(Lantana camara)*
Laurels *(Kalmia spp)*
Lily of the valley *(Convallaria majalis)**
Lords and ladies—see arum
Meadow saphron *(Colchicum autumnale)**
Mistletoe *(Viscum album*, Phoradendron flavescens)*
Monkshood *(Aconitum spp)**
Nightshades *(Solanum spp)**
Poison hemlock *(Conium maculatum)**
Pokeweed *(Phytolacca americana)*
Privet *(Ligustrum vulgare)**
Ranunculus *(Ranunculus spp)**
Soapwort *(saponaria officinalis)*
Spindle bush *(Euonymus europaeus)**
Spurges *(Euphorbia spp)**
Hemlock water dropwort *(Oenanthe crocata)**
Tubular water dropwort *(o.fistulosa)**
White snakeroot *(Eupatorium rugosum)*

Deadly nightshade

Dog's mercury

Enchanter's nightshade

Giant Hogweed

Soapwort

Spindlebush

Woody nightshade

Plants for Food

Unlike most other forms of wild food, plants cannot run away from you; which makes them the ideal first source of food for a survivor. The golden rule for wild foods and particularly edible plants is: ONLY EAT A WILD FOOD YOU HAVE POSITIVELY IDENTIFIED AS EDIBLE. This means you must learn the plants before you are forced to rely upon them. This is not as daunting a task as it may at first appear as in truth you can get by in most parts of the world relying upon a handful of the most useful and commonly occurring plants. Under no circumstances rely upon so called 'taste tests' often quoted as a reliable way to differentiate poisonous from edible plants. There is no safe short cut to learning your plant species.

When you are studying an edible plant, make a mental note of its taste and smell, the texture of its leaves, even the sound they make underfoot. I prefer my students to use their minds for storing this information rather than recording it in a notebook. This is the old way of teaching; to make notes you are using a valuable part of your concentration to write. Train yourself to absorb all the details of the plant received by your many senses. If it is edible, eat it, this is the best way to fix that information permanently in your head. If you learn the edible species really thoroughly and stick only to those you have learned, there is little or no reason to study the poisonous varieties. However, the ideal situation is to be able to recognise them when you see them, so I have listed below the common and most dangerous varieties you should familiarise yourself with. This list is far from comprehensive.

Preparing the Edible Parts

In general, wild plants require more preparation than the cultivated forms we are most used to; this is in most cases a labour and time-intensive activity. While many can be eaten raw some retain poisonous characteristics until prepared in a specific way or cooked. This chapter is specifically concerned with the gathering and preparation prior to cooking (see chapter ten). Before you begin to collect edible plants you must decide what your aim is to be. Are you gathering food for one meal or as part of a long-term diet? If the latter, you will need to concentrate your efforts on gathering the plants which will yield the most nutrition with a heavy emphasis on carbohydrate and sugar-rich underground parts. Wherever possible, plan your food stocks to complement any fish or game you are able to gather. Remember the old adage 'An army marches on its stomach'! Try to conceive exciting tasty meals and gather your groceries accordingly. Always bear in mind that while you gather your food resource you must also husband that resource, never denude an area of wild plants. Australian aborigines sometimes even leave behind part of each edible root they gather to grow again. When you have the opportunity help seeds to take root by bringing them into direct contact with soil. Along some of my favourite trails I have encouraged the local plants to grow especially the edible and utility varieties, although not to the exclusion of others.

The following are the preparation techniques you should be familiar with:

Making infusions: Infusions are made by steeping the plant material in water which can be cold or warm but never boiling. (Boiling destroys the ingredient you are trying to activate.) Teas should be infused using water just off the boil.

Making decoctions: Decoctions are made by boiling the plant material to release its active ingredients.

Boiling greens: Whenever boiling greens it is important not to use too much water, use just enough to cover the plant material. If you use more water than this you will lose much of the mineral and vitamin value of the plant. Of course this is not the case with soups and stews. Plants that are excessively bitter tasting may need several changes of water. In this case more water can be used initially.

Steaming: Steaming is preferable to boiling in all cases, except those where bitter flavours need to be boiled away with water changes. The plant material will need steaming in relation to its size and density; leaves need much less steaming time than do roots and fruits. A good way to use leaves such as tender beech or sheep surrel leaves is as stuffing for meat and fish that is being steamed.

Making coffees: Wild coffees, such as acorn coffee, are usually far less concentrated than commercial coffee, so greater quantities must be used in the brew. Infuse the coffee; boiling will make it more bitter as will over brewing.

Flours: Wild flours can be produced from many different plant sources, the best being cattails and acorns. Prepared flour is not always easy to store under survival conditions. Ideally you will need to store it in a clay pot with a lid. Acorns are better stored whole than as prepared flour. To grind up the flour you may need to use grinding stones, a smaller stone used to grind against a slightly hollowed larger stone or log mortar.

Extracting roots: Some of the edible roots listed below cling tenaciously to the ground: many of the most useful are so because of their resilience to drought and cold. To survive under these conditions they send down deep roots. To help in gathering these plants you should fashion a digging stick. This can be of any length or size, though I find a metre long and three to four centimetres in diameter is the most useful. Sharpen the point with a chisel-shaped end and fire harden it. Use this to pull the soil away from the root rather than trying to lever the root up as though using a fork. This process means that you will have to dig a larger hole than you bargained for. When you have finished replace the soil and add in some seed from the plants, or a neighbouring plant's seed head.

Useful Plants

Below is a list of useful plants for the temperate region with instructions on how to prepare and use them. I have not attempted to give any detailed description of the species although some of the more important species are shown in photographs. To use this list you will need to back it up with one or more field guides to aid you to a correct identification or better still visit a botanical garden to study these species. Those followed by an asterisk are commonly found in the U.K.

Agave, Century Plant, Mescal (Agave spp.): Agave leaves can be pounded to produce cordage fibres, and if cut cleanly at both ends, water can be drained out of them. But most importantly the young flowering shoot which rises from the rosette of spiky leaves can be eaten. This must be cooked before consumption. The native method is to gather the young stems just after they have emerged but before they have started to flower. These are then cut into suitable-sized lengths and steamed or roasted in a pit oven to produce a fibrous sugary brown mass. This is highly nutritious and sweet tasting. Agave stems can also be effectively dried for long-term storage.

Alder: *(Alnus glutinosa)*:* Alder is a light, easily-carved wood, but its greatest value is as a treatment for upset stomachs. Prepare a weak infusion from the bark.

Alfalfa *(Medicago sativa)*:* This highly nutritious plant is very rich in vitamins A, D and K. Washed, it can be used as part of a backwoods salad. Alternatively it can be dried and used by infusion for tea mixtures. It is not really flavourful enough to stand alone as a tea, so try mixing it with rose hip tea.

Amaranth *(Amaranthus spp):* This plant was used by native peoples as a salad plant although it is on the bitter end of palatability. To overcome this, boil the tenderest young leaves as a pot herb. Later in the year the plant carries heavy quantities of seeds which can be gathered and used for flour or gruel. Some of the tribes of the south-western U.S. cultivated the plant for these seeds.

Angelica, Alexanders *(Angelica sylvestris)*:* A member of the umbellifer family recognisable by its umbrella-like flower heads with stems reminiscent of celery and parsley-like leaves, which contains some highly toxic species (see poisonous plants). Care must be used in the identification of this plant. Growing near water and marshy ground, its bold round flower heads have a light pink tinge; the stems are hollow and downy. The major distinguishing feature is the inflated or swollen sheathing petioles of the small upper leaves on the stem. Cook the peeled stems in several changes of water or cook the tender young roots. This is a good last minute addition to a backwoods stew.

Apple, Crab *(Malus sylvestris)*,* **Apple, American Crab** *(Pyrus spp):* These miniature precursors to our cultivated varieties tend to be too sharp for eating raw. They can however be cooked by roasting or boiling into a mush and used in much the same way as sugar for flavouring other wild foods. Cut out any spoiled or wormy parts before cooking. If you have flour, they can be used to make an apple pie, or as I like them, used as a stuffing in wild game which is steamed. Apple pips should always be discarded as they contain cyanide; this is not normally a problem, but

in survival situations where you may be consuming unusual amounts, is potentially dangerous.

Arrowhead *(Sagittaria spp)*:* Growing at pond margins and in marshy ground, these species gain their name from the distinctive arrow-head-shaped leaf. These plants are a very important source of food for a survivor. The tubers can be gathered from the muddy ooze in which they grow from autumn to early spring, the native method being to wade for them, with bare feet acting as gathering hands. This is not always the chilly business it may seem since the mud at the pond edge is full of decaying humus and usually quite warm. When there is ice on the water you will find an improvised rake more effective. The tubers on average are slightly smaller than a golf ball. They are not palatable when raw but are fine tasty fare when cooked. For cooking treat them in the same ways as you would a potato: boil, roast, bake, mash etc.

Jerusalem artichoke *(Helianthus tuberosus):* Very similar to the wild sunflower, the Jerusalem Artichoke grows to 2–3 metres tall. It is the tuber that can be eaten. This should be gathered from late autumn to early spring. These are about the size of an average potato and can be eaten raw or cooked in all the same ways as a potato. Where it occurs this is an important survival food.

Ash *(Fraxinus spp)*:* The Sioux nation refer to this as weapon wood, or old smelling wood. Both are accurate descriptions of this wonderwood. Ash is straight grained, flexible and strong, especially resilient to shocks. It can be used for making bows, spears, clubs and bowls; the thin shavings make strong bindings and the growth rings of the tree can be separated by soaking and pounding for basket weaving. The keys (seeds) can also be eaten as an emergency food. The leaves can also be used as a compress for infected wounds.

Aspen *(Populus spp):* The leaves and bark of the aspen can be used in decoction for treating wounds and burns as an antiseptic.

Wood avens, Herb bennet *(Geum urbanum)*:* Wood avens is a humble trailside plant of shady woods. As a child it long fascinated me, and it came as no surprise when I learned that it has healing properties. In folklore it was reputed to ward off bad spirits a common association with antiseptic plants, which this plant is. The fresh flowering

Wild crab apple

Wild carrot

Herb bennet

Cattail

Blackberry

Chamomile

Burdock

Wild cherry

Coltsfoot

Japanese knotweed

Ground ivy

Lady's smock

Hawthorn

Mallow

Hazel

Pignut plant   Edible root

herb or dried and powdered root can be used as an infusion for cuts, sores and grazes. A weak infusion (1 teaspoon to a cup) was formerly used for stomach upsets and diarrhoea although I would not recommend that you self medicate internally without expert tuition. The roots of wood avens have a clove-like scent when bruised or broken and can be used as an alternative to clove spices. Wood avens was formerly used as an alternative to quinnine.

Bamboo: Easily recognisable, this grows in thickets, in clearings and particularly along the banks of streams in temperate regions. An extremely useful material, it does not reach the size of the tropical varieties. The young shoots which emerge quickly and in profusion after heavy rains can be eaten. Take only the soft tips and remove the protective hairy sheaths. All of the hairs must be removed as they are an irritant to the human digestive tract. Before eating, the shoots must be well boiled; they may need several boilings before they are palatable depending upon the species and local conditions.

Basswood and Lime trees (*Tilia spp*)*: The outer bark from these trees has been used as roofing material and the inner bark makes excellent cordage. The wood can be used for friction firelighting with drills and saws. The flower used in a cold infusion is used to treat headaches

Spanish Bayonet (*Yucca aloifolia*): see Yucca.

Beech (*Fagus sylvatica*), **American Beech** (*Fagus grandifolia*): Young beech leaves glowing a yellow emerald green always signal the arrival of summer for me. They are also a tasty addition to a backwoods salad or stuffing for a steamed fish. Beech leaf sandwiches are also very good. But it is the autumn harvest of beech nuts that is the most useful of all. The nut kernels which are rich in fat and protein can be eaten raw or roasted; they can be dried for flour or used as a coffee substitute. The only problem is that compared to other nuts they take at least twice the effort to prepare.

Bilberry, Blueberry, Huckleberry (*Vaccinium spp**, *Gaylussacia spp*.): No trailside nibble is tastier on a hot day than a bilberry, but as a survival food its only real value is its flavour. It can be cooked into a tasty morale-boosting drink which should be cooled before drinking, or it can be dried for inclusion in biscuits and soups.

Birch (*Betula spp*)*: The Native American Indians considered plants the 'standing people' each plant belonging to a tribe, each with its own unique features just like humans. Looked at in this way, the birch tree is one of the friendliest of all the standing people, providing us with firelighting materials, containers, glue, building materials, water, sugar, food, medicine and splinting. As mentioned in the water chapter, the sap from the birch can be collected in the spring, this can be processed for sugar in the same way as maple sap. In really hard times the inner bark can be gathered and dried for grinding into an emergency flour. The washed young twigs of birch can be used to produce an infusion which has stomach settling properties. The dried leaves have also been used for this purpose. The bark can be used rolled into a tube as a first-class splint.

Bistort (*Polygonum bistorta*)*: Common in damp upland meadows, this plant can be used as a salad plant or cooked in amongst other food stuffs such as stew or soup. The roots can also be eaten but must first be soaked and then roasted. However, the root is far more useful as a medicine. Dried and powdered it can be used as a dry powder or in an infusion to treat external cuts and bleeding. Infusions or decoctions have strong astringent and antidiarrhoeal properties. It was commonly used in Europe to treat snake bites and by Native American Indians for stings and insect bites.

Blackberry, bramble (*Rubus fructicosus*)*: Apart from the common uses of the edible fruit the brambles leaves can be dried to make an excellent tea substitute. They can also be used in infusion to treat stomach problems and coughs. Bramble stems can also be crushed and split to remove the pithy core for strong cordage fibres.

Bog myrtle, Sweet gale (*Myrica gale*)*: Occurring as a shrub in the boggy wetlands, it has a leathery grey-green narrow leaf. This is the fabled midge repellent used by Scottish ghillies who rub juice from the leaves on the skin. In my experience this offers little or no relief from the little biters but then neither do the most potent modern repellents. Dried, the leaves can be used to make a subtle tea. Unlike many other wild teas this one is very strong if you are not careful. The first time I made this tea my taste buds were knocked senseless by its strength; I had used too many leaves and steeped them for much too long.

Bullace *(Prunus domestica):* The forerunner to the modern cultivated plums, this delicious succulent slightly tart fruit is one of Nature's greatest gifts. As always discard the stone, and then eat it raw or cook it or even split it open for drying. This fruit is an excellent trail nibble once dried. It can be cooked in a pie or the dried fruit can be included in biscuit mixes.

Bulrush *(Scirpus acutus, Scirpus validus):* This plant of biblical fame (not to be confused with *Typha spp*) was providing men with food long before the Bible was written. The tips of the rootstock are rich in starch and sugar; they can be dried and pounded into flour or roasted and eaten. They usually need about three hour's roasting before they are really edible and do not taste like potatoes, having their own rooty flavour. The young shoots and the core at the base of the stem are also edible. While they can both be eaten raw I always boil, or even better, steam them. Bulrushes also produce sufficient quantities of pollen and seeds to make both worth gathering. Pollen is highly nutritious and can be cooked as a gruel or used to bolster wild flours.

Burdock *(Arctium lappa, Arctium minus)*:* Burdock is an important edible plant for survival. Its tender young leaves are rich in vitamins and can be cooked as a pot herb. But most important of all it has a large carbohydrate-rich root. Being a biennial plant its life cycle takes two years to complete. In year one it produces a small cluster of leaves close to the ground; these enable it to gain energy from the sun which is stored in the root as starch and sugar. In the second year it uses this stored energy to send up a flowering stem between 1 and 1.8 metres tall. It is the energy-rich first-year root that is of use to the survivor. This root extends straight down into the soil and can be very difficult to remove. To cook the root the thick rind must be removed before a long steaming or boiling with several changes of water until it loses its tough fibrousness. The root can also be fried but I find the best backwoods use is to include it as part of a soup or stew. The large broad leaves can be used for poultice wrappings and even water scoops or sun hats, and a section of the dried stem can be lashed to a straight hardwood stick for use as a hand-drill fireset.

Burreed *(Sparaganium euricarpum, Sparaganium erectum)*:* Growing amongst rushes and cattails at pond margins and marshes this is a difficult plant to mistake. The tuber can be cooked in the same ways described for the bulrush.

Wild carrot *(Daucus carota)*:* A member of the umbellifer family which includes some extremely poisonous plants. Although care must be taken identifying this species, this plant has a convenient way of identifying itself since in the centre of its white flower head is a single purple flower. It is unmistakable. The root is a cream colour and nowhere near as large as its cultivated cousin, but it is edible. It is best to include it in a stew.

Cattail, greater readmace *(Typha latifolia)*:* The cattail is one of the most important, if not *the* most important plant for survivors. It can be used to provide tinder, fire drills, cordage, basketry materials but most importantly of all it provides food all year round. Cattails, often mistakenly called bulrushes, are commonly found at pond and stream margins and generally boggy ground. They normally grow in extensive clumps which may also harbour the nests of waterfowl perhaps containing eggs.

In the winter the cattail rootstock which can usually be quite easily pulled up, can be used to produce a nutritious flour. Scrape the roots clean of any leeches and general boggy detritus. Now peel them to reveal the core. Crush and pull these apart in a large container of water. The water will become murky and milky as the starch in the root is separated from the fibres. Once the fibres are well washed, remove them and repeat the process with more fresh fibres until the water is very milky. Now leave the starch to settle and separate out from the water. The water can then be poured off and the whitish residue allowed to dry. Add more clean water and stir the mixture up to wash it. You may need to repeat this several times before you achieve a pure white residue. Once the residue has settled and as much of the water poured off as is possible, it can be used to make drop scones by simply mixing the flour with water into a runny batter and pouring it onto a hot stone. As they cook try dropping into the mixture some dried fruit.

In early spring the cattail begin to send up new shoots. These can be peeled and steamed, or lightly boiled for a tender meal. They are

Prickly pear   **Yucca**   **Wild strawberry**

Ramsons   **Thistle**

Wild raspberry   **Violet**

Rosehip   **Wood sorrel**

Yarrow

Jew's ear

Bladderwrack

Horn of plenty

Chicken of the woods

Inkcap

Dryad's saddle

Lycoperdon perlatum

edible raw but it is better to cook them in case they contain any parasites. These shoots grow rapidly into stalks which can be gathered and peeled for eating in this way until they are about half a metre tall.

By late spring the green flower spikes are beginning to emerge from a sheath of protective leaves. These can be collected and boiled, or steamed and eaten in the same way as corn on the cob.

By summer the flower heads have matured and are heavy with a protein-rich pollen. This can be gathered by bending the flowerhead over a basket and tapping them with a stick. Large quantities of this pollen can easily be gathered in this way. Dried, it can be stored for use as gruel or mixed in with rootstock flower.

As the wheel of the year turns full circle, cattails send out finger-size horn-shaped shoots from the base of the root stock. These can be collected and boiled for food. The rootstock to which they are attached is also edible if prepared like a potato. While good emergency food, I find this to be an acquired taste.

I have also heard of the ripened seed heads being burned to separate out the seeds from the down, but find this less practical and a waste of the down—one of the most useful parts of the plant. Down can not only be used as tinder, but is important as an absorbent dressing for wounds.

Do not confuse the root of the wild iris for that of cattails. This is an easy mistake for the tenderfoot to make and if in doubt taste a small piece of the root. Cattails should be virtually tasteless; iris tastes quite disgusting.

Cedar (*Thuja spp*): Cedar is a very useful wood. It can be used for making bows and building materials, and is very suitable for steam-bending. On the northwest coast of America the native inhabitants would steam-bend large planks of cedar to make cooking boxes. The bark has many uses for cordage and basket weaving. The wood is also a good choice for friction firelighting. The inner bark has also been made into flour in times of famine

Chamomile (*Chamaemelum nobile*)*:A familiar name from the shelves of herbal teas in a health shop. Chamomile tea has soothing and calming effects, easing a good night's sleep for the muscle-weary survivor who has struggled to construct his shelter. It can also be used in infusion as a mild antiseptic. Gather the plant in flower (preferably) and dry it in shade.

Cherries (*Prunus avium,* * *P. Virginiana, P. serotina*): Cherry trees contain prunasin, a cyanogenic glycoside which is particularly concentrated in the leaves and seeds (being most potent in dry years, and in Prunus serotina, the black cherry). For this reason all cherry pits (stones) should be discarded and preferably the fruit should be cooked. Most of the wild cherry species are too bitter for consumption raw in any case. The way I usually use wild cherries is dried and incorporated in pemmican.

Horse Chestnut and buckeyes (*Aesculus spp*)*: A hard wood which resists decay, it makes for good firewood and can be carved into beautiful bowls and containers. The fruit is poisonous but the wood can be used safely for cooking utensils.

Chickweed (*Stellaria media*)*: Chickweed can be used as part of a salad or used as a pot herb. It does however contain saponins so should not be consumed in large quantities. Because of its saponin content it can be used as a soap plant (see soapwort).

Chicory, wild succory (*Cichorium intybus*)*: The most commonly used part of the chicory plant is the swollen root which is roasted until brown and then ground up and used as coffee; this coffee is very bitter. In Europe the roots were forced in warmth and darkness to produce chicons, bleached stems which were a popular salad ingredient. You can achieve more or less the same by gathering the leaves where they disappear underground. The green tender leaves of the plant can be used as a pot herb.

Chufa, nut grass (*Cyperus usculentus*): This plant is common to many parts of the world from the temperate steppe to the tropical rainforests. The tubers spread out from the base of the stem, each ending in a small tuber just slightly larger then a large acorn. The rind on these tubers must be removed before consumption; they can be eaten raw or can be boiled if unpleasantly dry. These tubers can also be dried and ground up for flour. A cold drink can be produced by soaking the tubers and then crushing them in clean water, or they can be roasted and used as coffee.

Goosegrass, cleavers (*Galium aparine*)*:

The name cleavers comes from this plant's habit of cleaving to your clothes as you pass by; a walk through summer undergrowth where this plant is in residence will cover you in the small green seeds which cling like velcro. But this is an easy way to gather a coffee, for those seeds roasted and ground up make a coffee substitute. The sticky green stems of this plant before it goes to seed can be used as a pot herb when cooked like spinach, although they are not the best.

Coltsfoot (*Tusilago farfara*)*: Coltsfoot is a multifaceted plant for the survivor; its young flower buds, flowers and leaves can be added to salads. The leaves can be dried and used in decoction as an antiseptic or tea. They can also be burned to produce a salt-like seasoning, although in my experience this has a stronger charcoal flavour than salty flavour. In the bush on the move, this is one of the native warrior's medicine plants: a cut or wound could be treated by washing the leaf and then crushing it up before application to the wound as an antiseptic. Although scorned upon by modern medical practice, the natural way to accomplish this was to simply chew the leaf and then spit it on.

Dandelion (*Taraxacum officinale*)*: Medicinally the humble dandelion is greatly valued for its soothing effect upon the digestive system. As a stimulant for appetite it makes a nutritious part of any backwoods feast. The plant contains vitamins A, B and C. All parts are edible; the leaves can be eaten raw or cooked as greens, as can the root. The root of a large dandelion can be as large as an adult's finger. The most common use for the dandelion is the roasted and ground root which is a coffee substitute. The leaves are tasty raw.

Dock (*Rumex obtusifolius*)*: There was a time when every British school boy or girl knew that the dock leaf can be used to ease the sting of a nettle, but times have changed. The dock leaf is a common and useful plant; its tenderest young leaves can be cooked as spinach. To use the dock leaf to relieve stinging nettle stings it is no use just rubbing the leaf on the stings as most people do, as hardly any of the plants juices are released in this way. Instead, rub the leaf between your palms quite vigorously until the juices are released, and then smear this onto the stings. After a few seasons' gathering nettles for cordage and food, you will hardly notice their sting.

Elder (*Sambucus nigra*)*: Elder is another one of those especially useful plants for the survivor. As a food plant it is of very little use: the green leaves, stem, roots and fruit are all poisonous. The flowers and ripe fruit however can be eaten. The flowers can be dipped in batter and fried as fritters; batter can be obtained from wild flours. The berries contain important vitamins and minerals and despite their small size can be gathered easily in large quantities. Raw, they are foul smelling and tasting, but lose this disagreeable characteristic when cooked or dried. They are especially good dried and added to pemmican or backwoods drop scones.

As a utility plant the elder wins its spurs; it grows straight tall shoots sometimes up to two metres long. With careful management it is possible to ensure that a particular shoot grows straight and true, I once so managed a shoot over several years to make a blowpipe. The shoots are of a dense hard wood with a soft pithy core, this can be pushed out to make a drinking tube (SEASONED WOOD), or an inspiring straw for blowing a slow fire to life. But probably the most important use is as a hand-drill fire-starting drill. A dry, seasoned, elder shoot is just about the best hand drill there is, but even when it can only be had green, it is still useful. A short length of another fire-starting wood which is dry enough can be pushed into the pith of a well-lashed elder shoot. This is particularly useful as the chances of finding a short length of suitable wood are far greater than finding a long section.

Medicinally, elder flower when taken as an infusion has been used for creating a sweat.

Ground ivy, gill over the ground (*Glechoma hederacea*): Ground ivy is not to be confused with wood ivy trailing along the ground. In fact it bears no resemblance to wood ivy whatsoever. A small plant with lavender flowers, it makes a strong herbal tea when dried or the young shoots can be used as a salad ingredient or better still a pot herb; it makes a good addition for soups and stews.

Goldenrod (*Solidago virgaurea*,* *S. odora*): The dried leaves of these plants can be brewed for a liquorice-like tea. The flowering tops can be used in infusion to treat cuts and abrasions as well as burns.

Good King Henry (*Chenopodium bonus-henricus*)*: 'Good King Henry and the

You can always recognise those who have learned to make friends with plants.

Goosefoots' may sound like a sixties rock group but they are in fact the best wild greens that the survivor can find. The others include Lambs Quarters, Red Goosefoot and the Common and Spearleaved Oraches. The seeds from these plants can also be used as seasoning for soup, cooked with water into a nourishing gruel or even gathered for flour making. But the most important use of this plant is as a cooked green, boiled or best of all steamed. If you have backwoods flour available, try mixing some steamed and slightly dried and diced goosefoot with it before cooking on a hot stone as a savoury dropscone.

Ground elder (*Aegopodium podagraria*)*: This plant is a member of the umbellifer family, having a distinctive white umbrella-shaped flower head. It is difficult to mistake for the poisonous umbellifers; its leaves are very similar in shape to those of the elder, hence its name. Rarely more than a metre tall, it likes the shady conditions of the edge of woodland. For food, the tender leaves and shoots can be used as spinach. Medicinally this plant has a long history of use particularly during the medieval period when it was cultivated by monasteries and country herbalists. For backcountry use it is most valuable used in infusion for cuts, grazes and burns. It can also be used as a compress to ease insect stings.

Ground nuts (*Apios americana*): Found in dense cover, particularly along stream and river banks, ground nuts were one of the commonest emergency foods used by backwoodsmen in the early history of the U.S. On the famous St Francis raid by Rogers Rangers during the French and Indians war, it was ground nuts and lily roots that were the 'wretched subsistence' afforded to his men by the wilderness when they discovered that the rescue party they were expecting had paddled back to base leaving only a burned out fire. The tubers, which are about the size of a horse chestnut, occur along a thread-like root. They can be eaten raw although are better eaten boiled or included in a stew.

Hawthorn (*Crataegus spp*)*: Hawthorn is a very useful tree; its wood is dense and hard—although not resilient to shocks and blows—and it is prone to cracking. It is fine to carve and fashion into tools, (where the strength of ash is not needed) and is an attractive dark yellow colour, turning orange as it seasons. Producing a profusion of thorns, this is an ideal wood for making fish hooks. As the tree grows, the lower thorns die and become brittle, making ideal fire kindling. These brittle thorny twigs are traditionally called 'tinkers sticks' because tinkers, romanies and other folk of the road would use them for their fires; hawthorn being a common roadside tree. Tinker's sticks can be found dry under the canopy of a mature hawthorn even under the heaviest downpours.

This tenacious and hardy tree also provides food; the tenderest young spring leaves can be added to salads and the fruit or 'haws' can be added to pemmican once the stones have been removed. They are very bland though. Hawthorn thickets are also excellent places to trap: many rabbit-sized mammals rely upon the thorny cover for their homes and protective cover.

Hazel *(Corylinus avellana spp)*: The 'cob nut' tree (hazel) grows fast to give long straight shoots, which made it the natural choice for coppicing. Cut cleanly close to the ground—two or more shoots will rise from where one stood previously; in some parts of southwest Britain there are coppice 'stools' which are over a metre in diameter showing many years of successful coppicing. This wood is one of the most useful a survivor will find. Because it grows in straight shoots it is the natural choice for arrow wood; even the Californian Indians used this wood for arrows. Hazel can also be split for wattle and hurdle making. It makes ideal cooking material: split sticks for fish spits or meat, and tongs for moving hot stones. It can be easily bent into hoops and will retain its shape when seasoned. In the autumn it produces hazel nuts which can be gathered or eaten just before they fully ripen and drop. The nut can also be dried and ground into flour. Medicinally the bark and leaves can be used in decoction to treat slow-healing wounds.

Horse radish *(Armoracia rusticana)*: On first acquaintance this plant resembles dock but once you are fully familiar you will be able to recognise it from a distance at a glance. A quick test is to crush the juice from the leaf or stem; if you are right there will be no mistaking the overpowering horseradish smell. Because of its powerful taste and smell it is only the horseradish fan or hardy,

solitude-loving, gastronome who can stomach the flavour of young horseradish leaves in a salad. But one such leaf in an average sized backwoods stew will be a welcome flavouring, as will be a small amount of the sliced root. Beware overdoing it, the strength of the flavour is legendary. The dried powdered root can also be used in a poultice as an antiseptic, although frequent applications to one area of skin have been known to cause a rash.

Jack by the hedge, hedge garlic *(Alliaria petiolata)*: A strong-flavoured plant; a few leaves added to a wild salad make for an interesting flavour. When crushed the leaves give off a strong garlic smell. The juice from the leaves or a decoction from the leaves can be used for cuts and other slow-healing wounds.

Jewel weed *(Impatiens capensis*, I. pallida)*: The juice from this plant is one of the traditional remedies for poison ivy rash, although I am yet to be totally convinced of its efficaciousness. It can also be used for nettle rash. The young shoots of jewel weed can be cooked by boiling in several changes of water, which should be discarded.

Juniper *(Juniperus spp)*: In Britain, juniper used to be a plant associated with magic. Tied over doors and burned as incense, it was said to drive away evil spirits and demons. Dreaming of the juniper was considered extremely meaningful and various interpretations could be made concerning the detailed nature of the dream. The tree used to be common on the chalk hills in the south of England, but in recent years many of these bushes have disappeared, crowded out by an unstemmed tide of hawthorn.

As a survival plant, the juniper is very useful: its wood can be used for friction firelighting; its peeling bark can be used as grade one tinder, and in those regions where it grows as a tree, it can be used for bow wood. The finest junipers I have seen are those that tenaciously cover the sun scorched tops of the mesas in New Mexico. Even now if I use a juniper hand-drill hearth and the sweet smell of the smoke brings memories flooding back. For food, the juniper berries and the inner bark can be used. The inner bark is white and fibrous and can be dried and pounded into a sort of flour. The ripe blue berries, a traditional seasoning for game, can be rubbed into a roasting joint, or they can be split open dried in the sun and then ground up for adding to other flours or including as flavouring for soups and stews. Well-seasoned juniper wood can also be used for smoking meats, imparting its own flavour.

Kinnikinik, bearberry *(Arctostaphylos uva-ursi)**, **Alpine bearberry** *(A. alpinus)*:* A plant of the mountains, the berries can be cooked for food, but they are not palatable when raw. The dried leaves are the kinnikinik that the native American valued so dearly for his tobacco mixes.

Japanese knotweed *(Polygonum cuspidatum)**, *(Reynoutria japonica)*:* This species was introduced to Britain in 1825 as a garden variety since when it has escaped and taken root all over the country. A gardener I know once tried to reclaim a part of his garden from this voracious weed and only succeeded when he resorted to a chainsaw and flame gun! But for the backwoodsman this is a useful plant; the young sprouting shoots can be gathered and boiled or steamed like asparagus; they do not taste like asparagus but have a sharp flavour all their own. The rind and green inner walls can be scraped from the fibrous bamboo-like inner wall of the stem and used as a sort of rhubarb. The first time I tried this I followed a recipe for cooking a knotweed pie which specified using chopped peeled stems. The result was tasty but totally inedible as the filling was as woody as if I had used chopped mature bamboo. Prepare the knotweed carefully before use, scraping it and chopping it extremely finely; the flavour is remarkable and a welcome change from the usual bitter wild flavours.

Lady's smock, cuckoo flower *(Cardamine pratensis)*:* Lady's smock is one of my personal favourite flowers; a sure harbinger of spring. It is also a useful food plant, rich in vitamin C; it makes an excellent addition to backcountry salads bringing a delicate peppery cress-like flavour to the dish.

Lambs quarter, fat hen *(Chenopodium album):* Use in the same way as already described for Good King Henry.

Pond lilies *(Nuphar spp)*:* Pond lilies are an excellent source of food for emergencies. The large rootstocks can be cooked like potatoes, although they need four or five changes of water. Not my favourite food, it never seems to lose its strong flavour which is reminiscent of stagnant water. The seeds can be collected and dried for use as flour.

Water lilies *(Nymphaea spp)*:* Water lilies are also a first rate source of food if not a little better than their pond lily relatives. The seeds can be used in the same manner as above; the young shooting leaves and developing flower heads can be steamed, or best of all the tubers which branch off from the rootstock can be pulled out of the mud and cooked as potatoes.

Mallow *(Malva spp)*:* The beautiful flowers of mallow are one of my favourite sights in late summer, the young leaves of these plants particularly common mallow *(Malva sylvestris)** are a good green addition to soups and stews. The seeds called cheeses by country folk, are also a tasty nibble. The plant normally grows in large bushy clumps and is a particularly attractive habitat to many insects so the leaves must always be washed well before use.

Stinging nettle *(Urtica dioica)*:* This plant can even be found in the dark! Fortunately its stings disappear once cooked. The tender tops and leaves should be boiled with several changes of water and used as spinach. They can also be useful as the base for stews and soups. Dried, the leaves make an excellent herbal tea. The dried stems provide one of the best natural fibres for cordage.

Oak *(Quercus spp)*:* Apart from oak's legendary strength it produces one of the most important of all wild fruits: the humble acorn. The only problem is that the high concentration of tannin in the nut makes it taste bitter. There are several ways to remove this bitter taste: for example the nuts can be buried over winter until the taste has faded or they can be placed in a basket in a running stream for some days. The method I have found most useful is to shell the kernels and then crush them (not too finely), so that you have a granular mass. Now place this in a piece of clothing which is to act as a muslin cooking bag. This bag is then secured and boiled in repeated changes of water until the water no longer strains brown from the tannin. This done, the meal can be either cooked immediately into a nourishing gruel or dried and ground into high-quality cooking flour. Acorns can also be roasted and used for coffee.

Common orache *(Atriplex patula),* **Spear-leaved orache** *(Atriplex hastata):* Used in the same way as already described for Good King Henry.

Pignut *(Conopodium majus)*:* No relation to the pignut tree found in North America, the pignut is a delicate member of the umbellifer family and without any doubt my favourite wild food. It appears in the early summer in grassland and at the edges of woodland, or along the sides of woodland trails where the sun penetrates the canopy. It is the root of the plant that we are after. Despite its small size above ground, occasionally you will find a root which is almost the size of a golf ball, although for the most part they are about the same size as a hazel nut. Digging this root out of the ground is no easy task however as the stem turns a ninety degree angle at the root, narrowing to a very weak thread thickness. Great care has to be exercised as you follow the stem down to avoid breaking the stem off and losing your way to the root, You can easily identify the root: it is roundish and knobbly and if squeezed, the skin parts easily revealing a creamy white inner surface. Tasting like a cross between a radish and a cob nut these are a delicious addition to a salad or eaten on their own raw. They can be cooked but there is little advantage to be gained. The only preparation which needs to be carried out is to squeeze off the outer skin.

Pines *(Pinus spp)*:* **The pinon pine** *(p. monophylla):* Pine trees are one of the most important sources of wild food. The white inner bark when dried and ground into flour has been used for centuries as an emergency food in many widely varying regions of the world. This flour is highly nutritious but has an overpowering pine flavour when cooked so any other flavourings you can add will help. Young pine needles can be steeped in hot water to produce a popular herb tea, rich in vitamin C and A. Never boil the needles for the tea as this reduces the vitamin C content.

The pinon pine is even more important as it contains the famous pinon nut. These nuts are in fact seeds; every pine produces seeds from its cones which are edible but few are large enough to be worth gathering. The pinon cones are gathered in quantity and then roasted by the fire to loosen the seeds which are then simply knocked out. Once you have shelled them you can either eat them raw or parch them further in the shells and grind them up into a flour.

Greater plantain *(Plantago major)*:* This common trailside plant is a useful source of food because of its wide availability. The washed tender young leaves can be used raw

in a salad or boiled as a green but for the most part I find this a little too bitter for my palate. The seeds from the 'rats tail' seed stalk can be gathered for use in stews and soups. The best use the plant can be put to is as an antiseptic used in infusion or as a poultice.

Prickly pear *(Opuntia spp):* Despite its armour of thorns, the prickly pear is good fare. The ovoid fruit which occurs on the top of the pad can be eaten by slicing away the top and peeling away the thorny outer skin. The seed-filled interior of this fruit can be eaten whole or the seeds spat out dried and ground up into a flour. The prickly pear pads can also be eaten. Scrape away the thorns and peel the pad then slice it into thin strips; these can be eaten raw, boiled or best of all fried.

Ramsons, wild garlic *(Alluim urisnum*, A. spp):* Very strong flavoured, these members of the onion family can often be detected from their odour alone. The young tender leaves can be cooked as a pot herb or used in salads; the flower stalks make an excellent spring ·onion substitute; and the bulbs can be added to stews.

Wild raspberry *(Rubus idaeus)*:* A favourite wild fruit, it needs little introduction save to say that apart from the fruit being eaten raw or cooked, the leaves can be dried for use as a tea—the perfect wild tea combination being a mixture of blackberry and raspberry leaves.

Red goosefoot *(Chenopodium rubrum)*:* Use as already described for Good King Henry.

Reed *(Phragmites communis)*:* The seeds of the reeds can be gathered for use as flour and the young stems can be dried and ground for flour; this is very rich in sugar and can be heated near a fire until it bubbles up and browns like to marsh mallows. The stems can also be lightly crushed so that the plant exudes a sugary gum. After some days, depending upon the weather and moisture available, enough of this gum can be gathered from several plants to be used as sweets. Reed stems also make good light and fast arrow shafts.

Rose *(Rosa canina)*:* The wild rose provides an important source of food in the form of hips. These are extremely rich in vitamin C. They are however slow to gather and prepare for eating. Bright orange, they are easily spotted on the bush against the winter snow, a welcome sight for any outdoorsman or woman on the winter trail. The leaves and hips can be infused to give one of the best soothing herbal teas, and the hips can be eaten raw or included in other recipes. Before use however, the hips must be split open and the hairy pips inside removed as they can irritate the digestive tract.

Marsh samphire (*Salicornia europaea*)*: This tasty plant grows in the silt of salt marshes and tidal inlets; only the healthy emerald green specimens should be gathered. They are cooked by steaming or boiling in a small amount of water for about ten minutes. The succulent green parts are then pulled off the fibrous stem with your teeth. Be sure to warn your friends though as this plant is very rich in soda and can have interesting though not alarming effects on your digestive system.

Sorrel (*Rumax spp*)*: Sharper flavoured than dock, sorrel can be used in the same ways as already described, makes a very good addition to fish dishes.

Sea purslane (*Halimione portulacoides*)*: Another lover of the salt marsh, sea purslane grows in bushy clumps which usually require some wading to reach. Wash this plant thoroughly and boil in a little water as a green. If it tastes very salty you may need to change the water several times.

Soapwort, bouncing bet (*Saponaria officinalis*)*: This plant is poisonous yet very useful as a soap. The leaves and stems are crushed with water and used as a detergent; no soap that I know of leaves your skin feeling as clean and silky smooth as this natural alternative.

Wild strawberry (*Fragaria vesca*)*: This delicate fruit is even more tasty than its cultivated cousin although it is smaller. Its leaves can also be used dried as a herbal tea.

Sycamore (*Acer pseudoplatanus*)*: The sycamore provides wood for friction fire lighting and tool making and can be tapped for its sap just as can birches and maples. This sap is much less sugary than birch or maple but can be used as an emergency source of water in areas of heavy contamination, both for drinking and cooking.

Sea beet (*Beta vulgaris*)*: As suggested by its name, this is a plant of the sea shore, and believed to be the ancestor of the cultivated beets. The underground parts have no uses but the leaves can be cooked as a pot herb.

Sloe berry, blackthorn (*Prunus spinosa*)*: Blackthorn is a hard dense wood with a pinky orange color. It is a traditional favourite for poachers throwing sticks and clubs. The thorns can be used for fish hooks. In early spring this tree flowers with beautiful white flowers which look from a distance like little star-filled explosions of dazzling white. The sloe berry can be used for food. After the stones have been removed from the berries they can be dried for use in pemmican and flours or better still, cooked in just enough water to cover them. This removes the unpalatable tart quality of these berries, forming a sort of plum paste. This goes very well with backwoods drop scones and other fruit concoctions.

Thistle (*Cirsium spp*)*: Despite their ferocious spiny leaves and stems, thistles are an important source of emergency food: the tender young stems can be peeled and eaten raw and the young leaves can be boiled as a green (they lose their prickle when cooked). Like burdock, thistles are biennials, the roots of the first year plant can be peeled and eaten raw or better still added to a stew. Most novel of all the thistle foods is the flower button of the spear thistle (*Cirsium vlgare*)*. By opening the flower head up a button can be found at the base of the flower which is a creamy white colour discolouring quickly upon exposure to air. This is a tasty nut-like treat.

Violets (*Viola spp*)*: Rich in vitamins, violets are another useful edible plant. The young leaves can be used as part of a salad or cooked in stews soups or as a green. A tea can also be made from the dried leaves. Used in infusion, the leaves are an effective treatment for mouth sores and sore throats.

Watercress (*Nastutium officinale*)*: This is a first-class salad plant, though it must be well washed. It can be differentiated from fools watercress by its untoothed leaf edge, and less regularly ribbed stem.

Willow (*Salix spp*)*: A springy wood green, it becomes brittle when dry. Traditionally used for twitch up arms of traps and basket weaving it can also be used for friction firelighting. The bark of the two to three-year-old stems contain salicylic acid and can be gathered and used in infusion as aspirin. This is one of the most effective backwoods remedies, although it is very bitter tasting.

Rosebay willow herb (*Epilobium augustifolium*)*: Known as fire weed by the North American Indians because of its appearance on ground recently burned out, its distinctive flowers can be seen at a great distance. The young spring roots of this plant can be added to stews, the young shoots can be steamed or boiled. The older shoots can be peeled and the core used for flour dried and crushed. The young leaves can be used in infusion either fresh or dried to treat headaches. This tea is very rich in vitamin C.

Wood sorrel (*Oxalis acetosella,* * *Oxalis spp*): This small plant grows in clumps preferring shady spots of the forest floor. While it should not be consumed in any quantity, its apple peel flavour is a welcome change to the more common bitter-flavoured wild plants. It is best eaten raw as a salad plant although I have used it successfully to reduce the bitterness of soups and teas made from less palatable species.

Yarrow (*Achillea millefolium*)*: This is a very powerful medicinal herb, so much so that it would be very unwise to use it as an edible plant. Pregnant women should not use it under any circumstances. Used throughout the world from ancient Greece to North America, it is traditionally used for treating wounds, both to reduce the flow of blood as a haemostat and to prevent infection as an antiseptic. It can also be used to induce perspiration when used as a strong infusion and can reduce your natural protection from sunburn.

Having read about these uses I determined to put this wonder drug to my own test. Gathering the plant from amongst tall grass where it was forced to grow tall, I dried the stalks and leaves in the shade and then powdered them. As described in the second chapter I ended up using the plant to treat a worse cut than I bargained for, but it worked extremely well. The powder applied to the wound absorbed the blood and stuck tight to the wound forming an artificial scab, and so stopping the bleeding very quickly. Once I had returned to modern hygienic comfort I removed the scab to clean the wound. The scab did not break up as I expected but held together, coming off cleanly like a cast. The wound was clean and had begun to heal, I suspect that in the past such a scab may have been left in place. I then washed the wound with a strong infusion of the dried yarrow which I continued to use in place of conventional antiseptic with no ill effects. I relied upon a modern dressing to hold the wound closed but am certain the original scab would have done the job. This experiment was not scientific and I am not suggesting that you use herbs solely in place of modern medicine but if you have no other alternatives available to you, yarrow would seem to be a useful stopgap.

Yew (*Taxus baccata*)*: Yew is a poisonous tree especially the seeds, the green wood should never be used for cooking utensils or cooking fuel and while spoons and bowls can be made from this wood it should not be used for long term food or water storage. The wood is hard and springy an ideal choice for spear or harpoon heads as well as its traditional use in bowmaking.

Yucca, Spanish bayonet (*Yucca spp*): This plant of arid and desert regions has blade shaped leaves with a sharp spike at the tip. It is an extremely useful plant. The fresh leaves crushed and broken up in water can be used as a backcountry soap, and the fibres of the leaves make very strong cordage. But on top of this it also provides food; the waxy flowers can be eaten raw in salads and the succulent fruit can be cooked. To prepare the fruit cut it in half longitudinally and remove the fibre and seeds then steam the remaining parts.

Seaweeds

When gathering seaweeds for food gather only those healthy-looking specimens that are firmly attached to rock by a hold fast. Despite their unpalatable appearance seaweeds are a valuable food stuff high in mineral content. Gather them by cutting them half a metre from the hold fast, this will ensure that they grow back. For food, all of the seaweeds listed below can be boiled for use in soups and stews, the more tender varieties can be eaten raw. One of the best ways to use seaweed is to dry it and then grind it up into a powder which can be used to thicken and flavour soups and stews. Before use, all seaweeds must be thoroughly cleaned. Some of the seaweeds such as laver can be boiled until they break down or can be easily mashed into a puree or soup. Of the hundreds of different seaweed species only the sea sorrels *(Desmarestia aculeata, ligulate* and *viridis)* pose a problem because they contain sufficient levels of sulphuric to cause severe stomach cramps. It is unlikely that sufficient quantity will be eaten to cause death.

Edible kelp, dabberlocks *(Alaria esculenta)**

Kelp, carweed *(Laminaria digita)**

Sweet oar weed, sugar kelp *(Laminaria saccharina)**

Sea lettuce *(Ulva lactuca)**

Carragheen, Irish moss *(Chondrus crispus)**

Dulse *(Rhodymenia palmata)**

Bladder wrack *(Fucus vesiculosus)**

'No common name' *(Enteromorpha intestinalis)**

Laver *(Porphyra umbilicalis)**

Mosses and Lichens

The lichens and mosses listed below are edible. Like seaweed they can be dried and powdered for use in soups and stews acting as thickening and flavouring agents.

Reindeer moss *(Cladonia rangiferina)*: A survival food of the Lapps this plant can be boiled down into a jelly useful for thickening stews. Before use it should be soaked for several hours to lose its bitter taste.

Iceland moss *(Cetraria islandica)*: Used as for reindeer moss.

Rock tripe *(Umblicaria pustulata)*: Cook this in the same way as seaweed allowing it a slow simmer to cook.

Fungi

Fungi are surrounded in superstition and mystery which coupled with the fact that some species are lethally toxic has led to their being virtually completely ignored as a source of food in the U.K. Those few people who can recognise the edible varieties and appreciate their subtle flavours are regarded as being a little eccentric. In Europe, however many of the wild species are greatly valued for their culinary qualities and traded alongside the humble cultivated mushroom. In survival situations a knowledge of edible fungi will open a world of flavours otherwise closed to you.

Much nonsense is spoken about the value of learning fungi for survival purposes, so let us get it right. Fungi are a useful food supply but do not come before many of the plants already listed in importance because of their mainly unpredictable season and appearance. They are a resource which can only be taken advantage of when present, whereas plants can be more easily hunted for with greater certainty of success.

Poisonous fungi: The threat from poisonous fungi is very real, some species are extremely toxic and with no known antidotes. The death cap *(Amanita phalloides)** for example once ingested will not cause any symptoms of poisoning for up to two days, by which time the damage done is irreparable. Death from this species is regarded as being fifty to ninety per cent certain. The rule for gathering fungi is the same as for any wild food NEVER EAT ANY WILD FOOD YOU HAVE NOT POSITIVELY IDENTIFIED AS EDIBLE. Again, despite what you may have heard to the contrary there is no shortcut to learning the edible species from the poisonous species.

Before you begin to learn to forage for fungi you should acquaint yourself with the poisonous varieties listed below. Of these the most dangerous are those members of the Amanita family. They have certain characteristic features which should be considered danger signs and are a fungus to be avoided. The features to watch for are a notably bulbous base from which the stem rises, and a skirt or veil just below the cap which may in some cases have detached or fallen off. Any cap that has white gills should be avoided.

Poisonous Fungi

All members of the Amanita family *(Amanita spp)*: The following are particularly common:

The death cap *(Amanita phalloides)**

Destroying angel *(Amanita virosa)**

Panther cap *(Amanita pantherina)**

Fly agaric *(Amanita muscaria)**

All members of the Inocybe family *(Inocybe spp)*: *(Cortinarius speciosissimus)** and *(C. orellanus)** rare in U.K. These species have been confused with the chanterelle.

*(Gyromitra esculenta)**

*(Entoloma sinuatum)**

*(Paxillus involutus)**

The yellow staining mushroom *(Agaricus xanthodermus)**

The devils boletus *(Boletus satanus)**

The common earthball *(Scleroderma aurantium)**

Having familiarised yourself with these fungi you can begin to learn the edible varieties. The edible fungi listed below are chosen because of their common occurrence and difficulty to mistake with the dangerous varieties. Make certain that you remove the fungus you are examining from the ground intact so that you can identify it correctly. Apart from the obvious physical characteris-:ics your field guide will most likely rely upon relevant habitat details as well so if you are removing the fungi to another location for analysis take note of the habitat in which you found it.

Edible Fungi

Braket fungi: These are fungi that are commonly found growing on trees:

The beef steak fungus (*Fistulina hepatica*)*

The cauliflower fungus, brain fungus (*Sparassis crispa*)*

Chicken of the woods (*Laetiporus sulphureus*)*

Dryads saddle (*Polyporous squamosus*)*

The honey fungus (*Armillaria mellea*)*

The jews ear fungus (*Auricularia auricula-judae*)*

The oyster fungus (*Pluerotus ostreatus*)*

Ground fungi: These fungi will be found growing from the ground:

Field blewit (*lepista saeva*)*

Wood blewit (*Lepista nuda*)*

Ceps: This family of fungi are widely regarded as the safest for gathering by survivors or beginners. While some varieties have been known to cause upset stomachs, deaths are rare. Easily recognised by the sponge-like surface to the underside of the cap those species listed below are common and excellent eating. If you have any doubt with this family stick to those with caps whose underside is yellow or light brown in colour and avoid those which are orange or red tinged.

Cep, penny bun (*Boletus edulis*)*

Bay boletus (*B. badius*)*

Larch boletus (*B. elegans*)*

Slippery Jack (*B. luteaus*)*

'No common name' (*B. apendiculatus*)*

'No common name' (*B erythropus*)*

Orange birch bolete (*Leccinum verispelle*)*

Chanterelle (*Cantharellus cibarius*)*

Fairy ring champignon (*Marasmius oreades*)*

Field mushrooms: These are of the same family as the cultivated mushroom. Many are edible and good eating, however care must be exercised in identification and any that

discolour yellow when bruised should be discarded. The following are the best edible species.

The horse mushroom (*Agaricus arvensis*)*

The prince (*A. augusta*)*

The field mushroom (*A. campestris*)*

The wood mushroom (*A. silvicola*)*

'No common name' (*A. bitorquis*)*

Hedgehog fungus (*Hydnum repandum*)*

Horn of plenty (*Craterellus cornucopioides*)*

Shaggy ink cap (*Coprinus comatus*)*

Morels (*Morchella esculenta*)*

Common morel (*M. vulgaris*)*

Parasol (*Lepiota procera*)*

Shaggy parasol (*L. rhacodes*)*

Puffballs: There is a danger with this family that in identifying the smaller of these species, you will mistake the golf-ball-like early stage of a poisonous amanita for a puffball, or confuse an earthball for a puffball. Both of these problems can be avoided by cutting the fungus in half. If it is a developing amanita you will see a developing cap. If it is an earthball the centre will be brown or with the very youngest earthballs slightly yellowish. In both cases discard the fungus, even edible varieties of puffball should only be eaten when the centre is a pure virginal white.

When puffballs have become little bags of spores they have medicinal value, since the earliest times being used as a haemostatic, the powder being directly pounded onto a wound to stop the bleeding.

The giant puffball (*Langermannia gigantea*)*

'No common name' (*L. perlatum*)*

'No common name' (*Calvatia utriformis*)*

'No common name' (*C. excipuliformis*)*

Preparing, Using and Storing Fungi

Fungi should be collected when fresh and young and this is particularly important with the bracket fungi. If they are wormy or part eaten cut out the damaged sections, the fungi can now be used immediately or dried for later addition to soups and stews. When drying fungi string them on a wand of willow or similar wood and hang them in a dry part of your shelter they can even be smoked lightly, the more fleshy varieties such as the brackets and boletus varieties dry best if they are cut into 5mm thick slices and laid out in the sun. Only place them together in a container when they are thoroughly dry. Do not be afraid to mix varieties of dried fungus. Horn of plenty and the boletus fungi are exceptional as stew and soup additives when dried. All fungi used in backwoods conditions should be cooked. They can be sliced thin and fried or simmered in water or added to stews. Some are better than others—the Chicken of the Woods is a really exceptional fungus; slice this thin and sauté or stew it. Fungi can be used as stuffing to meat dishes and baked in a backwoods oven.

Fungi are, as I am certain you will discover, a fascinating and absorbing study. They have many uses beyond just food. Many have been used commercially for tinder, some for sharpening razors. One particular lady I have met, can actually manufacture leather from fungus!

Hunting

· 'He saw how if a man were to break a stick or shout or
otherwise betray his presence, the whole forest would freeze,
united in silence against the intruder. He saw that the
Indians moved silently, and were themselves as much a part
of nature as the animals they hunted.'

(Lovat Dickson writing of Grey Owl)

It is in hunting that the backwoodsman graduates, carrying his awareness and attunement as others carry their velum scrolls. For in the backwoods every sight, sound, smell, or movement is a piece in a great jigsaw. Every hunter or alert naturalist spends many years assembling and putting together the pieces of this mysterious jigsaw; learning to recognise the recurring patterns so that in the identification of one piece such as the cawing of a crow he can say with certainty that another piece, such as a hunting fox, is nearby. In this way native hunters are able to learn and take advantage of the keener senses of the wild animals around them.

This level of awareness is easily attainable by modern man; all that it takes is practise. Once you begin to make a point of noticing the patterns of disturbance, both near and far, of different events you will surprise yourself with how quickly you can predict the presence of different creatures.

For the native hunter without the advantage of modern hunting weapons, the difference between eating and starving was often a matter of feet and inches. To be certain of his kill he had to be able to stalk his quarry to within a few feet, pitting his cunning and ability to move invisibly across the land against his prey's heightened senses and instincts. Out of this competition the hunter

learned to respect the animal he was hunting and often the hunt was surrounded with taboos. Many native hunters will tell you that the animal being hunted recognises the hunter's need for food and sacrifices its body to aid him. In this sense any game caught is sacred and must not be wasted lest the spirit of the animal be insulted. On these occasions, hunting is solely carried out for the supply of food and resources, and nothing is thrown away, the inedible parts being fashioned into tools, cordage, leather etc. Whether or not you choose to believe the hunter's view of the kill it is a practical attitude in balance with the natural order which I think is still valid today. By the same token, should a hunter return unsuccessful from a hunt he simply accepts the fact and waits for his next hunting trip, when as always he will not pass up any game which might satisfy his need; when hunting to eat, in the wilderness you cannot afford to be choosy.

Although not immediately obvious hunting skills are probably the woodcraft skill of most overall benefit to an outdoors man or woman, being of value in both cosmopolitan metropolis and far flung desert. Learning to hunt need not necessarily involve the taking of any life; stalking can be practised using a camera; the use of hunting weapons practised against easily-improvised targets. In fact this is how many native children learn to hunt—they play games such as creeping up behind small mammals to touch them which develops their reflexes and hand/eye coordination, both of which are vital to the successful hunter. Native children all over the world learn to use hunting weapons by shooting blunt arrows and spears from miniature bows or spear throwers.

Seeing without being Seen

To hunt successfully requires a range of skills rarely employed in the modern world. In the outdoors you are competing for food with creatures whose senses are biased in a very different way to your own. Above all, you must remain alert and use to the full the sensory abilities you already possess: sight, touch, smell, taste, hearing. It all begins with the attitude you adopt to your surroundings. I think of the outdoors as a great river flowing gracefully yet powerfully with a mesmerising regularity. If you cast a branch into the current, after an initial pause it begins to move with the flow, but should the branch snag on a rock it will break the calm surface with a white spume. In many ways this is how nature is, in the mountains and forests there is a pace to life, a current, the speed and flow of which changes with the seasons and weather, and bound up in it are the lives and movements of all the wild creatures. If you walk into a forest or savannah in the same way as you walk in the city—heavy footed, bobbing up and down and in a rush—you will stand out like that snagged branch. The secret is to sit quietly and still for a few moments until you have absorbed the pace and can slip silently into the stream with a smooth action, unhurried and in sympathy with your surroundings. At first this will feel contrived but in time will be a natural and almost imperceptible action.

I have met those who make much fuss about stalking and claim almost supernatural abilities for ballet-like actions but find this to be mostly contrived to satisfy the imaginations of tenderfeet; the only real secret to being aware is acquiring a level of calm sufficient to allow your senses to receive an unscrambled picture of your surroundings. To see this at work watch an old game keeper as he goes about his chores. He moves freely and easily about his estate with no outward signs of alertness save for the fact that he is searching the surrounding cover with his ears, listening for the sound of fledgling kestrels in the tree tops, or any other tell-tale signs. His eyes are not fixed on the ground in front of him but look far and near and in those places that the deer and woodcock like to hide. These skills are most apparent when the keeper accompanies an apprentice. While the apprentice can walk through a wood and see nothing but the obvious, the keeper walking the same path, listening attentively, his gaze drawn selectively to sounds of interest, can gather a mass of information. The good woodsman also learns to appreciate silence, he should not feel uneasy without conversation on the trail; talk is best saved for the drama of the campfire.

Learn to see with your ears and hear with your eyes. Whenever you witness an animal doing something, such as searching for food or burrowing a den, memorise both the actions and the sounds so that if you ever hear that particular sound again your mind can play back the pictures. This is a very important aspect of your awareness skills—especially if you feel yourself walking at night, in dense forest or country where the local wildlife sports the most effective camouflage. In any situation where eyesight alone is not sufficient, you must heighten your hearing skills for your own safety let alone hunting.

It is vital that you learn to combine your senses. If you detect a faint sound, stop and listen more carefully, stilling yourself to produce absolutely no noise. Use the old school master's trick of cupping your hands behind your ears to magnify and focus your audio equipment. Check the air for scent with your nose; deer and many other mammals have very distinctive scents which are often well within the range of human sensory awareness. There is no set way that your senses must be used, but the most frequent way I use mine is as follows. As I move down a trail or across country my nose may pick up the odour of a scent marking. Finding this and giving it the scent test, it is often possible to gauge the freshness of the mark, especially if there are suitable tracks to use as a double check (see Chapter Eight). Then I have the option to either follow the tracks, or as would be more likely in the case in a non-hunting situation, make an educated guess as to the likely direction of the target and by viewing the landscape as though I was that creature, pursue the most likely course, checking occasionally for tracks to confirm the right choice of route. I almost always hear the animal first before I see it. If this is the case, then with the minimum of movement I turn my gaze in the direction of the sound, taking the widest view I can, until a movement is detected and I can focus my attentions on it.

These are the real skills of hunting, skills that enable you to approach and study wild creatures without disturbing them, thus enabling you to devise a cunning means of capture whether for the pot or to get them on film. To further disguise your presence you should use the prevailing wind conditions to your advantage (walking into the wind so that it carries your scent away from the prey) and take steps to minimise your body odours. Apart from resisting any temptation to splash cologne all over your body, the easiest way to do this is to smudge yourself with woodsmoke which effectively masks most of your other odours. You can also carry with you some strongly scented plants which occur in the area you are hunting, bruise them slightly to allow the odour to escape although do not overdo it. Your aim is to mask those odours which tell your prey 'the most dangerous animal is hunting nearby', not to lure them to your charming herbal perfume.

To further disguise yourself you can resort to camouflage, although with most mammals as long as you are wearing drab colours they are enough to break up the outline of your silhouette. A common practise amongst native hunters is to disguise themselves as their prey and then by mimmicking their movements and sounds, to approach them across open ground. I have never used this as a hunting technique but have experimented with it once to see how close I would get to a herd of deer. I was on a tracking expedition with a colleague at the time and we had trailed the deer to their resting area which was situated on the side of a depression in a secluded area of bogland. Improvising a crude disguise from two sprigs of Sweet Gale hastily pushed into my head band to represent ears, I approached the herd across the boggy ground, imitating as nearly as I could, the proud movements of a deer—much to the amusement of my colleague who almost blew the whole experiment with his loud chuckling! But he was as astonished as I with the results. At first the look-out deer signalled the

presence of an intruder to the rest and they all stood on alert, but after a moment of my mimicking them grazing they lost interest and returned to their own patches of food. Encouraged by the success of my unlikely disguise I carried on towards them to within thirty feet where I gave a loud deer call. I thought I'd gone too far when they moved a few paces uphill, but although thoroughly suspicious they returned to their grazing—as did I—although they paused frequently to squint in my direction. Even so, I was able to approach to within fifteen or twenty feet of them, before they finally decided that I was not a desirable member of the herd and trooped off in order of priority. While I have stalked right up to deer in woodland situations, this is the closest I have ever got to them in completely open difficult ground, where even with a very poor disguise I was easily able to approach within striking distance assuming a bow or atlatl. (I should point out that this took place well outside of the breeding season and that I would not normally disturb a herd of deer.)

Having learned how to increase your chances of approaching closely to wild animals you must practise. No skill is more rewarding on the trail than being able to get to within a few feet of a wild creature or close enough to fill the frame of a medium range zoom lens. In fact hunting with a camera is an excellent way to practise stalking; it allows you the opportunity to study wild creatures and their movements with the minimal investment of time, although it will not guarantee that you achieve the best photographic results. A classic example of this occurred last spring when early one morning I went hunting for a picture of a fox with a photographer friend. I would not normally hunt with anyone else but this friend knows the value of stealth and silence and is no more obvious than a shadow. After a disappointing sighting of a vixen sniffing the trail thirty feet ahead we opted for a more overgrown path which led into thick hawthorn woodland. On the woodland floor there was a carpet of white hawthorn blossom and the night's proceedings could be read from the gaps in the carpet where the blossom had stuck to the feet of the woodland folk. I sensed we were not alone and almost immediately detected a movement. Without signalling (I relied on my friend's ability to detect the movement also), we stood stock still as a dog fox trotted down the trail to a junction three feet in front of me where he paused, cocked his head quizzically at us as if to say 'that's strange I could have sworn those weren't there earlier!' and then hurried home leaving us with a picture imprinted in our memories but not on our film. One of many encounters too close to move the camera to the eye!

Hunting Weapons

Given the choice I would always rather hunt with a camera than with a weapon but we must be realistic. To survive in the bush we need meat and very importantly fat. Only in very exceptional circumstances is a vegetarian diet a feasible alternative. So if we must hunt for food let us make certain that we have the technology and ability to do the job swiftly and efficiently, causing as little suffering as possible. The following hunting techniques and tools have been used by native hunters for centuries for every imaginable prey and on nearly every continent. Some are

simple and were almost certainly employed by our most primitive ancestors, while others are complex in construction and have a longer range. Don't let the simplicity of a design deter you from its use in favour of the complex; some of the simplest weapons are the most deadly.

Sticks and stones: The first weapon a human learns to use is in most cases a stone. You only have to watch children playing to see this happening; from a very early age they learn to pick up and throw a stone to where they could not physically reach—and as they grow and their muscles strengthen the stone thrown becomes larger and their range greater. Used against small game the stone as a weapon can be very effective; its great advantage being its easy availability in many different environments. Technique varies from individual to individual as does a preference for size and shape of stone, though a swift punch or whip-like throw, using an egg-sized round pebble is one of the best. Try to throw instinctively without a complicated

Old English catapults made by the author; a simple hunting tool which fits into a pocket.

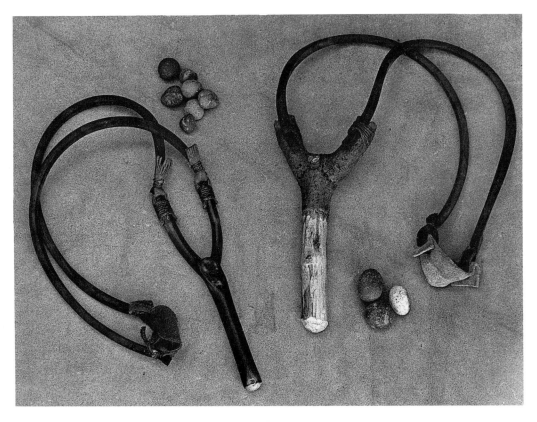

aiming system; I find that the harder I try to hit the target the more often I miss it, whereas if I am running or moving about (perhaps in search of plants or shelter materials) I can hit the target when forced to react quickly to a situation. Of course the stone you use does not have to be small or thrown; on several occasions now I have been able to sneak up and drop a large rock on unsuspecting rats. A very swift and efficient technique!

Sling shot: To increase the range over which a stone can be used, the sling shot was devised, and once you have used one, its giant-slaying reputation is entirely understandable. Essentially this weapon has been used in three forms; the small hunting version a larger hand-held form as an antipersonnel weapon during the medieval period (which threw a stone the size of a cricket ball particularly against siege forces) and the largest one which was a large mechanical version which threw very large stones indeed.

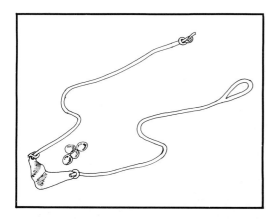

Often underestimated, the slingshot is a hunting weapon which takes some practice to learn to use, but is easily made and is a high-powered weapon.

Of course we are only interested in the hunting version which can throw a stone of any size ranging from a stone the size of a pigeon's egg to that of a hen's egg. Today this simple weapon is only in regular use in remote regions of the world such as Papua New Guinea—a fact which surprises me for it is very effective. The principle is simple: a suitably sized round pebble is placed in a fold of leather which has two thongs attached to it. One of these thongs has a loop in its end to fit over the thumb of the throwing hand while the other end is knotted for ease of grip. With the stone enfolded in the sling it is swung

forcefully around your head, the stone being trapped by centrifugal force. At the correct moment the knotted thong is let go, releasing the stone with great force at the target. In actual use you will only have time to swing the sling once, or at the very most twice, before releasing it as the action will alert the game. Of course this skill requires practise but if you persevere this weapon will bring down the largest small game.

The sling itself is best made from well softened rawhide although you could also weave an alternative from plant materials.

Bolas: Commonly used by the hunters of the arctic, the bolas was used to bring down principally water dwelling birds such as ducks, geese and gulls. It is made by attaching between three to eight weights to one metre thongs which are then joined together. The finest were joined together to form a handle which was further wrapped with a withe. The weights can be made of wood, bone or stones wrapped in rawhide. To avoid tangling, the bolas was carried by a hunter with the thongs loosely tied in a form of slip knot so that when needed for use the weights could be pulled and the knot would disappear leaving straight untangled lines. It was used by throwing it into a flock of birds on the ground or water where it had the greatest chance of striking or tangling a bird. It is not unusual for this weapon to bring down more than one target.

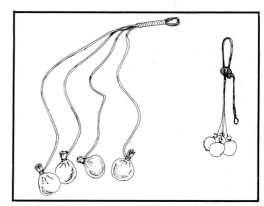

Traditionally used for waterfowl, the bolas can be used for any flocking birds. When not in use it should be carried tied with the slip knot illustrated to reduce snarls and tangles. It works best when thrown horizontally at about knee height.

Throwing sticks: Another weapon commonly used all around the world is the throwing stick. In England the throwing stick

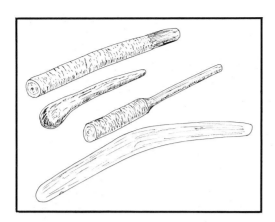

Throwing sticks are just about the simplest of all hunting weapons and yet they may be all that you need to stay alive. They vary from a simple evenly-weighted stick (top), to weighted varieties, to the aerodynamic non-return boomerang of the native Australian.

was one of the classic poachers' weapons, silent effective and easily discarded if surprised by the keepers. The shape of throwing sticks varies according to the way they are used, ranging from the English club-shaped stick to the Aboriginal non-return boomerang. In my travels I have come across at least eight different ways of using a throwing stick but basically they can be broken down into two basic techniques.

The first of these involves the throwing stick which has one end weighted heavier than the other and is thrown with force in such a way as to pin the prey flying like a bullet. The second is to use a stick which is evenly weighted, or even carved to an aerodynamic design. This type of stick is thrown in such a fashion as to spin around its centre of gravity like a helicopter blade. You will develop your own technique along these lines but remember that the throw must be executed with an explosive swiftness. The pinning type of stick is best suited to heavy undergrowth. I have even seen a game keeper stop a rabbit in the middle of a bramble patch with such a stick, while the rotating type of stick is better suited to open ground.

Spears and javelins: For ninety per cent of your needs the primitive weapons so far described will serve your needs, but for long-term survival or travel through areas where there are dangerous predatory animals, you may need a more effective weapon. Spears are the obvious choice; their great advantage is that they will allow you to bring down larger game which possess greater

amounts of fat—an essential requirement in a survival diet.

Spears can be divided into two types: 'spears' which are mainly used in the hand, and 'javelins' which are mainly thrown. While at a pinch each can do the other's job these two weapons are very different in design. Hand spears are heavy and strong, their length depending on the prey and your hunting technique, while javelins are of medium weight to allow them to penetrate at range.

At its very crudest, a spear can be simply a suitably-sized piece of wood sharpened at one end and perhaps hardened in a fire. Compared to modern hunting tools this is a crude and cruel weapon but its ease of manufacture makes it an important tool; early man was able to procure his needs in this way. Yew is a good hard wood to use. To reduce the suffering of the prey and make a weapon far more effective, you need to improvise a sharp point which preferably will cut, this can be made from a variety of materials such as wood, stone, bone or antler (see Chapter Twelve). The shape of the spear point depends upon the type of game you are hunting and the type of spear in general. Thrusting spears should be equipped with a broad cutting edge as there is sufficient force available for its use, whereas javelin points should be more streamlined to allow deep penetration at the greatest range.

The best way to use a thrusting spear is to wait in ambush for the prey, the problem with this is that it can be time consuming and is frequently fruitless unless you make a detailed effort with your camouflage and descenting. Javelins on the other hand can reach game when you encounter it even if it is in the midst of thick undergrowth, although their range and velocity are quite limiting. This was a problem for early man and as usual he came up with more sophisticated weapons to solve the problem.

Sophisticated Hunting Tools

These are the tools the native hunter most commonly used, and are a quantum leap forward in technology from sticks and stones. As soon as you pick them up you can sense their potential, boosting your confidence and reducing your fears. They change the hunting experience from that of a long careful stalk

Spearheads made by author: left to right, a close-range spear with a broad flint point. An atlatl dart with a barbed antler point. A very primitive close-range spear with a point of yew.

with an anything but certain outcome, to a more instantaneous activity, freeing time from the hunt for other chores.

The Woomera or Atlatl: This is the spear thrower, the precursor to the bow and arrow. Today it still finds use with the Australian Aborigine who never evolved the bow and arrow. In Europe the hunters of the Upper Paeleolithic used these weapons to hunt a wide range of game from woolly mammoths to reindeer. The obvious pride they placed in these tools can be seen from the intricate and very beautiful carving they lavished upon them (in my experience hunters only decorate in detail their favourite and most prized possessions). Of all the hunting tools I have chosen to include this is the most practical for survival purposes. It is easily made, can be quickly mastered and has easily enough power to bring down efficiently the largest

game you are likely to need to hunt. In fact I believe this to be the most under rated of all hunting tools.

The principle is simple. The spear thrower acts as an extension to your arm, effectively lengthening the leverage you can apply to the spear. The easiest way to make the thrower is to cut a straight tree limb of about thumb thickness which has a suitable off-shooting branch that can be carved to locate with a depression made in the base of the spear. If you search hard enough you can sometimes find suitable branches growing from the scar of a severed branch that are the perfect shape for the job. However, such spear throwers are only really suitable for the short term, because the amount of force generated when the spear is launched is considerable and concentrated on that one spot. Far better is to carve the throwing arm from one piece of wood and fit

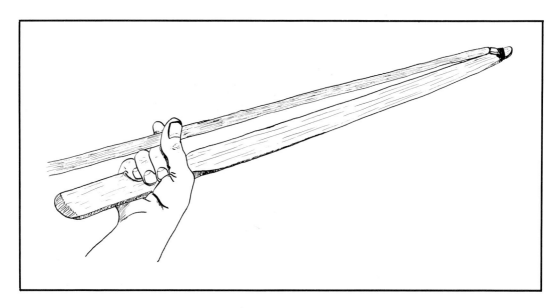

The atlatl acts as an extension to your arm accelerating and magnifying the cast of a spear. This is probably the most undervalued survival weapon. The atlatl may also double as a digging stick or fire saw.

a bone or antler peg into it, or to carve the thrower completely from antler. My favourite spear thrower is carved from hawthorn to an aboriginal design and has a peg of antler fitted and lashed into place with sinew. The peg is recessed and shaped so that the loading it receives in use holds it tightly in place, minimising the strain placed on the sinew.

The size and weight of your spear thrower can vary according to your preference. Aboriginal woomeras come in a wide range of shapes and sizes from long and narrow to short and very broad, the early European spear throwers seem to have been relatively short while atlatls used in the Americas were long, sometimes even with an additional weight fitted to the articulating end. Some of these weights are formed from beautifully carved stones drilled to slip over the main shaft of the thrower. To use the thrower the base of a medium weight javelin (or fishing harpoon (is fitted on the peg and held by one or two fingers of the hand which holds the atlatl. The spear is then projected forwards towards the target with a graceful throwing action which accelerates into a wrist action as the spear thrower boosts the spear on its way. When you first practise this movement concentrate on developing the technique first, you can build up the power once mastered.

Similar but not quite the same are the harpoon throwers used by the waterborne arctic hunters. These are shorter than the spear thrower and carved intricately to allow for careful finger placement. Because they are used from a kayak they have to be used with far more wrist and finger force than arm force, to avoid upsetting the balance in the boat. This may seem strange—after all these are expert canoeists—but on land when you use a spear thrower you are actually using your whole body in the action predominantly with a rotation of your upper body. The kayak technique is more linear.

To improve the accuracy of this weapon you can attach flights to the tail of the spear to stabilise its flight. The spears you use can vary in size from the largest javelin to fast, very high-powered light darts, halfway in size between a small javelin and an arrow. My favourites are made from straight elder stems fitted with a short foreshaft of hard wood fitted with a suitable stone point. The atlatl was also used for fishing and many other purposes; sometimes the atlatl doubled as a digging stick or fire saw. When the great storm of 1986 left a lot of debris to be cleared I found an unusual use for a spear thrower when a tree which no one could find a solution to clearing had not fallen cleanly and

In general use the atlatl is used in a quick over-the-shoulder action. But it can also be used to cast a fishing harpoon.

was caught up in the branches of another. No amount of pulling on ropes or chopping was going to free it leaving no option but to cut it free above ground. Climbing the tree was out of the question because of the tangled mess, so the answer seemed to be to prussik up into the tree and cast a rope over the one suitable limb. But here again the tangle seemed to make that task impossible. And then it dawned on us; we made a makeshift spear and thrower and attaching some strong line from the ditty bag to the spear we were able to accurately cast the spear through the tangle and over the desired limb. It was then a simple task to tie the rope to the line and haul it over the branch. Who said ancient hunting tools are obsolete!

Bows and arrows: England has a long history of archery going back to Robin Hood and battles such as Agincourt; many well preserved bows were salvaged from the *Mary Rose* ship. In fact in the days of chivalry, so feared was the archer that he was branded unchivalrous and if captured was frequently put to the sword without question. Having practised archery weekly by law from youth

the archer was not easy to mistake since the sheer strength of his arms gave his trade away at a glance. But as archers were superseded by the musket, so the bow became reserved for sport and occasional hunting. In the process the more powerful war and hunting bows became less popular and now the bows that could pin a knight to his horse despite the plate armour and saddle, have been almost forgotten.

I started making bows and arrows as a child when although they were very crude, they fascinated me. By a process of experimentation and reading I was soon fashioning my own flighted arrows and remarkably powerful bows using the simplest of tools: an old saw and a blunt metal file. In the process there were many failures with bows snapping sometimes when in use with alarming results. However luck was with me; bows are in my opinion the epitome of woodcraft, especially the English long bow which is a self bow (made solely from one piece of wood) gaining all of its awesome power from the way in which the wood is carved. In the process of learning to make a bow you have to learn to listen to the wood fibres speaking to you and follow the grain coaxing it gently into the finished tool. You need to know which woods have the characteristics which make them a suitable choice for the bow and how to select them. Most importantly of all you must appreciate the sheer mechanics of the wood structure itself. These things are not learned over night and you can expect many failures in the process of bow-making as you discover the secrets of the craft. When I teach primitive bow-making I am constantly reminded of the many comical mistakes I made in the early days, it is a sort of natural apprenticeship.

Bows are not made quickly; the fastest I have ever made a hunting bow was four hours working flat out with perfect materials and a metal knife; the best bows are those made slowly over a period of some weeks. The very best bows—the sinew-backed horn bows of the Turks—often took several years to make. So why have I included the technique when the atlatl is so easily made? Simple: making a bow is the best way I know of learning the intricacies of woodcraft and developing patience, a vital and declining quality. For youngsters on a campout or for a father-and-son project, none is more rewarding at the

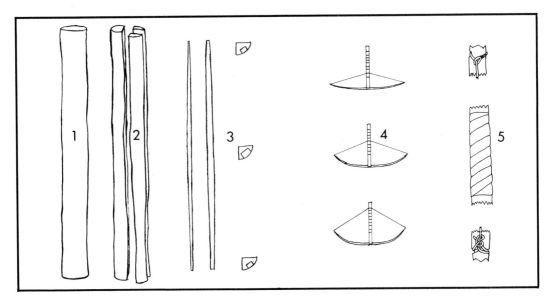

The stages of bowmaking: 1. Find a suitable piece of wood. 2. This is quartered. 3. The quarter with the straightest knot-free grain is rough hewn to a bow shape. 4. Shave it to the final shape. 5. Finally the grip is marked, the bow greased and the nocks cut.

end of the day, and in real terms if you do ever venture into the backcountry and your rifle fails, the ability to make and use a bow will be invaluable.

There are many designs of bow which you might choose to make, but the one I have chosen to explain is the self bow (a bow fashioned from a single piece of wood), common to the plains tribes of North America. I have chosen this for two good reasons: it is simple in construction, and it is short—usually no more than 125cm long—which means that you will more easily be able to find suitably straight raw materials. The only difficulty you may face is maintaining the power of the bow without it developing any cracks, but if you follow my instructions carefully you should succeed.

Making a bow: Bows have been made of many woods: the English longbow was traditionally made from yew which is one of the best bow woods, while in America the Osage Orange wood was preferred. In general, bows made from hard woods are the strongest and most resilient. This does not rule out the use of soft woods, which (excepting yew) need to be carved broad and thin to prevent the grain splitting. For your first bow choose a wood which is easily worked (ideally ash) and has an obvious straight grain which is easy to follow as you carve.

Ideally the wood should be dry and seasoned. In my experience the best naturally found bow staves are those suspended in the branches almost horizontally. Vertical standing wood is often seasoned in different degrees from one end of the stave to the other, not an insurmountable problem but one that will cause unevenness in the manufacture which is a complication best avoided in your early attempts. If you are unable to find suitable wood which is dead there are two options: either to cut green wood and season it before carving, or to carve the green wood and season the bow for use by smearing it with fat to slow down the drying process and prevent cracking. Generally, seasoning before carving is the best option.

You are searching for a stave of wood about three inches in diameter and straight for at least five feet. The best wood will always be found in dense woodland on a slope where the trees have been forced to compete for light, growing tall and slender with a straight knot-free grain. Assuming you have found suitable wood, do not remove the bark. This will help protect the most vulnerable fibres during manufacture. Should you have to store the stave any length of time, keep it dry and horizontal.

The first step in the manufacturing process is to split the wood to take best advantage of the grain. The wood which occurs nearest to the bark is called the pith wood; the fibres in this part of the wood stretch well and will be used to form the back of the bow (the side which faces the target when used). The fibres in the centre of the wood are called the heartwood, these fibres do not stretch well but do compress well, so this part of the wood is used to form the bow's belly (the part which faces the archer when in use). By carefully quartering the bow stave you should have enough wood to make four bows, although you may find it easier to halve the stave until you are more proficient at wood splitting. The best way to split the stave is not the conventional 'frueing' from one end as carried out by the expert woodsman. This takes a great deal of practise to master and bow staves are too valuable to be learning such rudimentary skills on. Take a small axe or tomahawk and hammer it through the centre of the stave, being careful to keep it in line with the sides. Then remove it and by a similar process either side of the initial split, work the split to the stave ends. If you are careful this should perfectly bisect the stave. If you do not wish to risk quartering you are ready to progress to the next stage, but if you

are feeling confident repeat the process on one of the halves. Be sure to cut through from the bark side otherwise you will find the split difficult to direct.

With your quartered stave you are ready to rough out the bow. Working only on the heart wood, carve the bow to the dimensions shown in the diagram. You can remove the bark at this stage to better gauge the wood thickness but on no account carve the pith wood. With the carving go steady, avoiding too deep a cut. Use your eye to judge the proportions and try to gain empathy with the piece of wood you are working. This is very important. Remember you are coaxing the best out of the wood, not following some magic formula for success; no two bows are ever alike. You should try to visualise the bow within the piece of wood you are working. Once you have reached the outline plan you are ready to put the magic into the bow. This process is called tillering the bow and is where you fine tune the bow to draw evenly to the maximum of its power. You will need a length of strong cordage as long as the bow roughout and a tillering board which might simply be a one metre straight branch with a forked end

Tillering a bow: the process of gradually testing the bow's pull; never rush this process.

into which you can carve notches for the tilering process. Tie the ends of the cordage to the ends of the bow and fit the forked end of the tillering bar to the centre of the bow belly and draw the bow string back to the first notch you have carved in the bar about 15cm from the fork. Prop this up and stand back. You should be able to see any unevenness in the drawn bow limbs. Taking your time, you gradually carve the bow down keeping the surface smooth until the string can be drawn back to a notch about 50–60cm along the tillering board. With practise you will be able to achieve longer draws but this is a perfectly adequate draw length to aim for. This process cannot be hurried since to do so is to risk ruining the bow. Once this is done you can carve the notches to receive the bow string and smooth the bow down with sand and buckskin, finally coating the bow with warm rendered fat to help protect it from the elements. Apart from fitting the string, the bow is finished. These bows tend not to have the range of more sophisticated versions but shoot hard and straight. The art of native hunting after all is being able to stalk close to the prey rather than to fell it from a distance.

Once you have mastered the manufacture of this simple self bow there is no reason why you should not attempt more complicated designs incorporating recurved limbs and sinew backing (see Bibliography).

Bowstrings: The hardest part of primitive bow making is forming the string. A bow string must be thin and yet strong enough to resist snapping when the bow tries to snap back to the straight. Very few plant fibres are strong enough to resist this even when very carefully prepared; the best are dogbane, stinging nettle, yucca and rattan. For speed and convenience I usually always opt for a hide string, here you can use either gut which has been stretched and twisted, sinew or rawhide. Sinew will make the best string, but beginners will find rawhide much easier to work with.

There are two techniques you can use to fashion a rawhide bow string—either a two strand string as described under cordage (Chapter Eleven), or the single strand variety, which I prefer to use. The single strand has the advantage of being quick and easy to make and less sluggish than the two strand—although what it gains in speed it loses in strength. To make a single strand bowstrand

choose a piece of rawhide that comes from a part of the hide that is strong (see Chapter Thirteen). You will need a circular piece of hide at least 20cm in diameter and preferably 30cm. Cut this into a strip 6mm wide in the usual spiral fashion, until you have a rawhide whang twice the length of your bow. If you are short of rawhide, one and a half times the length will suffice. Soak the rawhide and attach one end to a branch or similar fixed point and begin twisting the whang until it has a round cross section evenly all the way along its length. Now stretch the string and let it dry. That is all there is to it if you were careful in your choice of hide and cut the whang evenly. Before I attach my string I usually smoke it and give it a slight greasing, then soften the ends by soaking to facilitate easier tying of suitable knots.

Making arrows: Arrows if they are to fly straight and fast and bend without breaking when they have reached their target can be harder to make than the bow. Modern wooden arrows are made from large pieces of wood cut down into many smaller arrow-sized sections which are then turned to shape. This method can be applied for backcountry arrows but is unnecessary when shooting saplings can be found of the correct diameter; besides in my experience sapling arrows tend to warp less.

The best native arrows are made from reeds or wood which has been seasoned, in fact hanging high in the tepee of most plains indians would be a bundle of a hundred or more suitable shoots for arrow making, seasoning for use. In fact amongst these organised tribes there were specialist bow makers and specialist arrow makers. According to some contemporary accounts ten good arrows were valued as being worth a horse. I most often use hazel for my arrows, not because it has any special strength but because it is easily available in a serviceable size. The traditional arrow woods of English archery are poplar and alder.

I usually collect suitable hazel wands in February when the sap is down, but in survival situations you will not be able to be choosy. Select the straightest shoots you can find, by doing so you will save yourself hours of labour. Look especially for wood which has been forced to grow straight in competition for light, and cut them as cleanly as you are able near to the ground, covering the open wound with soil. With care you should find that the sapling will shoot again. This is how coppicing begins. If you are able, gather the wands into bundles of ten and lash them together for seasoning. If you are not able to season them, try to give them at least a day to dry. Don't go overboard with your gathering efforts though, collect only a number of arrows you can deal with. Even with seasoned wood it takes me a whole day to make four or five good arrows!

The wands you have selected should be about 10–12mm in diameter including the bark, which should now be scraped off. The first step in the arrow making process is to straighten out any obvious kinks; this is achieved by gently heating the wood over a slow fire to make it supple and then gently bending the arrow straight with your hands. Hold the wood until it is cool and it should remain straight. Carry out this process from the centre of the arrow and work first to one end and then to the other. If the wood scorches it is overheating. Some natives preferred to use a wrench for removing awkward kinks from an arrow but I find that doing it with my fingers is more than adequate for the task.

With the primary straightening complete you can begin reducing the shaft to the desired diameter. For this task I use a stone scraper knapped (see Chapter Twelve) to a concave shape, for the rough shaping followed by a pair of sandstone blocks for smoothing. This is a laborious but not unpleasant task which by choice is a good activity for a sunny afternoon in camp. The arrow must now be cut to the desired length, assuming the bow is made, measure it to be 5cm longer than the draw of your bow.

Effectively the difficult part of the arrow making process is now complete, all that remains is the fitting out. First you will need to cut the notch. This can be accomplished in one of three ways—either it can be sawn in, using a saw of the bow string diameter or, it can be cut and broken out or—and this is the way I notch all of my arrows—it can be drilled and cut using a stone drill. The important thing is to shape the nock so that the arrow does not split when cast by the string. Notch the arrow at the opposite end to accept the arrow head, this notch should be cut at ninety degrees to the other so that when the arrow is fitted to the bow the arrow head

Securely lash the arrow head in place with plant fibres or sinew. Pine resin or hide glue helps.

Fletch the arrow with halved but untrimmed feathers. Smooth the bindings down flush with the shaft.

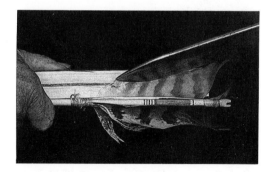

Trim the flights to a long slender profile. Trim off any loose ends of sinew.

The finished flight will have its own natural twist.

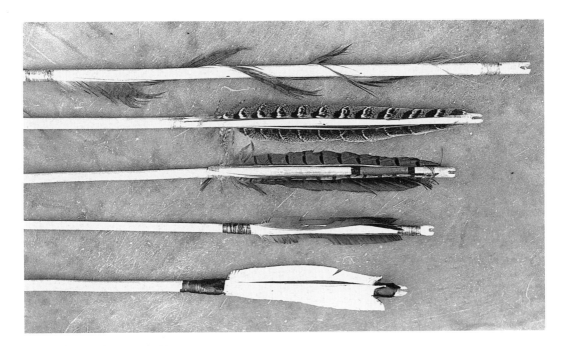

The type of fletching you choose will depend upon the use to which you intend the arrow to be put. The spiral fletching top is intended for blunt pointed arrows used to bring down tree dwelling game (see 'f' below). If the arrow lodges in the branches the slightest movement causes the shaft to spin increasing the chances of its falling to the ground. Below this is a fishing arrow (see 'a' below) with two fletchings. Used at close range this provides enough stabilisation. Below this are three conventional three-feather fletched arrows for general hunting.

Arrow heads come in many shapes and sizes. All these were made by the author:
a) Fishing arrow, hazel shaft foreshafted with yew point fitted with antler barbs. b) Neolithic-style European arrowhead affixed with pine resin. c & d) What are popularly referred to as war arrow heads made of flint hafted with sinew. e) Serrated edge flint hunting point hafted with butterbur fibres. f) Bone pointed arrow left, blunt for hunting tree-dwelling game. A sharp point would pin the game to the tree out of reach of the hunter. g) Barbed antler point typical of design used for hunting amphibious mammals. Like a fishing arrow this arrow would be attached to the bow with a long, thin but strong cord. h) Simple bone hunting point. i) Simple antler hunting point.

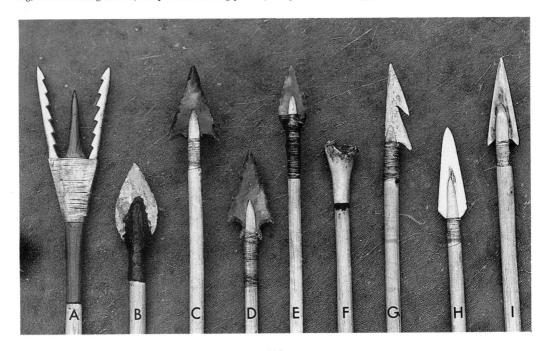

The secret to bowhunting is being able to stalk to within a few yards of your prey. Strike silently and unobserved to avoid panicking the prey.

is horizontal, and at ninety degrees to the bow. This is not as some traditionalists insist to make the arrow pass more easily through the horizontal ribs of a man (the arrow rotates in flight) but is to help prevent the arrow splitting should it strike bone. Fit the arrow head into the notch securing it with pine resin or hide glue (see Chapter Eleven) and lashing it securely in place with suitable fibres.

To enable the arrow to fly straight you will need to flight it with split leaves or preferably feathers. The favoured feathers for flighting hunting arrows have traditionally been owl feathers as they are silent in flight, but you will have to use whatever comes your way; no bird need ever be injured for the purpose of arrow flighting as they leave plenty lying around on the ground for the hunter. The best flight is that made from three feathers. If using wing feathers make certain to use feathers that are from the same wing—all left or all right wing—as otherwise they will bend in different directions.

Bow Hunting
Hunting is never a beautiful activity, but can be exhilarating which is why it is carried on outside of necessity. Hunting with a bow from a hunter's view point is the most challenging of all as it tests the hunter's ability to stalk with a limited range weapon. There is no kudos to be gained from a long shot. But the bow does have one deadly advantage over the rifle: it is virtually silent and even at a range of only two or three metres will afford you in most circumstances two shots. I do not propose to cover at great length bow hunting technique as it is really about the close stalk, except to say that when I have quizzed other people who have hunted with primitive weapons out of necessity they all agreed that it is the stalk which is exhilarating rather than the kill, which even when absolutely necessary leaves a sense of remorse.

The techniques I have described here are included for the sake of completeness. By choice I would always rely upon food carried in to an area when possible. It is a sad human who finds pleasure in the needless slaughter of his four-footed brothers—though we must also recognise the need to manage wildlife populations by selective culling, an unpleasant reality forced upon us by the damage we have already wrought on many species.

Tracking

'. . . I mean the tracks in the dust, the mud, or the snow. 'These are the inscriptions that every hunter, Red of White, must learn to read infallibly. And, be the writing strong or feint, straight or crooked, simple or overwritten with many a puzzling diverse phrase, he must decipher and follow swiftly, unerringly, if there is to be a successful ending to the hunt which provides his daily food.'"

(Ernest Thompson Seton, 'Animal Tracks and Hunter Signs')

Sometimes I wish I had never become interested in tracks, for the art of tracking is totally addictive. Be warned, for once you have successfully trailed a creature you will no more be able to pass by a footprint or disturbance than a bloodhound ignores a scent. In the early morning and evening the ground transforms itself into a library of true wildlife adventures as the low light picks out the fine nuances and details of every disturbance. Just as the radio operator can decipher meaning from the dots and dashes of morse code that travel the airways, so can the tracker decipher the slots and slashes on the land. In really perfect tracking conditions it is easily possible to build up a very detailed picture of life in a particular area of country. Even the caution and wariness of wild creatures at places of danger shows clearly, enabling you to make the ultimate tracking transformation and step into the mind of your quarry seeing the terrain as if through its eyes. It goes without saying that it is the ultimate aim of any hunter to become as one with his quarry and that if you can achieve this it makes the difference between success and virtual unfailing success. But this ability does not come cheaply; it takes time and much study.

It would be easy to fill volumes on tracking but here we are interested only in tracking for survival purposes, so that it is enough to know what creature made what run, and how long ago it last passed by. But tracking is one of those subjects where it is difficult to separate basic technique from more advanced technique because they are so closely intertwined. For example you might study the trail left by the mammals in your most common hunting grounds, but then find a sign you do not recognise and you are lost because you have not learned why some creatures' tracks have five visible toes and others only four. So my aim here is to introduce you to the subject from the grass roots yet leave you to read more specialised books for the finer details.

Learning to Track

It was many years after I had learned to track that I actually realised I had succeeded. While I knew that following most trails was within my capability I did not believe I could match the fabled skills of trackers until I met others who also could track. Now I realise that tracking is one of those subjects much glorified, though seldom exaggerated, by Hollywood. Films are full of tall tales and grizzly stories of 'man tracking', and there are many larger than life characters who make great efforts to live up to such comic book images. Tracking is not a mystic art, it is simply a logical process of intelligence gathering by detailed observation, well within the capabilities of anyone with the inclination and dedication to learn how. There is no need to have been suckled by a she-wolf and raised by savages to master tracking; invariably the better trackers I have met are quiet unassuming folk who shun loud claims of tracking skills. They would rather be on the trail than talking about what they have done.

Tracking is a complicated business and involves several distinct activities; the identification of sign, interpretation of sign, and following of sign. So where to start learning? This is not an easy question to answer. I first became interested in tracking by learning to identify the tracks of foxes from the multitude of local dog tracks when there was snow on the ground. As time passed I was able to identify the fox runs, and as the snow disappeared and the ground hardened, my tracking abilities increased. As the weather changed the runs also changed, although they would still meet up at fence crossings and marking posts so that I could pick up and follow the new trails. This new information also gave me a detailed insight into the mind of my quarry. I learned for instance how a fox will always try to use thick cover to approach something that has caught his attention, disappearing only to reappear cautiously much nearer to whatever it is. I was able to spend many hours watching a vixen guarding her cubs while they played at springing on each other with their unique and delicate hunting pounce. I have spent many nights sitting in a tangle of hawthorn scrub listening to the sounds of carnage as a fox has caught an unsuspecting bird, rabbit or vole and watched as it has hidden the meal before vanishing. On one occasion I stole the fox's meal for my own so that it did my hunting for me. When in close contact with such a beautiful and intelligent wild creature you gain a powerful feeling of kinship.

In all this trailing I never once considered that I was learning to track but that is precisely what I was doing; I regret now not having kept a naturalist's notebook or taken any photographs, for now when I would keep a record and use a camera to supplement my income, I have fewer opportunities to spend time on the trail.

Learning to track can start at any time of the year; it is a slow business which involves a gradual improvement of observation and a tuning in to the finest signs. Tracking is much less about following obvious tracks than most people would imagine; anyone can follow a string of tracks. Tracking is about spotting the scuffs and minor disturbances where to an untrained eye there are no discernible marks of a creature's passage. The absolute rule for learning to track is to do so in the outdoors; books can only be a guide to identifying what you find and targeting what to look for. Start slowly, do not try to run before you can walk; pick a particular area of country to study tracking on; try to choose an area with ups, downs and level ground with a wide variety of different vegetation although don't be over ambitious. It is better to choose a less ideal area that you can travel to easily and frequently, than an area with very diverse conditions that is too far away.

Next, from the guidance below, choose a specific aspect of sign to concentrate on to the exclusion of all others. If you can make the aim even more specific by targeting a specific animal that lives in the area you have chosen, you may decide for example, to concentrate on finding hairs, and more specifically badger hairs. Each time you hit the trails in your training area pick a different aspect of tracking to concentrate on—remember to the exclusion of all other aspects! The aim here is to discover just how much sign is available to you and how much can be learned from one source. Do not break the exclusion rule until you have searched for each aspect of sign listed below. When all these aspects have been studied at least once, hit the trail in search of sign, any sign. Having found a sign—perhaps a dog hair, try to find the other types of sign which match up with the hair and begin to build a mental picture of the animal you are following. Now you can begin spooring as described below.

Sign

Sign is the term used by trackers to refer to the subtle hints they follow. The largest difficulty you face when learning to track is that you are likely to be training in an area near a town or village that is therefore relatively heavily frequented by people. If this is so you face being bombarded with sign and the likelihood of the trail you are following being obliterated by other passers by. This is an everyday fact of tracking, but don't let it discourage you; this is good training. By the time you start your first backcountry trail you will find the going astonishingly easy, as with much less competition from confusing and obliterating sign you can concentrate solely on the trail you are following.

I think in terms of sign in two categories: 'definite' sign and 'indefinite' sign. On a difficult trail you will find that for much of the time you are following indefinite sign, marks which by themselves are not evidence enough to indicate a specific target. Only occasionally when conditions allow will you find a definite sign to confirm you are still on the correct trail. Always as a general rule search for more than one piece of sign to corroborate the evidence you have already found.

Footprints: These are the most obvious of all signs and barely need any explanation save to say that they should be very carefully studied when found in good conditions as they may be your best opportunity to really come to terms with the individual target or targets you are following. Often scars and unusually worn claws will show in the print. In many cases these are also a good clue to the species that made them.

Partial Prints: Here it may or may not be possible to identify the individual but there is nearly always enough information to indicate that you are following the correct species, although you will need to use some care here since for example, a partial print of a British badger can very easily be mistaken for a cat track. *Don't jump to conclusions.*

General Ground Disturbance: Although tracks and signs are part of the overall picture of the outdoors and their absence would seem unusual, put in their context they are in fact out of place variations in the pattern of the ground and vegetation. Any anomalies in the ground pattern must be carefully scrutinised to determine whether they were made by a passing creature or falling vegetation. Look also for colour or texture changes.

Transfer: Anyone who has played football or rugby will be familiar with the casts of mud piled outside the changing room door, each of which shows the unmistakable impression of the boot studs it has left; these are transfer tracks. Likewise, the muddy paw prints across

the living room where a faithful pet has come indoors are transfer tracks. A transfer track or sign is therefore any sign where one material has been picked up in passing and transferred onto another. I also include in this category the 'sign' of where the material has been transferred from, i.e. the muddy hole or the gap in an otherwise even sprinkling of blossom on the floor or a hawthorn wood in spring.

Sometimes a transferred sign is too fine to be picked out by sight alone; a classis case is on the sea shore where the target has walked from sand onto pebble or rock. At first you will see obvious damp partial prints and transferred sand, but then the trail will begin to fade so that the further you follow the trail the less sand you will find. If you can guess or think you know where the next track might be you can lick your palm and press it on the rocks at that point. Any really fine grains of sand will adhere to your palm, indicating a transferred sign. Now, taking your other hand repeat the process, but on a rock where you can see no sign and think that there is little chance of there being a track. Depending on the freshness of the trail you are following, your first attempt should show a higher concentration of sand than the second 'control' attempt—indicating you are on the trail.

Reflection: This sign is only visible in certain lighting conditions; it is caused by the passing of the target altering the ground or vegetation so that where it passes there is either a shiny trail or a dull trail in a landscape that would otherwise catch the light. There are two classic occurrences of this sign, the first of which is the field of long grass where the angle of the depressed grass is different from its neighbour's (therefore reflecting the light differently). In this situation you can either follow the individually disturbed patches of grass or you can follow the reflection sign where you can read large distances of tracks at a time and which is therefore quicker.

The second classic reflection sign is where there is a smooth surface and the dust has been lifted on the feet of the target leaving shiny patches. This is not a transfer track because without the unique lighting consideration you would not have detected the transfer (see also Dew).

Fall out: Nothing to do with radiation or atomic bombs, 'fall out' is literally what it sounds like—items which have fallen or been dropped on the trail. The classic human fall out sign is the discarded cigarette, while in the predators world it is the downy feather or wing from a captured bird. The most amusing fall out sign I have ever come across was a perfect trail of cornflakes which led to a scout who was carrying a cartoon-like load of a rucksack with a kettle swinging on the outside and a large, leaking family-sized packet of cornflakes pushed haphazardly through the straps.

Droppings: Believe it or not, droppings are one of the most useful signs for any tracker or hunter. Many species of animals have very distinctly shaped and sized droppings. But more than this, they will also reveal the animal's state of health and much about its diet. All this is invaluable information for the trapper. See below for details.

Feeding signs: Other vital signs for the trapper are feeding signs; these show *where* the target prefers to eat and *what* it prefers to eat. These signs range from food stashed away, to the actual feeding site. By carefully studying the material which has been eaten it is often possible to identify the species responsible, by studying the marks left by the teeth and the way in which the meal has been eaten. For example, the sparrow hawk leaves a very distinctive kill site of a carcass of a small bird such as a robin or sparrow with its head severed and frequently missing. The flesh is plucked clean of the spine, usually leaving the spine and wings attached to the tail.

Dens: Dens are an excellent starting place for your tracking activities as you are able to follow one of a variety of exit trails and study where the target goes and what it does—vital information for naturalist or hunter alike.

The home or sleeping place of an animal is not an easy place to hunt however as the creature will be cautious entering or leaving the area although it can be a useful site for a trap which may lie idle until the creature has accepted it as non threatening. There are exceptions though, once you have found a rabbit's burrow for example, you should be able to fish him out by wrapping a stick in brambles, pushing it into the den and turning it to snag in his fur enabling you to pull him out.

Above ground disturbances: Broken flowers, fallen petals, snapped twigs and thorns, torn cobwebs or snow brushed off the tips of branches which overhang a trail. These are all signs which may prove valuable as corroborating information. It is all too easy when tracking to only search the ground for sign and forget anything above. If we consider the location of sign on a vertical scale, based around a six-foot-tall human being, about 65% of sign will be found on the ground, 20% between ground and waist height, 5% from waist height to top of the head and 10% above head height which will mainly be sign from birds and tree dwelling creatures. This being the case, it is all too easy to only look at the ground, but remember this is a serious tracking fault and try to always look above as well.

Debris damage: On most trails there is a greater or lesser amount of fallen leaves, twigs and branches, decaying fungi and other debris lying on the ground. Depending on the weight and foot size of the target, a varying amount of damage will be done to this debris in passing. Learn to become aware of this and to recognise individual signs such as the puncture marks made in a leaf by claws as opposed to the holes eaten by a caterpillar or insect.

Tangled leaves: In areas of dense or tall vegetation, particularly crops and long grasses, look for signs of tangled stems and leaves. As an animal pushes through these areas the vegetation is pushed aside and swings back after the animal has passed by. In this way the material is fanned and tangles itself with an action similar to shuffling cards. Depending on the vegetation, strong breezes can either free it or make the tangle worse.

Scuffs: Unlike the paved trails of the urban environment, backcountry trails weave in and around trees and bushes and are full of bumps, raised roots and half-buried rocks. Inevitably, as an animal passes by these protrusions they become scuffed and bruised—particularly roots which may lose their bark or moss covering. At first glance the scuff may seem unimportant but always take the time to study it closer; there can be a surprising amount of detail recorded there.

Dew: This is the classic tracker's sign. As a target moves through an area covered in dew it wipes the dew off on to its feet or other part of its body, leaving a dark patch in an otherwise highly light reflective surface. In good conditions it is often possible to follow a dew trail with great ease for some distance. I

The dog family. Tracks, droppings and trails, left to right, of dog, wolf, fox.

once followed the dew trail of a man who was following the dew trail left by a confused roe deer. Eventually the trail led into a wood where I noted the man had lost the trail and had taken the wrong turning; he had missed the 'transfer' sign of water droplets which had been deposited in passing, on nearby dog's mercury leaves. Remember that the dew is picked up by the passing target and is highly likely to show up as a transfer when the terrain changes.

The Art of Tracking

So far we have glimpsed the range of sign or spoor available to the tracker, but this is only the information a tracker uses to pursue his art. There are three basic stages in learning to track once you can spot the available spoor. These stages also represent the general order in which a track analysis is carried out.

Stage One—Track Identification

In a survival situation you may be faced with the trails of unfamiliar animals, but under all other circumstances you should familiarise yourself with the target and learn to recognise its habits and the way it lives its life. Make certain you can recognise its tracks, its droppings, its hairs, as well as the type of home it builds.

The first stage of learning to identify tracks is to learn to differentiate between the trails of various families of related species—such as the cat family and the dog family. Once this is done you can then learn to differentiate between the individual species within those families. This is not always easy. For example, it can be impossible in some circumstances to differentiate between the tracks of a large dog and those of a wolf. In such instances you must fall back on corroborating evidence.

The following are the generalised track and dropping characteristics for the principle species families. Space does not allow for a more detailed exploration of the family members, but given the ability to differentiate

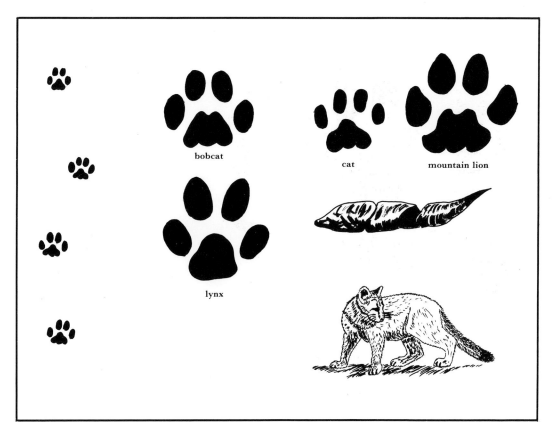

The cat family. Tracks top left to right: bobcat, domestic cat, mountain lion, bottom left lynx. Cat droppings show distinctive carnivore's tail and some segmentation.

between the tracks and droppings of the principal families and the ability to recognise sign, you should be able to piece the rest of the picture together through careful observation and interpretation (Stage Two below). By principal families I refer to those directly relevant to a survival situation that involves either food or safety.

When I come across a track or dropping I compare it to an archetypal track design I carry in my mind. This is a compilation of the major distinguishing features. In reality the track that you are studying may appear very different from this, either because of the individual characteristics of the target's foot or due to distortions attributable to the ground conditions. Despite this, at least two of the key features are usually represented, which when backed up by further substantiating evidence or local knowledge should give you a positive identification of the species.

Note: Never handle droppings with your bare hands. Always use a probe or, under ideal conditions, disposable gloves. Always wash your hands afterwards.

The Dog Family (dog, wolf, fox)

The tracks of members of the dog family tend to be longer than they are wide, and are generally an oval shape overall. Commonly four toes will show for both fore and hind feet, with accompanying claw marks. As a general rule wild dogs and working country dogs leave sharp claw prints whereas domestic dogs that walk frequently on paved surfaces will leave blunt claw prints. In general, dogs register but not directly. This means that they place their hind feet on top of the track left by their fore feet but not so perfectly as to totally hide or obliterate it. Those members of the family that are good hunters, or working dogs, such as sheep dogs, will more directly register than domestic pets. The classic 'direct registering' dog is the fox who frequently leaves a trail which shows only the hind

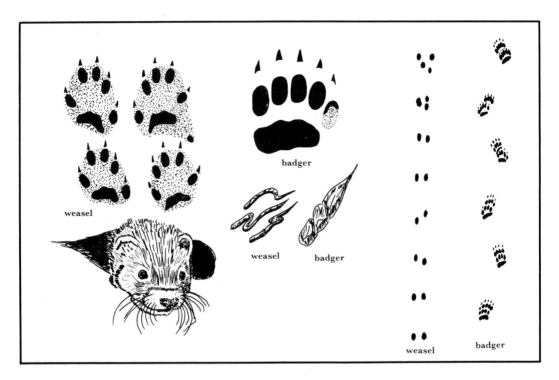

Above: The weasel family. Top left: the left fore print of a weasel. Next to it the right fore print and below respectively the left and right hind prints. Middle top is the badger's track; the fifth toe frequently does not show. Weasel family droppings are squiggly, smelly and often very liquid. Far right: badger trail; left of this, weasel trail in snow.

Below: The rabbit order. Individual rabbit tracks rarely show although you can often see the scratches from their claws. Rabbit droppings are distinctive pea-like pellets comprising fibrous plant material. In snow you will often come across the distinctive rabbit trails like double exclamation marks.

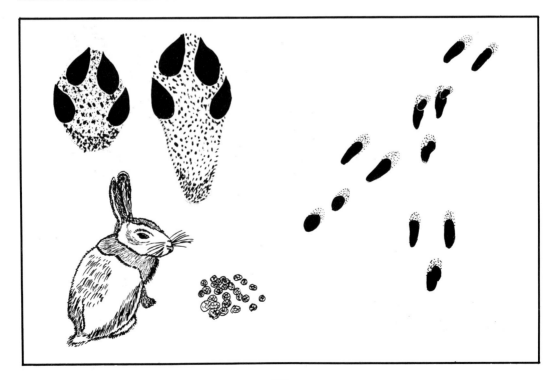

prints. This has been the source of many stories told by gamekeepers of the fox tip-toeing into the hen house on his hind legs.

The droppings of the dog family vary widely in size, and are relative to the size of the species. They are probably the most familiar dropping to modern man, being cylindrical in shape usually in one piece, and often with a tail. The colour of the dropping will vary greatly according to diet. For example a fox dropping is often white during the spring when he enjoys a glut of unwary young mammals, which supply him with plentiful quantities of calcium in the form of their bones. During the autumn however berries play a more predominant part in the fox's diet, turning the dropping black. A typical feature of a fox's droppings is the frequency with which they are found on a raised mound which he uses as a marking post.

The Cat Family (wild cat, civet, lynx, mountain lion)

Proud feline grace and menace show clearly in the tracks of the cat family. From a tracker's perspective no other four-footed animal is so well adapted to stealth and stalking. Cat tracks are round tending to oval in their overall shape, and are generally wider than they are long. Similar to members of the dog family, their tracks show four toes front and hind but only show their claws in exceptional circumstances such as very soft snow. A characteristic very typical of a cat track is the way in which the interdigital pad is cleft. Unlike dogs, cats directly register most of the time when walking, placing their rear foot onto the depression left by the fore foot with absolute precision and almost in a straight line. In snowy conditions you could almost swear that the cat was using a pogo stick to avoid cold paws. I once found a line of evenly placed cat tracks in soft snow, which when examined, showed the cat's claws. The odd thing was that the claws showed both in front and behind the track, indicating that the cat had travelled first one way and then returned retracing its footprints absolutely perfectly.

Cat droppings are cylindrical (like dog droppings) but are more frequently segmented; they also show a tail though less often than dogs. Colour varies widely with diet and

The deer family. The individual tracks are, from left to right: Red, Fallow and Roe Deer, and respectively for the droppings. The most noticeable difference between the tracks is size. Often you may find the droppings stuck together into an elongated mass called a fewmet.

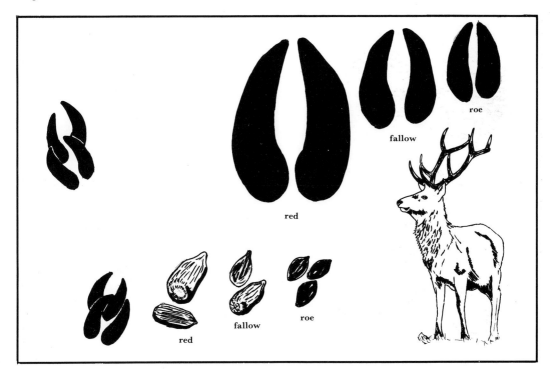

fallow

red

fallow

roe

red

undigested remains in the dropping may often indicate the cat's carnivorous diet. Depending on specific species characteristics, the droppings may be wholly or partially buried.

The Weasel Family (weasels, badgers, stoats, ferrets, polecats)

The weasel family contains a wide range of species each of which can vary enormously in size from the other (i.e. the weasel and the badger). In all cases the track is longer than it is broad although often it appears broader than it is long due to only a partial impression being visible. The distinguishing feature of this family is the five toes with claws showing on both fore and rear feet. Under imperfect conditions it is a common mistake to miss the fifth digit and mistake the track for that of a four-toed creature. But even when the fifth outer toe cannot be seen, you should become suspicious when you see the inner digit widely spaced from its neighbour's while remaining more or less parallel, indicating a wide foot.

The members of this family are as tough as nails. I have often found useful stone working materials in prodigious mounds of flint excavated by local badgers, while the ever-alert weasel—a pure hunting machine—will sometimes tackle prey larger than itself. The droppings of this family tend to be long and squiggly with a characteristic carnivour's tail, and a very distinct weasely smell. The badger, fastidious house keeper that it is, will often excavate a latrine into which it lays its droppings. Sometimes these are more runny than solid although the odour remains.

The Rabbit Order (hare)

Rabbit tracks are best studied in the grouping of their stride as this is how you will most often find them. But for survival purposes this is not the most valuable sign to search for. Better by far is to look for the close-cropped vegetation and raised, dropping-covered sentry mounds. Rabbits will graze an area to the smoothness of a golf course using their razor sharp incisors. It is important that you study the vegetation the rabbits are feeding

The bear family: The tracks of very wide-bodied heavy animals are large, often deep, and frequently overlap. Their droppings are large and full of plant and insect remains as well as berry stones. You may also come across scratching posts which will give you an indication of how tall the bear stands at full reach.

grizzly

on if you intend to trap or hunt them—they are immune to deadly nightshade for instance but if you eat a rabbit that has eaten it, you can be poisoned. Rabbit droppings are easy to recognise: they are brown spherical balls of fibrous plant remains that dry and eventually crumble to dust. These droppings occur widely in any area grazed by rabbits or hares.

A hare moving fast across deep snow can leave very confusing tracks especially if making a turn. It is generally true to say that inexperienced trackers under-estimate the stride length of many creatures; this is certainly the case with hares who are really able to leap using their powerful hind legs. In deep snow the traces of this galloping motion are greatly enlarged, leaving huge sweeping footprints with long distances between them.

The Deer Family

Deer have been a challenge to trackers and hunters for centuries. I used to know a game keeper who managed a herd of deer and could identify each member of the herd by its tracks alone. In Britain the tracks of deer are by tradition called slots and this is a very apt description. Deer are cloven hooved and in most cases leave two, more or less parallel slots for each foot with a slight register. In soft ground such as a stream, bank, mud or snow, the 'dew claws' may also leave a mark; these are found much higher up the deer's foot. The size and general shape of the slots are an indication of species but this can be very confusing, especially when there are young deer moving with old. Always try to substantiate your suspicion by corroborating evidence.

Deer droppings are a far more reliable guide to the species than are their slots. In general you will find small mounds of droppings in deer country. Because a deer will leave droppings as it moves along, you can very often find a pile of droppings with a gradually decreasing trail of droppings leading away from it; an excellent indication of the direction which the deer has taken.

Deer also leave other indications of their presence—such as obvious feeding signs where they have browsed vegetation to the full height of their reach, or bruises where stags have been rubbing away the velvet from their antlers. Not all species of deer shed their antlers but those that do will leave a very useful commodity for the backwoodsman

each spring; usually during the first three weeks of April.

The Bear Family

I can remember the heart-pounding excitement of finding my first bear track while on holiday in Yosemite; it was both the most exciting track and yet the most disappointing for there was not time to follow it to see where it led. To an untrained eye a bear track which shows five toes with claws fore and hind, can be confused with those of a barefoot man; particularly the black bear's forefoot track. But as a bear is a four-footed creature and walks with a distinctly flat-footed, toed-in posture typical of heavy weight four foots, this mistake should not be made.

Bears can cause considerable problems in the backcountry. When you are in bear country you are in the bear's domain and must pay due respect to these much maligned creatures. The great problem is that humans tend to expect bears to think like a human, but to a bear things are very different. His major preoccupation is finding food and no creature that I have ever observed is more industrious in this labour than the bear as he grubs up roots and ants' nests to meet his insatiable appetite. Should he smell that tastiest of all morsel though, the sizzling meat on a barbecue, or any other camp fare for that measure, resign yourself to the fact that he will compete for it. Never argue with a salivating bear; that is the number one rule. In bear country keep all your food suspended high out of bear reach and take every effort to reduce smells, both when cooking, or just in your own personal hygiene. Women must also take great care during their menstrual cycle as there is evidence to suggest that this has attracted bears. If you do have the misfortune to fall into bear claws the general advice is to shield your throat and genitals with your hands and no matter what happens, to play dead. There are enough scarred but living survivors of bear attacks to attest to this policy. A bear, even grizzlies, usually attack because they feel threatened; if you fight back they will only bite harder, but if you play dead the theory is that you lose your threat value and they will lose interest and leave.

Better still, avoid being mauled in the first place. In some parts of North America and Canada, hikers are encouraged to wear a bell on their sack to let the bears know they are

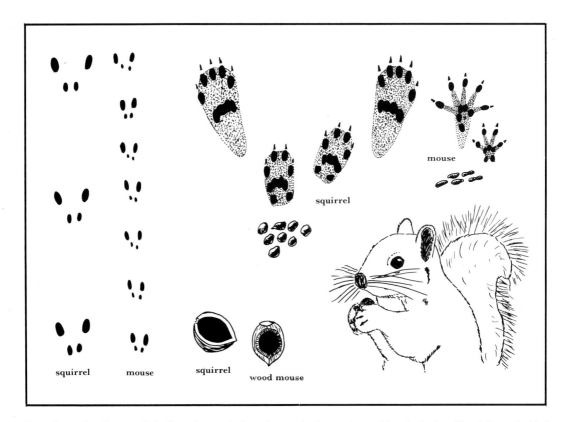

squirrel   mouse   squirrel   wood mouse   mouse

The rodent order. Characteristically, rodent tracks have five toes in the rear foot and four in the fore. Top right are the hind and fore track of a mouse, left of this are the tracks of a squirrel. Most rodents have cylindrical droppings but the squirrel has moist pea-like droppings.

there and give them time to move away. If you have no bell try singing; a rousing chorus from Gilbert and Sullivan should do the trick.

After all this talk of bear attack you probably expect bear droppings to comprise the mangled torsos of unfortunate hikers, but that is not the case. Despite their fearsome reputation bears are omnivorous and would rather be eating berries, insects and small game than people. Their droppings are large and cylindrical, often found in piles, and contain the remains of all manner of foods. Also look out for bear marking and scratching posts.

An interesting point to note is that all across the world native people have revered the bear as a good luck symbol. Particularly in Native American societies the bear was believed to be able to impart supernatural strength and power by appearing to a warrior in a dream. This led to bear cult societies in many tribes, where warriors would dress and paint themselves to represent bears. Also the bear was believed to be a teacher of herbal medicines and many native American plant medicines are claimed to have been learned from observing bears curing their own ailments.

The Squirrel Family
(rats, mice, water rats)

Squirrels are rodents and as with the weasel family there is a wide range of different sized members. The key to identifying their tracks is that they show four toes on the fore feet and five toes on the hind feet, with claws present for both. The family includes rats which prefer to live near water. This can cause serious problems for the travellers as rats carry a disease called Leptospirosis (Weil's disease) which they pass into the water through their urine. This disease is a killer unless correctly diagnosed early on; it is contracted by the disease organism entering your blood stream through an open wound or through the membranes of your eyes, nose, mouth, or ears as well as by drinking. For this reason never trap or kill rats for food, and learn to recognise their sign so that you can avoid any nearby water. It is unlikely that you will be using a large body of water or stagnant pool for your water supply but you may be searching for edible plants in the vicinity of such an area, in which case the plants must be washed and preferably cooked.

Rodent droppings show a variety that matches their order. Squirrel droppings for instance are pea sized and pea shaped whereas rat and mice droppings are sausage shaped and vary in accordance with the size of the maker. All though comprise finely chewed matter which is plasticine-like in texture when first dropped, hardening with age.

Stage Two—Track Interpretation
This is where you have the chance to be Sherlock Holmes, for track interpretation is a process of logical deduction. But to be successful, you must have done your home work and studied the behaviour and lifestyle of your target—for now you are not only attempting simple identification but you are trying to determine what went on and in some cases what the target's immediate future intentions are most likely to be. To be able to make these deductions you need to be able to take in the whole scene yet remain aware of all the detail. When I look at a track or a trail I am not able to tell at first glance the full story, it takes a few moments for the tracks to register in my mind. Rather like watching an old TV screen warming up, or a photograph emerging from the developing tray, only the obvious features are apparent at first but then the finer details begin to reveal themselves until the full record can be scanned and absorbed ready for analysis. Now you can build a mental picture of what went on; to do this you should use your mind's eye to picture the animal making the tracks. Of course this ability only comes from much study of the way animals move.

Each animal has its own distinct way of moving or standard walking gait, which registers as a distinct pattern on the ground. If the animal's mood changes or it changes speed from its normal gait, so too will this pattern change. Watch a dog or better still a cat, see how it walks then watch as it breaks into a run. Study it as it stalks and plays. You will notice if you study the tracks that a dog

runs very similarly to the way a rabbit walks. Spend as much time as you can studying these patterns because they will enable you to decide where the next track on the trail should be—a vital skill for following the trail.

To help fully understand the meaning of the tracks you are studying you will also need to know at what time of day they were made, or how fresh they are. This is not an easy skill to learn—again requiring much diligent study—but with practise you should be able to estimate the age of a track to within minutes—although you must remember that each soil type ages at a different rate. The easiest way to estimate the age of a track is to make a similar mark next to the track for comparison and then estimate the age using your observations for how quickly the track will fade, taking into account the prevailing weather conditions. Don't be dismayed if your early attempts at ageing are inaccurate; this is a very difficult task which even many experienced trackers get wrong. Generally though your ageing estimates will improve with your tracking experience as you increase your subconscious data bank.

Stage Three—Following Up
The last stage in the tracking process is 'following up'. This is simply the process of finding every track on the trail. It is easy to skip a few tracks that are not so easy to see but this is poor tracking. Once you have identified a trail stay on it, follow every sign and make interpretations whenever you can or need to, such as at trail junctions, or changes in gait. Your aim is to get inside the mind of the target. Remember to look around and view the terrain from the target's height; sniff the air. A common fault with tracking students is to fail to interpret the points on a trail where the target stopped to sniff either the ground or vegetation; this for him is an important part of his information gathering, which is not available to us. We may smell the scent mark but cannot unravel the code of its maker and other complex signals it most likely holds. We have to second guess this by studying the target's behaviour changes.

As you follow a trail make certain you keep the track between you and the light source and be careful not to carelessly obliterate sign you have not yet read. The general rule is not to move until you have spotted the next two sign. This cannot be overstressed; careless movement is the cause of most tracking failures. If you do lose the trail, return to the last positive track you found and carry out a detailed sweep search of the vicinity. If the animal has leapt ahead or sideways this should be indicated in the last track you could find. Don't give in, it is the difficult sign which teaches you the most!

I have had the great fortune to have tracked alongside many tracking experts in many different areas. Each uses a different system for following tracks and has a different mental approach to the task. But the above is the kernel of skill common to all. It would be easy to fill several volumes on this subject but it is better that you make your own discoveries through experience. Remember you will gain more by learning the movements and habits of one animal really well, than by learning the movements of many not so well.

Trapping and Fishing

'We had no cattle, no hogs, no grain, only berries and roots
and game and fish. We never thought that we would be
troubled about these things, and I tell you my people, and I
believe, it is not wrong for us to get this food. Whenever the
seasons open I raise my heart in thanks to the Creator of His
bounty that this food has come.'

(Chief Weninock of the Yakima Nation from the 'Proceedings of the New Jersey Historical Soc', New Series Vol 13,
1928)

Despite its more macabre aspects, trapping is a fascinating study of both wildlife and engineering. I have yet to meet a skilful trapper who traps to feed his family who does not have a great love and respect for his prey. This comes from many hours watching and following the prey. It is one thing to sit at home and watch wildlife documentaries, another altogether to sit and shiver in the wind and rain as you share the sounds and smells of wild living with the creature you are watching. No matter how cold hearted a man is, he cannot fail to be moved by the essence of the wild. Many people do not realise that it is not the trapper who should be feared but the person who has not learned to appreciate the living soil beneath his feet or to listen for the sounds of a changing season, or the songs of the feathered family. Hunting and being hunted is part of nature; they are an inevitable part of the cycle of life, an everyday fact for survivor or native alike.

The great advantage of traps is that they free your hands for other tasks and enable you to be hunting at night when your senses are less effective. But they are not as simple to operate as they first appear, you cannot just set a trap and hope to find it has been successful. A correctly set trap is placed with precision with as many factors of chance eliminated as possible. Wild animals are not stupid; all of their senses have been honed by natural selection to enable them to survive the many hazards in their path. Above all, they have learned the smell and mark of man, the most dangerous of all their enemies. To succeed at trapping you must, just as in hunting, be able to see and think like your prey, and be practised at constructing the various designs of trap you may elect to use.

I place faith in my reader's integrity and the strict laws which control the use of trapping devices. The use of the traps here described is only acceptable to procure meat in real wilderness emergencies out of dire necessity. However, even if you do not ever think you will need to use a trap don't pass by the subject; it has much to teach the outdoors person and you need never kill or hurt an animal in any way to benefit from trapping skill. At the end of the trapping section you will find a diagram of how to adapt a primitive trap trigger to trip the shutter release of a camera. By using this technique you will absorb the finer points of the trapper's art and gain field practise, without killing animals unnecessarily.

You will find below a large number of trap

designs, cunning and ingenious triggers developed over centuries of experimentation, to meet a wide variety of prey and conditions. But trapping is only ten per cent a mechanical skill. The real secret of successful trapping is a detailed study of the prey's life. An understanding so perfect that you can see and think like it does.

Siting

The most important aspect of trapping is knowing where to site the trap. It is no use just setting a trap and hoping that you will be lucky; the trap must be placed either where the animal is likely to pass by or where it will arouse his curiosity without causing too much suspicion. The simplest and one of the most effective places to locate a trap is on a 'run', a frequently-used animal trail which is easily spotted as an area with compressed and parted vegetation. Very often runs are used by more than one species so try to select a smaller run leading off of the more well used one which is more likely to be the preserve of the species you are after. Look especially for hairs to help you in your identification.

So long as your trap is not obvious, a run is an excellent place for siting an unbaited trap such as a snare. The best placing for your snare along a run is near the run's end where the prey will be preoccupied with the dangers of crossing open ground or a more well-used run. It is absolutely vital that the trap be correctly camouflaged, blending unobtrusively into the surroundings de-scented or the cent disguised. Place some twigs and small sticks either side of the snare or trap to act as a funnel (see below) to help prevent the prey passing around the side of the trap. Your aim is to completely surprise the prey, catching him when his mind is preoccupied or he feels confident. This means' that you must be at great pains to avoid disturbing the surrounding vegetation when you are setting the trap. Any broken vegetation will give off scents which will alert the prey, as will any major changes to the run itself. A really expert trapper will use the caution and curiosity of creatures to his advantage by setting a decoy to distract the prey's attention as it nears the trap. One game keeper showed me a rabbit snare which he claimed never failed. It comprised a simple 'wire' sited on a run which led onto a field. About a metre in front of the snare was a sapling, bent so that as the rabbit

passed by it, a trigger bar would release it causing it to spring straight against a log. This startled the rabbit so that it sprang to flight through the run opening where the snare was ready and waiting.

Baited traps must be sited in a different way; they make their mark by actively luring the target to them. In general they are better sited away from trails and placed instead near areas where the prey feeds, or marks its territory. The bait must also be correctly chosen for the intended prey.

Talk of bait and immediately the question arises what does your prey eat? But this presupposes you intend to bait the trap with a tasty morsel. Baiting need not solely be accomplished with food. In many ways a scent is a more practical bait than food. A scent is more pungent and has a greater range than food. Above all else it is far more irresistible, often catching the attention of an animal even when it has eaten. A scent bait is also easy to obtain and will attract many visitors during the night. To obtain a scent bait the old fur trappers would save the scent glands from their prey, but in a survival situation there is a much easier way. Having found a scent marking post (if you have done your homework this should not be difficult for you to locate), tie or otherwise fix a large bundle of dry plant material (similar to a tinder bundle or dew mop) to the marking post. Leave this for a few days until it has been marked and absorbed the scent. Now site your trap and bait it with the scent bundle.

If you are relying upon food for your bait it must be tailored to suit the prey. Carnivores should be attracted using a suitably sized piece of meat or better still a small fish. This is about the best way to turn an earthy fleshed bony fish into a decent meal. Herbivores however must be attracted to the food they prefer to eat. Here you must study their feeding signs carefully to determine what to use for bait. In general it is better to use neck or leg-hold spring snares with this type of bait. This is because the animal tends to snip the vegetation cleanly or tear it by tugging, making it difficult to guarantee a clean kill with a deadfall snare.

Funnelling

As its name suggests, funnelling is the

technique used to guide a target into your trap, though the technique varies according to whether you are using baited traps or unbaited traps. With an unbaited trap you are trying at all stages of the setting to avoid drawing attention to its presence. All that is needed are a few carefully positioned sticks to convince the prey that the easiest path to follow is that which leads into your trap. If you were to build a rigid wall of sticks with a single opening you will only scare the prey away. After all if you were walking home your usual way and suddenly found a brick wall across your path with one opening in it wouldn't you be suspicious?

Baited traps though are a different proposition. Because you can more or less predict your prey's movements when it reaches the bait you can build a more substantial wall which funnels the prey into the trap precisely. You may need to wall in the bait to prevent the prey circumventing your snare or deadfall. An obvious wall is feasible in this situation because of the strong enticement of the bait which will overcome the prey's natural caution. This does not mean though that just any wall can be built: it remains important to build as small a wall as will successfully do its job.

Choice of Trap Design

The choice of trap you decide to employ should be the result of deliberate and careful planning. Limited by the materials available for its construction, it must be designed to carry out its task swiftly and efficiently. This means that you must know as much about your quarry as possible: its weight, height at head and shoulder, and have a rough idea of how strong it is. Never underestimate the strength and determination of wild creatures; rabbits have been known to bite their own leg off to escape from gin traps.

Your aim is to kill the prey as swiftly and cleanly as possible or to catch it in such a way that it is unable to gnaw itself free. Despite the macabre nature of trapping, if carried out efficiently, it is a clean and humane method of killing: the prey goes about its daily routine until suddenly it is all over. For a quick clean kill it is essential that your trap is built strong enough for its purpose; spring snares should ideally be powerful enough to both break the prey's neck or back and carry it far enough aloft to be out of the reach of scavenging predators who will as surely as you take advantage of unguarded food. Deadfalls on the other hand must be heavy enough to break the prey's back cleanly; ideally they should fall swiftly from some height and act with a scissor or hammer action against a solid anvil—such as a log or rock—rather than against soft earth. It is also important that the trigger remains firmly set so that the prey doesn't have time to escape or shift position and thereby become maimed.

In conditions of extreme cold, some triggers may lose their efficiency by freezing or becoming weighed down by snow. Spring snares in particular, which rely upon a bent sapling as the twitch-up spring, should be avoided as they will freeze solid. Rely instead upon the counter balance tossing bar method.

Setting a Trap Line

To trap effectively you need to approach the subject in an organised manner, moving into your preselected area with prefabricated traps and setting them quickly, quietly and efficiently, to cause the minimum disturbance. Always set more than one trap to maximise your chances, a usual number for survival purposes would be between five and ten. It is no use trying to learn to make trap triggers when you actually need to use them; it is a simple matter to practise setting traps without any need to actually catch anything. Making traps is a slow process; they cannot just be quickly made as is suggested by the drawings below. In real situations you do not have perfectly straight wood to work with and you will most likely be alone without any helping hands to steady heavy deadfall weights while you set the trigger. The man who said that traps are a means of hunting without effort was obviously no trapper. It is a slow, tiring, strenuous and frustrating business.

Before you start to manufacture or even gather the raw materials for your traps, wash and disguise the scent on your hands and cutting tools. I usually wash my hands with a natural soap of some sort and then dry them in the smoke of a fire. Woodsmoke does not overly bother wild creatures as it is a natural odour familiar to them. I will also de-scent my feet or shoes before entering the trapping area in teh same way. This may be unnecessary, but it is a tradition I have always followed. In the process of making the traps, handle the materials as little as possible and darken any exposed cuts with soil, (more to mask the scent of the cut than disguise the blaze.) Be methodical and precise.

Once you have manufactured the trap components, carry them to the area. Try if possible, to lay your traps out in a line which is easy to check. Do not dot them around in the bush where you may lose them or cause a disturbance when checking them. Set the traps as quickly and quietly as you can without drawing attention to yourself. Wild animals are not stupid. Once set, the trap line should be checked twice daily if possible. Try if possible to check the traps from a distance without approaching them. To this end some trappers affix a sprig of leaves to twitch-ups to act as a signal to show that the trap has been set off.

Trap Designs

Traps vary very little. In principle their greatest differences lie in the design of the trigger which is tailored for a specific prey and a specific set of circumstances. If you are familiar with a fairly wide range of trap designs you will find it much easier to conceive your own from the natural materials available to you. The traps which follow are all extremely effective and cover a wide range of trapping principles. However I have deliberately decided not to include any spearing or impaling traps as they are unnecessarily barbarous; there is always a better alternative. Besides if you are trapping for food the only result of puncturing the prey will be to attract the unwanted attention of scavengers, or more dangerous competition.

Snares: The snare is nearly as old as man himself and has been used all over the world. It consists of a noose which is tethered so that it will tighten around the prey's neck or leg—or in the case of some monkey traps, even the hand. The simplest snare of all is the running noose or as it is known in Britain the wire. This is a noose secured to a post which is set on a run at a height suitable to allow the prey's head to pass through. The noose however is only wide enough for the head and will not allow the shoulders or body to pass through as well. The noose comprises a slip knot which tightens and chokes the unfortunate victim. I have seen the same device used to take rabbits alive; the noose was prevented from tightening enough to choke or strangle by tying a stopper knot a few centimetres in

The pressure bar spring snare is attached to a spring branch or bent sapling so that when triggered the snare whips upwards tightening and in some cases lifting the prey out of the reach of other predators that might rob you of your meal. It is ideally suited to catching animals which like to leap through gaps or are inquisitive.

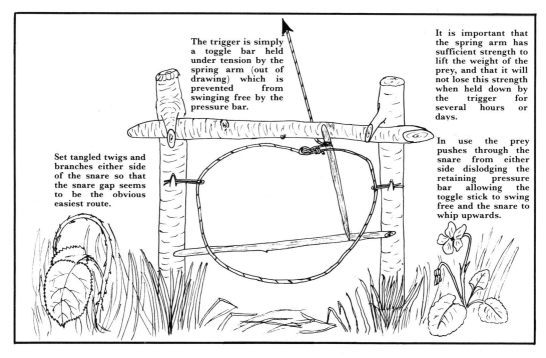

The trigger is simply a toggle bar held under tension by the spring arm (out of drawing) which is prevented from swinging free by the pressure bar.

Set tangled twigs and branches either side of the snare so that the snare gap seems to be the obvious easiest route.

It is important that the spring arm has sufficient strength to lift the weight of the prey, and that it will not lose this strength when held down by the trigger for several hours or days.

In use the prey pushes through the snare from either side dislodging the retaining pressure bar allowing the toggle stick to swing free and the snare to whip upwards.

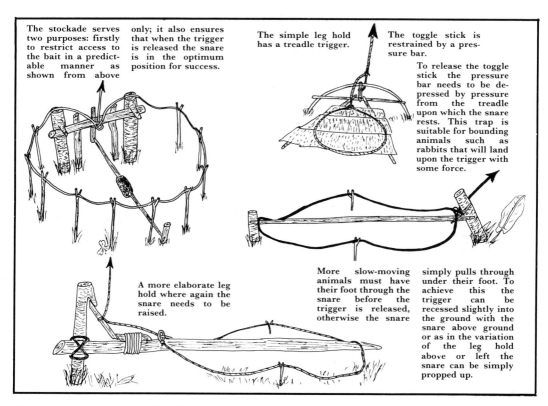

The stockade serves two purposes: firstly to restrict access to the bait in a predict-able manner as shown from above only; it also ensures that when the trigger is released the snare is in the optimum position for success.

The simple leg hold has a treadle trigger.

The toggle stick is restrained by a pres-sure bar.

To release the toggle stick the pressure bar needs to be de-pressed by pressure from the treadle upon which the snare rests. This trap is suitable for bounding animals such as rabbits that will land upon the trigger with some force.

A more elaborate leg hold where again the snare needs to be raised.

More slow-moving animals must have their foot through the snare before the trigger is released, otherwise the snare simply pulls through under their foot. To achieve this the trigger can be recessed slightly into the ground with the snare above ground or as in the variation of the leg hold above or left the snare can be simply propped up.

All pressure bar snares also rely for effect upon a spring arm which pulls in the direction indicated by the arrow. Top left is the neckhold with baited trigger stick. This trap works by the restraint of a toggle stick with a baited trigger stick. It is intended for mammals that reach down to feed or for birds that reach down or which might hop into the stockade.

In really cold weather spring arms and triggers have a tendency to freeze up. To overcome this use a counterbalance instead of a spring arm.

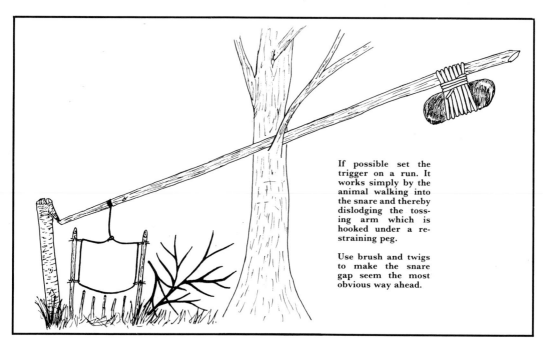

If possible set the trigger on a run. It works simply by the animal walking into the snare and thereby dislodging the toss-ing arm which is hooked under a re-straining peg.

Use brush and twigs to make the snare gap seem the most obvious way ahead.

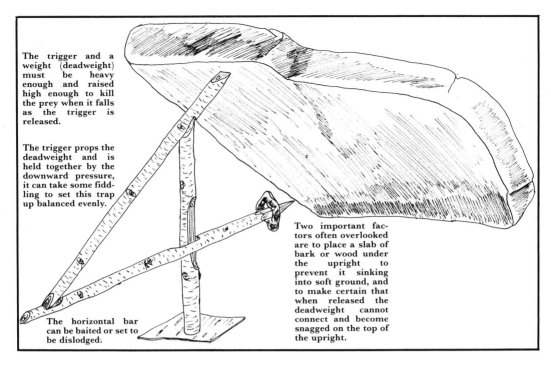

The trigger and a weight (deadweight) must be heavy enough and raised high enough to kill the prey when it falls as the trigger is released.

The trigger props the deadweight and is held together by the downward pressure, it can take some fiddling to set this trap up balanced evenly.

The horizontal bar can be baited or set to be dislodged.

Two important factors often overlooked are to place a slab of bark or wood under the upright to prevent it sinking into soft ground, and to make certain that when released the deadweight cannot connect and become snagged on the top of the upright.

The figure four deadfall is a classic survival deadfall yet more incorrectly described and drawn than any other survival trap. The best way to understand it is to make it.

The paiute deadfall is a variation to the figure four deadfall which incorporates a toggle stick and baited prop. This is a much more sensitive arrangement than the figure four; so much so that it can be set off by strong winds.

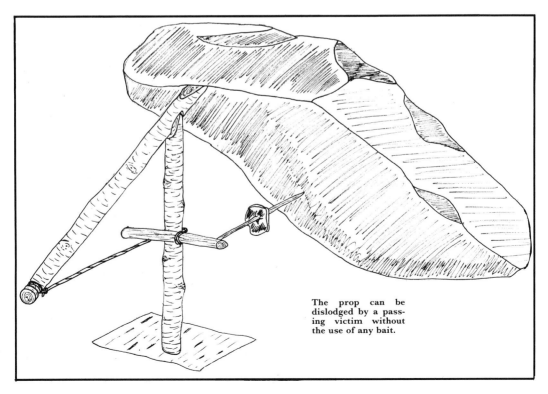

The prop can be dislodged by a passing victim without the use of any bait.

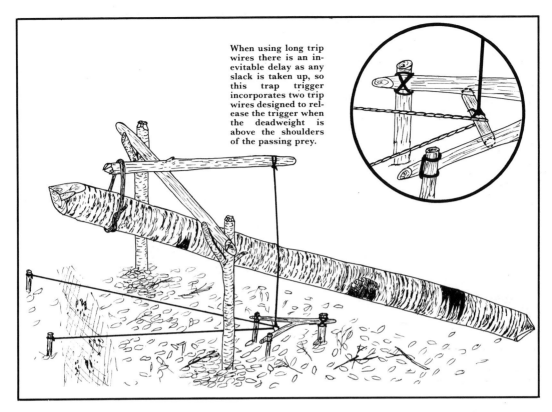

When using long trip wires there is an inevitable delay as any slack is taken up, so this trap trigger incorporates two trip wires designed to release the trigger when the deadweight is above the shoulders of the passing prey.

The Nootka overhung deadfall is designed for larger mammals; as with all deadfalls it is essential that the deadweight is heavy enough to kill swiftly.

The kicking bar deadfall. Similar in principle to a toggle-based trigger, this trap utilizes the mechanical advantage of a long lever (kicking bar) which is held in position by a pressure bar.

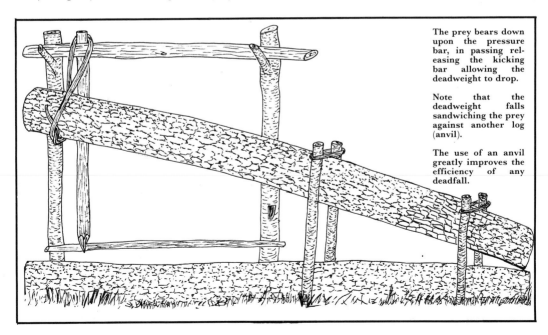

The prey bears down upon the pressure bar, in passing releasing the kicking bar allowing the deadweight to drop.

Note that the deadweight falls sandwiching the prey against another log (anvil).

The use of an anvil greatly improves the efficiency of any deadfall.

front of the slip knot. Not only is the wire the simplest snare, it is also probably the most effective of all traps—particularly in the hands of novices. I believe this is because no other trap can be set as easily and with as little disturbance. Personally though I would not use this trap; it is slow to kill and does not remove the prey from the reach of other predators. Try if possible to use a twitch-up stick or tossing bar which in most cases will facilitate a speedy dispatch.

Some snares are designed to take the prey by the leg. These do not necessarily kill but simply detain the prey. These are less humane than traps which kill outright, but are sometimes easier to set successfully. Of these the Apache foot drag is the least distressing. At first appearance it looks like a nasty barbed wait-a-while leg-hold, but this belies its true method of operation. A shallow hole is dug and the hubless wheel placed over this—not to trap the prey's foot, but to snag it. A noose is placed on top of the wheel so that when the prey steps through the wheel it also steps into the noose. The wheel then snags, causing the prey to try and shake it loose allowing the noose to tighten. The wheel is usually successfully shaken off. In fact any jumble of sticks that will serve the same purpose can be used for this job. The noose is attached at its other end to a weight which detains and occupies the prey's attention, so that it does not take any drastic action to free itself. The hunter must always take great care when dispatching the prey as a wayward kick or bite could in the case of larger prey cause an injury with fatal consequences.

Deadfalls: Many survival experts claim that the deadfall is the ideal type of trap to teach a novice trapper because it is swift and simple in operation. I do not agree with this. It is my experience that students underestimate the size and strength of trap required to kill the prey swiftly. A snare in the hands of a beginner will either work or fail but a badly-set deadfall will most probably maim. The advantage of deadfalls is that they require the minimum of cordage and are well suited to use in barren arid areas of scrub where twitch-ups or tossing bars are hard to improvise. They are also very well suited to use in arctic regions for taking large fat-carrying prey even to the size of bears. Before the introduction of wire and commercial traps, deadfalls were used extensively in the arctic. If in doubt as to the strength and size of your prey it is better to overweight the deadfall and crush rather than maim.

Deadfalls are very easily improvised in most situations. In the North of England some of the stone wall builders would incorporate small tunnels through their walls which were designed to be used as deadfall traps for rabbits, rats and other small mammals.

Pitfalls: Pitfalls were also incorporated into stone walls—usually in the form of a tunnel with a tilting floor which acted as a flap-closing lid to the pit. Pitfalls are easy to make and can be very effective for catching small prey such as rodents and snakes, which will keep you alive short term. However I would advise you to avoid handling the rodents as they may be carriers of Leptospirosis or Bubonic plague (still prevalent in many areas of the world including the USA).

Dead ends: These are very archaic traps best suited to use by groups rather than the individual. They consist of a dead end into which the prey can be lured or driven and then culled.

Stickups: If you have ever spent much time in a coniferous forest you will have come across the pine resin which finds its way onto your axle helve causing blisters. In warm weather this natural glue can be put to good trapping use for catching birds. Pre-bait a patch of ground with short sticks sticking upright out of the ground. Once the local birds have come to trust the area, coat the sticks in resin. This will stick to the birds feathers and prevent them from flying away.

On Trapping

It should be obvious by now that trapping is not a pleasant business. I find that explaining the basics of trapping to students is a very useful exercise. It dispels any romantic notions of an idealistic Crusoe-like adventure, bringing home the reality of survival techniques and the responsibility that comes with them. It also enhances their attention to detail when studying wildlife and improves their ability to improvise and adapt other survival principles.

The best way to practise trapping is to set up a camera with flash gun so that a primitive trigger is used to release the shutter. In this way you will have to carry out the 'trapping' of the photograph with exactly the same care, forethought and preparation as for any other

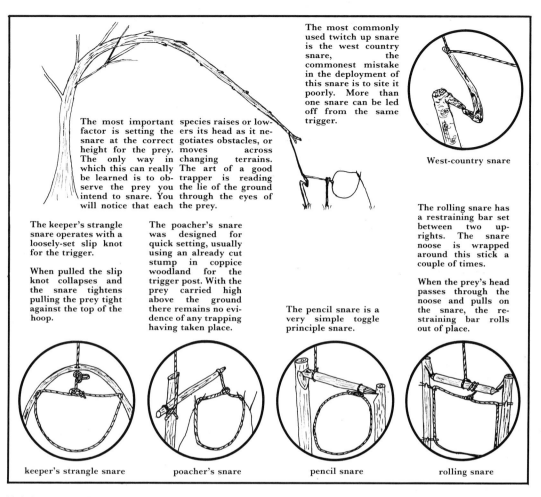

The most commonly used twitch up snare is the west country snare, the commonest mistake in the deployment of this snare is to site it poorly. More than one snare can be led off from the same trigger.

West-country snare

The most important factor is setting the snare at the correct height for the prey. The only way in which this can really be learned is to observe the prey you intend to snare. You will notice that each species raises or lowers its head as it negotiates obstacles, or moves across changing terrains. The art of a good trapper is reading the lie of the ground through the eyes of the prey.

The rolling snare has a restraining bar set between two uprights. The snare noose is wrapped around this stick a couple of times.

When the prey's head passes through the noose and pulls on the snare, the restraining bar rolls out of place.

The keeper's strangle snare operates with a loosely-set slip knot for the trigger.

When pulled the slip knot collapses and the snare tightens pulling the prey tight against the top of the hoop.

The poacher's snare was designed for quick setting, usually using an already cut stump in coppice woodland for the trigger post. With the prey carried high above the ground there remains no evidence of any trapping having taken place.

The pencil snare is a very simple toggle principle snare.

keeper's strangle snare   poacher's snare   pencil snare   rolling snare

Twitch up snares. Ideal for small mammals, these snares are quickly and easily constructed.

The ojibwa bird snare is a simple and effective snare which can be used with and without bait. The snare is tensioned either with the springy top of the snare post or by a separate heavy weight.

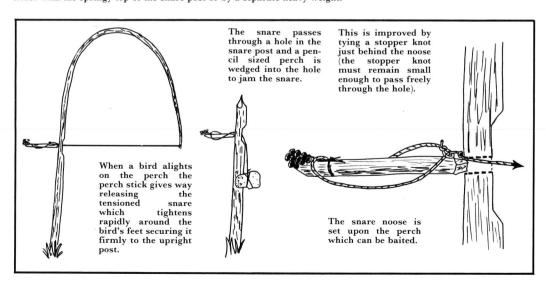

The snare passes through a hole in the snare post and a pencil sized perch is wedged into the hole to jam the snare.

This is improved by tying a stopper knot just behind the noose (the stopper knot must remain small enough to pass freely through the hole).

When a bird alights on the perch the perch stick gives way releasing the tensioned snare which tightens rapidly around the bird's feet securing it firmly to the upright post.

The snare noose is set upon the perch which can be baited.

trap. Make certain that the trigger does not cause too much camera shake, and be aware that the flashgun will gradually drain of power, so set it up at a time which gives you the greatest chance of success.

Some time ago I was visiting a friend who was having trouble with a mouse in his larder, and the suggestion was made that I try to trap it. So for interest we set up four traps, each baited with peanut butter, an irresistible bait. Three of the traps were fashioned from containers propped up with miniature deadfall triggers so that they would drop and enclose the target. The fourth was the simplest of all and was quickly improvised from materials available. A food funnel was set over a long tupperware container and a trail of peanut butter smeared tantalisingly down into the funnel tube (food funnels have a bore of about five centimetres). The next morning the little culprit was found languishing in its tupperware jail. As is so often the case, the improvised trap had worked best. After a last minute plea for clemency from my friend's two sons we conferred, and with all due solemnity, the mouse was taken a more than sufficient distance away and released into a suitable habitat. **Note:** Primitive trapping is illegal is most cases, excepting genuine emergencies.

Fishing Techniques

Fishing as a hunting sport is as popular today as it has ever been, but fishing to feed yourself in the wilderness is somewhat different. You must learn to improvise your own fishing tackle and to catch in quantity. Very often the fish you catch will be boney even muddy tasting, but it is food! To make the best use of this bountiful resource you will need to learn the ingenious methods of fishing used by native peoples. The following techniques are not sporting methods, they are poaching techniques outlawed on controlled rivers, because of their effectiveness.

Tickling

The simplest of all primitive fishing techniques is that which requires only a sharp eye and a steady hand. Tickling is usually portrayed on TV adventures by a country lad reaching over the river bank with one hand to fish out a wriggling salmon. But this is not quite true to life; I have yet to meet the man who had a hand broad enough to tickle a fish in this way. Tickling is an activity which requires you to wade into the water after the fish. It cannot be carried out in all streams; you need a wide shallow stretch of stream, perhaps with some eddy pools which can be dammed off.

Despite tradition, most fish that occur in these types of river can be tickled, although it is only really worth the effort with the larger game species such as the trout. Keep your eyes peeled for the deft flick of the tail which keeps the trout in the rippling oxygen-rich water breaking over stones or some similar obstruction. Once you have found the fish you are after you have two choices: you can either try to tickle him where he sits, or chase him into an eddypool which you have prepared as a holding pen. The first of the options is the traditional technique and requires considerable skill and stealth, while the second is better suited to emergency situations.

To tickle the fish you must slowly approach the fish with your hands already in the water, moving very smoothly and with great calm. You may find that your initial approach makes the fish move forward slightly. Don't let this deter you. Start again, moving slowly towards the fish, stopping occasionally to let him settle down. You should find that after a while you pick up the technique and get right up close to the fish. A tip here is to try and avoid your shadow moving over the fish. Now, very gently, with your hands palms up your little fingers touching and your thumbs pointing upwards, slide your fingers underneath the fish. Now you are poised to strike. With a bending lifting action, grasp the fish to your stomach and then cast him onto the bank, making sure he lands well clear of the water (all too often they wriggle back into the river.) That's all there is to it! It isn't quite as easy as it sounds but neither is it difficult.

If the fish swims under a bank or you are trying to catch him in an eddypool where the water has become silted up you will have to rely upon your sense of touch. The first time you feel a fish in your grasp in these circumstances is quite strange and most people flinch with surprise causing the fish to escape. Sometimes it feels as though the fish likes being touched and leans against your hand. When you feel this, it is time to strike.

Spears and Harpoons

In former days in North America, even the noble sturgeon was hunted with harpoons, sometimes in water more than 10 metres deep. But for survival purposes you can consider using spears and harpoons for those times when you can see the fish in shallower water. Using these weapons requires considerable practise; your strike must both be accurate and adjusted for the refraction of the water. To do this you must aim low by an amount that will correspond to the depth of water. The best way to learn this is to carry out some experiments.

Using spears and harpoons will soon teach you that river and stream bottoms are not the most welcoming of environments for them. Breakages are commonplace while you are learning. Make your spear light and strong and fit it with a hardwood or bone point. The problem here is that the point must be small enough to spear the fish without totally destroying it. This makes your fishing gear delicate. For smaller fish a spear like one of those shown will do the job perfectly well, but for larger fish they are not really strong enough. The very action of his thrashing around when speared, is easily strong enough to snap your spear head. To save your spear fit it with a detachable head, which is tied to the spear shaft. This will allow him to move around as much as he likes without escaping (usually) and without damaging your spear point.

Harpoons also have detachable heads but are thrown instead of thrust. They can also be fitted with more than one point to maximise your chances of success. To help in the throwing you can fit them with a finger grip, or notch the end for use with a woomera.

Gaffs are sort of reverse spears that have a backward pointing barb and are jerked upwards from underneath the fish. These can be a better bet when you are hunting a river with rocky pools.

But of all these spears, harpoons and gaffs, my favourite fishing spear is the leister spear which combines the best qualities of all three of the other designs. A leister spear can be fitted with a detachable head. Its success comes from the fact that it has one central barb with two gaff barbs either side which serve to guide the fish onto the central barb and prevent it slipping free. Ideally the gaff barbs should be slightly springy. I was once

demonstrating the way this spear functions using my hand to represent the fish when by accident I harpooned myself. I can assure you that it's not a pleasant experience; the grip of this spear is remarkable. Even so, many times when this same spear head has been used against trout they seem to almost wriggle free. Never underestimate the strength of a fish.

Any of these spears can be used from the land, from a canoe or from a wading point in the river. The length you make the spear will be determined by its intended use. In general, make the spear longer rather than shorter. For cordage (see Chapter Eleven) use plant fibres wherever possible as they resist soaking better than their hide equivalents. Pine resin can be used to waterproof and stick joints. At night, fish can be speared by attracting them to light. Natives hunted this way both from land and by canoe; the important thing is not to allow your shadow to fall on the water surface. When hunting by canoe a fire or lantern would be set on a fireproof platform laid across the gunwales and a screen erected to prevent the hunter's shadow being cast forward. From land the task was a little easier; a long torch would be fashioned from birch bark and then fastened to a long stick which could be held out over the water. Any shadow cast by this method would fall away from the water. A good modern method of such hunting is to use a head torch.

Another common way of luring fish to the spear or harpoon is to carve a fish-shaped lure from a piece of wood such as cedar or willow. This lure can then be pulled towards the hunter. Carved or bent to a slight curve, the fish would be attracted to the lure and follow it into striking range. There is endless scope for experimentation with different designs of lure.

Traps and Nets

Fish traps are an excellent method of catching fish in quantity with a minimum expenditure of effort. The basic principle is to create a coral or basket that the fish can swim into but not back out of. These are most effectively used on tidal rivers where all that needs be constructed is a crescent-shaped wall of rocks or sticks about eighty centimetres high against which the fish become trapped as the tide recedes.

In fast-flowing streams and rivers, simple basket traps can be set with funnelling walls of interwoven saplings to guide the fish in which they then become trapped by the force of water working against them. Even simpler are walls which guide fish into eddy pools which have been blocked off to prevent their escape, allowing you ample opportunity to spear or dip net the fish.

Nets require a considerable investment of both time and labour. The major problem is producing sufficient cordage. While time is something you have plenty of in most survival situations, it could be more efficiently spent making basket traps. Of the types of net you might make, the least ambitious and best suited designs for solo application are dip nets and the poacher's gill net. Dip nets are exactly as they sound. If possible fit them with a purse opening which can be opened and closed by a separate cord. The gill net is light and small; it works very simply by catching in the gills of the fish which swim into it. Often used at night, the net is usually secured to land at one end and then swung out into the river with evenly spaced floats and sinker weights to hold it vertical.

Hooks

Fish hooks have been a reliable way of catching fish for many centuries, although improvising them from natural materials is not an easy task since it is difficult to find materials small enough yet strong enough to do the job. The simplest and one of the most effective improvised fish hooks is the gorge hook which is simply a straight piece of hard wood or bone. This is sharpened at both ends and tied to the line at its middle. Baited in such a way that the gorge is held parallel to the line, the fish swallows the bait which then toggles inside his gut causing the hook to lodge fast.

If you have time, more elaborate hooks can be fashioned from briar thorns and a feather stem as depicted. Or bone can be abraded to make fish hooks of a more conventional design. The most beautiful fish hooks are those made by the fishermen of the north west coast of America whose steam bent hooks work remarkably well, seemingly reducing the fight the fish puts up. These are still in use today although now made of metal rather than wood and bone.

Even if you have made the best fish hook in the world it is totally useless without a suitable line. These can be made from a variety of materials ranging from algae to skin. Using plant fibres such as stinging nettles, surprisingly strong lines can be made (see Chapter Eleven) but for speed you will probably be better off using a rawhide line. Take a piece of rawhide which has been dried from the rack and therefore shrunk without weakening the fibres of its structure. Soak it and cut a line in the spiral fashion used for bowstring manufacture. The line you cut should be about just a little wider than the skin's average thickness. It is better here to use skin from the animal's neck; summer doe skin seems to be best. Cut the line until you have enough for your purpose and then stretch it and give it a rolling between your palms and a slight twisting to make it round. I prefer to then hang it over a smoky fire to dry though that is not necessary. Like all rawhide this line will be wiry when dry, but after a short soaking and flexing in water will be ready for use.

Poisons

Poisons have been made by natives in slow shallow streams to stun fish which can then be gathered downstream. But this is only really effective in warm water. Under suitable conditions this is possible in some temperate areas using a variety of poisons made by crushing and leaching out the poisons from plant stems or barks. However the use of this technique under survival conditions in temperate regions is unnecessary. Again it would be better use of your labour to devise another method of catching fish. The following are the species which have been used for this purpose: walnut bark, clematis, horse chestnuts, buckeye. The poison only works for a short while, stupifying rather than killing the fish, and soon becomes too diluted for use as it passes downstream. Any fish that you miss will recover. In general these fishing techniques can be swiftly learned and when coupled with patience you are on your way to easy fishing. Of the many fish I have caught for food not one has ever been caught with a conventional rod and line. I mention that because some students have doubted the validity of some of these old techniques compared to modern techniques. As I mentioned earlier, most of these methods have been outlawed because of their effectiveness.

Cooking, Preserving and Storing Food

'In my investigations I was unable to ascertain positively
why they were called Snakes, but one of their old men
claimed that it was because they formerly ate serpents . . .
Many of the bands living in the interior formerly had only
the rudest kind of lodges—at times only a pile of sage brush
to shelter them from the wind—and they subsisted on reptiles
and insects, in fact, whatever they could find alive, and such
roots, seeds, and berries as grew on the alkaline deserts and
in the mountains. With them rabbits were considered large
game. Some of the bands living near the streams and lakes
abounding in fish subsisted mostly on them, and they
exhibited some skill in the manufacture of grass nets, and still
others were energetic enough to secure ponies and hunt large
game.'

(W.P. Clarke (Captain 2nd Cavalry) The Indian Sign
Language 1884.)

'Come and get it!'

That was the cry of the camp cook, a cry
that could make or break the crew's morale
depending on the culinary delights on offer.
Yet this cry, born of a pioneering frontier, is
rare now. Instead all that can be heard is the
crinkling of packets of freeze dried food being
torn open. While there are those who apply
the old frontier flare for cooking to these
strange new foodstuffs, on the whole the skills
of backwoods cooking are in a sad state of
decline. Yet with an increasing number of
young men and women striking the trail on
expeditions for science or pure adventure the
ability to cook a camp meal can win you
many friends.

Even under survival conditions great
culinary delights can be prepared from the
most unlikely materials. The following skills
are the essential skills of backwoods cooking.

While covering cooking without utensils I
have also included cooking with a set of billies
that you will most likely have on an expedition or wilderness hike; cooking is a
fundamental outdoors skill. For ecological
reasons I have not at any stage included
cooking with aluminium foil, for while useful
in the home kitchen, it has little or no place on
the trail since its usefulness is short lived and it
is difficult to dispose of because it does not rot
away.

Attitude

Almost invariably in backwoods situations,
you will be faced with unfamiliar foodstuffs to
cook. This is especially true of survival
situations. Adopting the correct mental attitude to eating such foods is essential. I know
of several people who have eaten meals of the
most disgusting nature when in remote parts,

and many of my friends have sampled snails, slugs, lizards and large grubs, although they have not always been aware of the fact. On one particular photo demonstration day for a magazine, we found a yearling fox who had just been run down; a sad end for such a beautiful creature. But not to be wasted this windfall was put to good use—while the skin and sinew was saved for later use, the meat was prepared for cooking and the carcass returned to the soil in the traditional manner. Lunch was a quickly broiled slice of fox meat and grilled parasol fungus. The photographer who had not seen what was being cooked began to salivate as he smelled the meat cooking. I handed him a choice piece of the backwoods steak and he took a bite re-marking how good it tasted, especially with the slight flavour of woodsmoke, and asked what it was. When we told him it was fox he turned a very strange green colour and found he couldn't eat any more. I relate this just to reinforce the point: in emergency situations we must lose our predjudices and open our minds (and eyes). What in our everyday situations we might consider inedible, in many other parts of the world may be considered a delicacy. One old World War 2 soldier I knew was a prisoner on the infamous Burma railway and claimed to have survived by supplementing his meagre prison ration by cleaning and eating worms and other small creatures. He said that he watched his fellow prisoners who could not bring themselves to eat these unpleasant-looking foods waste away and die from disease made more dangerous through malnutrition.

The first place to start to enjoy foods which are unusual or unfamiliar is to stop trying to draw comparisons with those foods you are more used to. If a student asks me what squirrel tastes like I will always reply it tastes like squirrel. If you are continuously drawing comparisons with a Western diet you are at the same time grading the food by flavour and texture, but as your preferences are born from years of eating a small selection of foods it is unusual for wild foods to always compare favourably. You can soon become disheartened by such comparisons and can lower your own morale. At home, when I can afford to be, I am a very fussy eater, but when on the trail my appetite helps me to overcome prejudice, and I will eat anything that will keep me alive.

But that does not mean that wild food meals need to be anything less than a feast. One of my favourite outdoors challenges is to try to prepare four course meals from only natural products. With practise and given time to collect the foods, you will be surprised just how good a meal you can produce. Although most hiking meals need to be quick and easy to prepare, and in survival situations you are better off eating a little often, you will be surprised just how much enjoyment and satisfaction can be achieved from preparing a successful feast. Just thinking about some of the backwoods meals I have enjoyed is making me hungry, but before we consider making some, there is one absolutely essential aspect to deal with.

Hygiene

'A clean camp is a healthy camp' is an old scout phrase which is true—but what comprises a clean camp? Watch a docu-mentary about native Australians cooking goanna in the traditional way, simply slung onto a fire and turned occasionally by its tail, and you will probably think that this is un-hygienic. But in many ways this is a more hygienic way to cook than some of the methods employed by many western campers. While the meal may look dirty and ash covered, it has been well cooked in the sterilising heat of the fire and has suffered the minimum of handling in cooking and prep-aration. This highlights the first rule of out-doors cooking reduce the food handling to the absolute minimum and cook the food well to kill bacteria. Even if you can see your face in a brightly polished billy it is still going to be covered in bacteria which is too small to see with the naked eye. If you have washed your billy or are just about to use it to store some food, heat it over your fire to sterilise it.

Before you handle food make sure you have washed your hands; this is very important. In some desert areas where water is short, sand can be used for this task. Food—especially wild plants—should be washed before cooking or consumption; make certain that you do this washing with purified or sterilised water. Wherever possible use only fresh food or meat you have killed yourself. Without the advantage of a modern kitchen with easy-wipe work surfaces and cupboards, you will need to be highly organised in your cooking. Before you even start to wash the ingredients of your meal think the cooking process through so that you can make full use of your limited cooking utensils. Mats can be woven to act as makeshift tables to prevent loss of utensils and the contamination of food from the ground. If you are cooking for a group or in a camp, try to define the cooking and food preparation area. I always try to have a separate fire to the group's campfire to cook on. The last thing you need is idle hands and feet milling around the kitchen area—outdoors cooking isn't that different to indoor cooking!

If I am travelling I do most of my cooking on a simple fire—maybe an Indian fire, a star fire, or a criss-cross fire. But in a fixed camp the order of the day is a more elaborate set-up for your cooking gadgets and utensils. A spit or crane arrangement for suspending a billy over the fire at a variety of heights is an excellent innovation as is a simple table, which need only be a few inches above the ground. Make sure you have plenty of water to hand and fuel for the fire. For cooking, your fuel needs are better met from small sticks rather than logs and thicker fuel. A first class arrangement is to arrange your wood by thickness. Some campers prefer to arrange a rack for their different fuels but this is an unnecessary labour since no sooner have you racked the fuel than you are unracking it to burn. A simple but pleasing way to keep your kitchen clean and tidy is to fashion a small besom from springy twigs and to sweep the kitchen area clear of leaf mould and debris. It is very important to avoid dropping waste food on the ground; this will encourage the unwelcome attentions of rodents and other wild creatures. An old jungle traveller once explained to me that when rats enter a camp for food, snakes are certain to follow. Since then I have twice seen this happen both times in regions with venomous snakes. If you do have left-overs, either arrange for an old tree stump some way away from camp to be a left-overs post, or if you are in an area where there are dangerous predators, burn or bury deep this surplus. Keep this area clear and tidy, also tidying the fire each day.

Preparing your fire is an important step in the day's cooking. In a well organised camp the tasks of fuel gathering and water bearing are allocated to the other camp members by a rota system, so that the cook is free to prepare the food. For a camp of two days or more,

assuming you have the fixings for bread, an oven should be constructed next to the main cooking fire. Keep all of your needs in close proximity.

The cooking outfit: Without the advantage of modern cooking utensils, containers will have to be made—such as waterproof baskets and bowls for rock boiling (see Chapter Eleven)—and the techniques which do not require containers, made full use of. If you are equipped with a set similar to that described in Chapter Two you are handsomely equipped. For a fixed camp I would use three pots: small, medium, and large, and a mug. If transportation is no problem a box oven and a large billy are also useful. Utensils need not be elaborate: a spoon and fork are convenient for a one-person outfit although a spoon and improvised chopsticks would also serve the same purpose. On the whole, utensils can be improvised or carved to order although for large groups or expedition cooking, a ladle is exceptionally useful. The last piece of equipment which is extremely useful is a cloth for wiping your hands on; this should be washed frequently. If you are using metal billies it is perfectly alright to allow them to blacken on the outside and some would claim it even improves their performance. Just make certain that the insides and rim are clean before use. Wooden cooking containers and utensils are much harder to sterilise; the best policy here is to heat them to nearly scorching point over the fire, making sure it is the surface which will be coming into contact with the food that you are heating.

If these precautions seem at all fussy just ask anyone who has had food poisoning what it was like, and you will see their importance. While you may feel less persuaded to take all these precautions when cooking for yourself, they are absolutely essential if you are cooking for anyone else.

Latrines: This may seem an unlikely place to talk of toilet arrangements but it is in fact absolutely logical. When you are travelling alone a latrine may simply be a shallow depression dug in the ground or a rolled back stone or log, but in an organised camp this is in no way practical, here a proper latrine pit should be dug, preferably four feet deep if possible. The way in which either is used is important to reduce the risk of contamination by flies travelling from the latrine to the food preparation area. On expeditions this is an often overlooked aspect of field hygiene, which if neglected, can result in the whole camp becoming ill through picking up the infection of one member.

Firstly any latrine should be constructed well away from the camp itself, preferably in dense cover. After use, any stools should be covered with soil and toilet paper and preferably burned; then hands *must* be washed. In a large camp a bowl and washing facilities can be positioned by the latrine. Here again the task of keeping the latrine tidy and well maintained should be part of the camp rota, this is the best way of gaining the camp's co-operation in using the system properly. Never pour disinfectant into such a latrine to reduce smells—if everyone is covering up after use, the smell should be minimal; disinfectant simply destroys the putrefying bacteria, slows down the decay and prolongs the problem. The best way to reduce odours is to fill in the latrine and dig a new one. When this is done make certain you mark the location of the old latrine pit clearly.

Meal Planning

In the bush, living from the land is not easy as there is no guarantee that you will find food. You soon learn to make full advantage of many food resources and to reconcile yourself to those times when your gathering efforts have not been successful. In general, when on the move, food is prepared quickly and simply as it is found, but if you are working from a fixed camp or shelter you have the advantage of being able to discover the full food potential of the area you are inhabiting, and thereby plan meals, especially if you are able to dry or smoke meat and fish. If on the other hand you are hiking with food, your meal planning can be carried out before your departure, and should be done meal by meal.

The secret to successful backwoods cookery is simplicity and variety. If I am backpacking with rations they usually comprise as much fresh food as weight allows. The meals are also designed to match the cooking method I intend to use and will vary accordingly; hiking rations, for example, where I plan to use a stove, are designed to require the simplest cooking method and to produce very little clearing up, thereby allowing more time on the trail and for relaxing, with less time spent over chores. Very often I will include some tinned food. Many lightweight backpackers may be horrified at this, but planning meals around a rice base with a tinned topping such as sardines or chicken pieces is a menu worth its weight.

No matter whether your food is carried in or procured from the land, you should try to devise interesting meals which contain a variety of food stuffs and flavours. In survival situations, the nutritional value of meals is not easy to balance, because of your limited resources. Even the native inhabitants' diet may be beyond you as they would have had the advantage of being able to store the seasonal gluts to provide a year-round balanced diet. Calories and protein are the hardest of your needs to supply. The richest source of calories available to you are those contained in fat; unfortunately those small mammals that are easy to catch generally provide a very lean meat. Fattier meats mean catching larger game or water fowl or four-footed creatures who carry a layer of fat for insulation. Carbohydrate is another source of calories and this can be found in edible roots though in less quantity than fat. If you eat only lean meat, you will find you soon become quite ill, and for this reason it is very important to eat the fat on wild meat, avoiding cooking techniques such as spit roasting which destroy most of the fat.

If you are faced with the prospect of eating unfamiliar foods which are unappealing, you have two options: you can either hold your nose, close your eyes and swallow hard, or you can disguise the foods in the way you prepare them, combining them with other foods you are less put off by. Should you ever find yourself in the position of having to feed a number of people with unfamiliar foods, there are again two options: either you dish up a cleverly disguised meal and say nothing, or better still involve them in the food preparation and cooking.

A classic example of this happened a few years ago when I was instructing a camp of scouts. We had decided the camp should eat a survival meal which they would prepare and cook themselves in their patrols. We provided them with a variety of meats from rabbit to venison, and to help things along some rice for the meal base. All the other ingredients had to be procured from the campsite itself, having already scoured the site carefully, I had found a wide variety of edible plants and several deadly poisonous plants present. Selecting only those edible plants occurring in large quantity I gathered an example of each and briefed the teams on what they were to gather and how to proceed. Ingredients were only to be collected from the area I had reconnoitred and the poisonous plants (both woody ones and deadly nightshade were present), were shown and explained to each scout individually.

Before any cooking or food preparation was allowed the ingredients they collected were very carefully vetted, just to be on the safe side. A stew was the order of the day and each patrol helped prepare and cook their own, before dishing it up onto a base of rice with stinging nettle tea and acorn coffee to follow. Even I was surprised when every scout ate the meal heartily with expressions of approval only twelve year olds can make, but I am certain that if the meal had simply been placed in front of them and they had been told what was in it, they would have complained. Participation is a very important aspect of outdoors enjoyment.

The successful expedition or galley cook soon learns about that other key to successful cooking—flavourings and sweetenings. A small container of sugar or honey goes a long way to smoothing the passage of unusual foods as does a bottle of hot or savoury sauce. For example if I am baking in a camp oven, a nutmeg will enhance the flavour of pies immeasurably. Even when hiking, tomato puree included with pasta rice or mashed potato is a tasty surprise. There are no brownie points for acting the hard man and eating unnecessarily bland food—we can all do that—but transforming dull uninteresting food into a treat to look forward to, is a great and respected skill.

Food Preparation

One of the strangest things I came across when I first began to teach backwoods skills was how poorly tenderfeet prepare wild foods. Given a fish or small mammal they often have no idea of where to start, let alone know how to dress game for cooking. This unfamiliarity is almost certainly due to the pre-packaged nature of modern food.

Food should be prepared in keeping with its condition and how you intend to cook it; it never ceases to amaze me how many different ways there are of carrying out these tasks. The following are my favourite food preparation techniques: most of them are native in origin and all are perfectly suited to the special conditions of backcountry cooking—although they work equally well in the modern kitchen!

Meat: Whether faced with a deer or rabbit the principles of skinning are the same. I will describe below the process for a deer as this is the larger animal. There are many ways to skin an animal—as hunters are quick to demonstrate with a deft hand and flashing knife—but points are not won for the speed at which the skin is removed, but how well it is removed. A careless cut and it is spoiled. Small mammals can be skinned in the hand or laid on the ground, but it takes a lot of skill to skin a deer in this way without ending up with dirt-covered meat. More usually, large game is suspended off of the ground for both skinning and gutting. If you do not have cordage for the suspension, the legs are cut so that a stick or branch can be passed between the bone and tendon for wedging in a forked branch or some similar process of improvised suspension. Whether you suspend the animal head up or head down is a matter of choice—head up the gutting is easier, head down the skin is easier to remove from the neck area. If you are just beginning it is probably better to opt for head down.

With the game suspended, you have the choice of gutting before skinning or skinning before gutting. I prefer to gut first as the skin then acts as a protective layer against contamination from any of the stomach contents. Gutting is carried out by cutting open the skin along the belly but without opening the inner skin which encloses the stomach. To do this pinch up a small fold of skin in the belly, above where you can feel the internal organs have slumped, and using your knife, cut carefully horizontally. Your aim here is only to create a small hole just large enough for your finger. With this done insert just the tip of your knife and cut vertically upwards towards the groin. This may take several small cuts and you should be able to see the inner stomach wall which you must avoid cutting. The art of good skinning is to use a cutting tool as little as possible. With this cut made, extend it down to the breast bone. This is the opening cut complete.

You can now either gut the carcass or continue skinning. With small game it is quite often the case that the body is gutted when caught for skinning later; if this is the case it is a good idea to work the skin away from the flesh for about an inch either side of the opening cut, as later with the guts removed it will be difficult to carry out this separation. Also with small game and game suspended head up, it is a good idea to empty the bladder before the opening cut is made. This is accomplished simply by squeezing on the stomach and standing well clear of the obvious stream of urine. Suspended head down this is not usually necessary, but if in doubt carry this out as described before suspension.

Gutting is never as unpleasant as it may seem. The stomach wall is opened in much the same way as for the skin and all of the contents removed; be careful not to cut or damage them. Many of these parts are edible or useful. Keep your eye open for the gall bladder which is attached to the liver in which bile is stored. This must be removed intact to avoid contaminating the meat. Warriors traditionally smash this once it is removed or save it to produce arrow poison.

With the guts out you can clear them away and continue with skinning. Treat the skin as a jacket and cut it away from the body by slitting it up each of the limbs. Then using mainly persuasive force applied with your hands or fist, pull the skin away from the flesh; occasionally you may need to resort to your knife to ease the process. A good skinner can remove the skin from all parts of the animal including the head, but to start with you can simply finish at the top of the neck. Take the skin away for defleshing (see Chapter Thirteen).

Before you butcher the carcass remove any sinew you may need (see Chapter Thirteen). Butchering is essentially the process of sectioning the meat into a size and form you can easily handle This can be done to suit your plans in any way you see fit. An important consideration here is the cutting tools you have available; if you have a large knife or a tomahawk you can easily quarter the carcass without causing any dangerous splinters in the meat. But if you have only a small flint you may have to butcher the meat Indian style, laboriously cutting it away from the bone.

Poultry can also be skinned although in doing so you remove much of the fat. To keep insects away while you're doing this, skin in the smoke from a smudge fire. The alternative is plucking, which is made easier by scalding the flesh before plucking. As you remove the feathers you can pour a couple of cups of boiling water on the local area you are working. The feathers can be saved for arrow fletchings and insulation.

Internal organs: The liver, kidneys, heart, and brain are the most valuable edible internal parts of the carcass. The brain especially is rich in fat although it is also useful for tanning the skin. The remainder of the internal parts can be used as bait in your traps to catch other game.

Fish: Fish are one of the easiest of wild foods to prepare, the only problem being that they are slippery to hold, although with experience you will be able to hold them securely. Fish should be gutted as soon as possible as they begin to putrefy very quickly. To do this insert your knife in the belly of the fish just below the gills and cut down to the tail. Insert a finger in the belly and repeat the action with your finger scooping out the entrails. Cut off any dangly bits inside the fish and burst the swim bladder, which may be inflated inside. Particularly scaly fish can be descaled by scraping the scales off with a knife or flint flake; scrape from the tail to the head. Fish which do not have scales can be skinned; work from behind the gills to the tail.

If you intend to eat the fish straight after catching it, split it straight down the middle, lay some clean hardwood ash inside it and then drape it over a piece of hard fire wood for cooking in the coals of the fire. The flesh should not take long to cook through so keep a careful eye on it. If the skin is still attached—as for a trout or salmon—it is cooked when the skin slips easily away from the flesh.

My favourite way to cook fish uses a native American technique. For this the fish is best the day after it was caught, as the nerve endings have had time to die, making the filleting easier—although if you wish, a fresh fish can be suitably prepared by carving steaks off of its flanks. To fillet the fish, first cut off all of the fins and the tail. For this you will find a knife with a coarse edge is best, and use it with a sawing action. The next step is to cut down to the spine of the fish just behind the gills, but do not sever the spine. Extend this cut down and through the sides of the fish behind the gills, then with your hand grasp the head and spine and carefully lift it away from the flesh. You should find that the fish's skeleton lifts virtually cleanly from the flesh. With the steak so prepared, it can be fitted into a split stick as shown and broiled by the fire. This method of butchering is also suitable for smoking and drying (see below).

Sea shore edibles: All wild foods that come from a wet habitat are prone to going off very quickly but none more so than shellfish and the other delicacies waiting on the sea shore. While shellfish are on sale in the city this is no guide to their safety in the wild. Commercially-sold shell fish are thoroughly screened and vetted by health inspectors with the full benefit of modern science. In the wild you must be extra careful to avoid food poisoning. The most care must be exercised in the case of filter-feeding bivalves such as mussels, as they filter bacteria and toxins from sea water along with their food which then become concentrated in their bodies.

There are three particular problems connected with shellfish poisoning. The least dangerous is enteric bacterial infection from sewage. These pathogenic bacteria cause severe stomach upsets, and are particularly associated with mussels, oysters and cockles. This infection can for the most part be avoided by collecting shellfish away from areas of habitation or sewage outlets and by the thorough cooking of the shellfish. Under no circumstances should any shellfish gathered in the wild be eaten raw.

The most dangerous problem facing the gatherer of shellfish is the so called 'red tide'. This is caused by some single-celled algae which when absorbed by filter feeding bivalves (particularly mussels), concentrate toxins in the liver of the shellfish which can cause the often fatal Paralytic Shellfish Poisoning (PSP). The effect of these toxins is to paralyse the autonomic nervous system, leading to respiratory failure, leading in turn to heart failure. There is no known antidote to this toxin, PSP is *not* destroyed by cooking. Occurrence of the red tide is more or less seasonal, peaking around May to July, although it can be present several months either side of this period depending on local conditions. In seasons of extreme outbreaks of the red tide it can be seen as a red bloom in the water, but an absence of this colour is no indicator of the water's safety. The algae which produce this problem most commonly occur in regions of cool water, particularly when combined with a nutrient-rich upwelling current. There is no connection with the occurrence of this organism and polluted waters, it is just as likely to occur in clean water.

Another problem similar to PSP is Diureal Shellfish Poisoning (DSP). Less dangerous, it none the less results in severe stomach upset. It occurs for the same reasons as PSP, so to avoid it, it is best to remove filter feeders—and mussels in particular—from your survival menu.

Those shellfish which are not filter feeders are a much safer option, although care must still be exercised in their gathering, particularly in the summer breeding season when they are out of condition. Wash the shellfish you have collected before cooking. If possible leave them in clean sea water for twenty-four hours, then before cooking check that they are all alive, discarding any that may have died.

On top of these natural problems comes modern pollution from oil and other chemicals. Always keep a wary eye out for signs of this when gathering.

All these hazards aside, though, the most commonly encountered danger is that of becoming cut off by the rising tide. Because the best places to search for most of the seashore edibles are below the tide lines you must remain alert to the changing tide. I speak from experience when I say that it is all too easy to become so engrossed in your foraging that you misjudge the tide's return.

Listed below are the most commonly found seashore edibles for seaweeds (see Chapter Six) for both Great Britain and North America (many species that occur on the British coastline also occur along the North American shore). To become proficient at gathering seashore edibles it is important to understand the way each species lives; many of the listed species burrow into the sand, some leaving tell tale signs on the surface. To be fully efficient at gathering these species I strongly advice you to obtain a detailed field guide. Besides being an important part of your outdoors training, a few days spent exploring a coastline is always a rewarding experience.

Seashore Foods

In the following lists those species marked with an asterisk can be found within the British Isles.

MOLLUSCS
Gastropods

These are the safest of the molluscs as a source of food. They occur commonly on rocks and can be relatively easily removed for cooking by boiling, steaming or even baking.

Limpets (*Patella vulgata**):* These creatures cling tenaciously to rocks even in the strongest surf, and can be difficult to remove for cooking. The technique I most commonly employ is to sneak up on them and give a sharp sideways tap with a rock. Once they know you are after them they clamp down with a stubborn determination, so if your first attempt fails move on to another limpet preferably on an undisturbed rock.

Winkles (*Littorina littorea*)*: A traditional sea food, winkles are easily removed from the rocks on which they occur, and should be dropped into boiling water and cooked for about ten minutes. They are most easily removed from their shell by the judicious use of a pin or wild thorn.

Whelks (*Nucella lapillus*): Whelks can also be used for food, in fact all sea snails of temperate waters are edible. Treat in the same way as for winkles.

Black Abalone (*Haliotis cracherodil*):

Bivalves

These are filter feeders and because of this are apt to concentrate toxins and bacteria in their tissues. It used to be a common practise in British coastal communities to remove the mussel's stomach, siphon and gills which were believed to be where the poisons were most concentrated. While this practice may reduce the risk of becoming ill it does not remove it altogether. Better to avoid mussels completely. This preparation technique should be used for all other edible bivalves you may gather. An interesting fact is that the practice was also common amongst the native inhabitants of the North-West coast of America.

Mussels (*Mytilus edulis*): These are easily gathered from the rocks to which they anchor themselves. Most of the other bivalves listed here are to be found below the surface of sand, mud or gravel. Those which are found near the surface such as cockles often leave a distinctive pattern of little raised bumps over the bed where they lie. Others, particularly the clams, are less obvious and can be buried several inches deep, though empty shell cases occurring in an area should be a good indicator of their presence. With practise it is possible to develop an uncanny knack of knowing just where to dig, which I have several times seen demonstrated by beachcombers.

Oyster (*Ostera edulis*)*
Pacific oyster (*Crassostrea gigas*)
Portuguese oyster (*Crassostrea angulata**)
Cockle (*Cardium edule*)*
Scallops (*Pectens maximus*)*
Quahogs (*Venus mercenaris*)
Little Neck Clam (*Protothaca staminea*)
Clam (*Mya arenaria*)*: This shell fish is particularly gritty and often requires two days' cleaning in clean sea water.
Surf clam (*Spinsula solidissima*)
Bent nose clams (*Macoma nasuta*)
Razor fish (*Ensis siliqua*)*: *These are traditionally hunted by sprinkling salt in the hole in the sand and snatching them when they emerge.*

Cephalopods

The **Common octopus** (*Octopus vulgaris*)*: The North American Indians call this the 'Devil Fish'. It can be found in rock pools with deep overhangs and crevices. To capture this resilient creature it was speared with a gaff until so weakened that it could be extracted from its niche.

Arthropods

Most notable as a source of food amongst the arthropods are the crustacea which includes the shrimp, prawns, crabs and lobsters. While it is possible to collect shrimps under survival conditions your efforts will be better directed in collecting other forms of seafood; not least the following which can be trapped, speared or more easily collected from rockpools where they may be trapped.

The fiddler crab (*Portunus puber*)*
Hermit crabs (*Eupagurus bernhardus*)*
Edible crabs (*Cancer pagurus*)*
Jonah crab (*Cancer borealis*)
The lobster (*Homarus vulgaris*)*
Crawfish (*Palinurus vulgaris*)*: Treat as for lobster.

Like all marine food the meat of these creatures will go off very quickly if allowed to.

Cirripedia

The goose barnacle *(Lepas anatifera)*:* These float around on driftwood and flotsom and were utilised as a source of food by the North American Indians who would steam them and then peel away their skin before consumption.

Echinoderms

The unpleasant prickly surprise of many unwary bathers is the sea urchin, a valuable and important seashore food that provides fat, the commodity most lacking in a wild diet. The urchins can be collected with a three-pronged spear or carefully lifted by hand. If you are unlucky enough to be speared by their spines an acidic juice such as lemon or vinegar will help draw them out. To prepare the urchin for eating, smash it open and remove the roe which is the orange or white star-shaped meat inside. This can then be steamed to eat.

The common sea urchin *(Echinus esculentus)**

The green sea urchin *(echinocyamus pusillus)**

Cooking Shellfish

The technique most frequently used to cook shellfish is boiling, although under survival conditions, steaming or roasting are a more practical solution. Shellfish can also be preserved (see below).

Dressing out a crab: A crab must be carefully prepared to remove the poisonous internal organs, this is not the mysterious or difficult task some people seem to think it to be. To kill a live crab boil it for ten to fifteen minutes, large crabs may take longer, the guide here being fifteen minutes per pound.

Once this has been done twist off the large claws; these contain edible meat. Next remove the small claws and separate the crab's body from the shell, this should not pose any difficulties but if you do find some resistance here you can insert the point of your knife between the shell and the body and give a twist to effect leverage. With the body separated from the shell remove the small sac which lies in the big shell, along with any green matter. Then remove the lungs, affectionately known as the 'dead man's fingers' because of their shape. These are the parts which must be discarded.

From the sides of the shell extract the brown creamy part. This can be mixed with the white meat which should be extracted from the claws and other half of the body. The sides of the shell can then be broken away and the main part washed to serve as a plate to serve the meat on.

Having cooked the crab remove the claws.

Separate the crab's body from the shell.

Remove the lungs, sac and green matter.

Serve the brown and white meat in the shell.

Dressing a lobster: The lobster is prepared for eating in a different way to the crab. To kill a lobster you can either boil it in a similar way to a crab although allowing twice as long per weight than for a crab, or more humanely push a spike on the point of your knife through the top of the lobster's head at the point with the little cross mark. Make sure you are holding the lobster firmly. It is worth mentioning at this point that both crabs and lobsters are capable of making the saltiest seadog's eyes water if they catch your finger with their pincers. With the lobster dead carry out the boiling.

To dress the lobster cut through the top of the head and then down towards the tail. Open up the two halves and take out the dark string-like intestine and the sac which you will find in the top of the head. These are the parts of a lobster which should be discarded. The meat will be found in the claws and tail.

* * *

Unmentionable Edibles

In real survival emergencies or when you are travelling, the best source of food available to you may well be the smaller creatures. In most cases these are easily hunted even if you are injured. Some of the smaller creatures are proportionately high in nutrients.

Grubs, larvae and caterpillars: Most smooth-skinned larvae are edible although you should avoid those species which are hairy or brightly coloured as they may have chemical deterrents to predators that taste bad. I'm afraid I cannot tell you what these taste like as I have always respected nature's warning symbols. Some grubs contain fat well as very high proportions of protein—sometimes as high as fifty per cent. They can be easily found by searching under rotten bark or decaying logs; one of the largest grubs I ever found in Britain was almost two inches long and half an inch thick. I found it while pulling a decaying log apart in search of punk suitable for firelighting. Cook the grub by roasting it near or over a small bed of embers, I usually skewer mine on small slivers of wood and kebab them.

Insects, grasshoppers and crickets: The exoskeleton of insects is comprised of chitin which is undigestible to the human, but the juicy internal parts are edible. Pull off all the hard fibrous parts of the insect that you can such as legs and wings, and cook the remainder for a crunchy delicacy. Amongst the Californian Indians, grasshoppers were an important source of food and were hunted in a number of ingenious ways. Sometimes areas of grass land were burned and the roasted greashoppers collected and eaten, or in other cases they were driven into a corral or pitfall trap. On two occasions now I have been asked by a student if a grasshopper or cricket is edible only to see them swallow the captive alive before I could tell them to pull the wings and legs off and cook it.

Worms: When I was about four years old, I can clearly remember it still, one of my fellow playmates ate a worm whole without suffering any ill effects. But the advice on cleaning worms for food that follows is the process mentioned earlier, by prisoners working on the Burma railway. Clean them by storing them for twenty-four hours or more in clean water that is preferably salted. Then squeeze them to clean out their thread-like gut. Now they can be added to stews or generally mixed in with other foods. I am reliably informed that they can be used for creative cooking. In my experience they are virtually tasteless.

Slugs: Even the most open minded student of survival techniques has a personal revulsion, and for me it is eating slugs, even though when cooked they don't taste half so bad. There is really only one way to cook them and that is to kebab them. If you boil them, a most disgusting scum settles on the surface of the water just making the whole business even more repugnant.

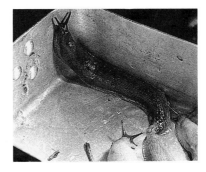

We all have a pet hate when it comes to food, and for me it is the slug. But in an emergency these are fair tucker, best spit roasted as a foul scum is produced when they are boiled.

Snails: While I may not like eating slugs, snails are a completely different story. Snails

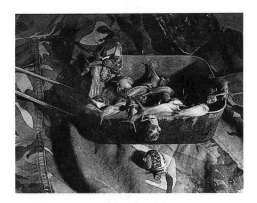

Snails are a survivor's delicacy! Escargots are tasty and nourishing. Hunt for them early morning or evening when they come out onto dewy grass.

are just about the finest survival delicacy I can think of; they can't run away; they are full of nutrients, and when cooked properly are chewy and flavourful. Many a student is astonished with the enthusiasm that comes over me when I spy a big white land snail. To cook them rake out a small bed of embers and place them still in their shells amongst this, with their openings up. With a little experimentation you will soon be able to judge when they are perfectly cooked (5 minutes is average), although if in doubt always over-cook them. Extract them from their shells with a sliver of wood.

Eggs: Another survival delicacy are eggs which need little or no introduction. The easiest places to hunt for them are in hedges and reed marshes. Blackbird and robin eggs are just as tasty, though smaller than duck or moorhen eggs.

Crayfish: Now a rare find due to pollution, I would suggest that given a choice you shouldn't eat them. But in the case of a real emergency they are the fresh water lobster and can be dealt with in the same manner as their salty relatives. They prefer fast-flowing, clear-water streams that run over chalk or limestone. Being nocturnal hunters they are often best hunted by night with a torch.

Frogs and toads: Frogs are an easy source of food to hunt. In the day, a quick hand and sharp eye are the tools of the trade. But at night you will have the greatest chance of success with a torch and trident spear. Listen for the distinctive croaking to guide you to them. The frogs' eyes will sparkle in the light from your torch enabling you to spear them not with a dramatic cast but from close prximity with a quick flick of the wrist. Be

careful not to allow the shadow from the spear to fall on them, I prefer to move the spear low and parallel to the ground, keeping the light high. A head torch is excellent for this purpose.

Some frog species have glands in their skin which produce toxic substances to deter their predators. These 'paratoid' glands are located just behind the frogs' eyes and in some species such as the South American arrow poison frogs, produce extremely dangerous toxic substances. For this reason always skin and wash the frog's flesh before cooking. As a general rule if you stick to eating members of the Rana genus, which can be found in most parts of the world you will be safe.

Frog's legs are tasty although only rarely do wild frogs have much meat on their legs.

Toads possess paratoid glands too and for this reason have for the most part been considered poisonous, although I have come across several references to toad pies being considered a delicacy among poor farming communities in rural Britain during previous centuries. Presumably they carefully skinned the toads before cooking, although I would not suggest you take such a risk.

Snakes and lizards: Snakes and lizards are good tucker, and can be easily caught particularly during the early morning. Being reptiles they are very sluggish until they have

139

been sufficiently warmed by the morning sun. Snakes have a somewhat undeserved reputation for evil, and in some parts of the world are hunted in large numbers for an annual mass execution born out of an almost paranoid hysteria. Particularly the rattlesnake is so persecuted, an ignominious end for the one venomous snake that is equipped to warn you of his presence. For survival purposes it is no good walking in fear, it is important to understand these beautiful creatures if you want to catch them for the pot.

Not all snakes are venomous and you should make every effort to learn to recognise the species occurring in your region. But if you are in an area where you are unfamiliar with the local species, consider them all as dangerous. Most snakes will avoid humans at all cost and will either disappear into the undergrowth of their own accord, or can be persuaded to leave the trail with a carefully thrown stick or stone. The real danger lies in surprising them by stepping on them or moving a log or rock under which they may be sheltering. Under these circumstances rattlesnakes have been known to strike first and rattle later! If you have to lift rocks in snake country, lift them so that the opening faces away from you. In fact most bites occur on hands, feet and faces.

If in doubt about the nature of a snake it is best to leave it alone. To catch a snake for food there are two techniques. The most practical is to pin it to the ground with a long stick held flat against the ground and then club it to death, after which the head and first two inches of the neck should be chopped off immediately and buried. It would not be very comfortable if later on you sat on the discarded head of a venomous snake! The other method is to catch the snake with a noose on the end of a long stick. I once met an old jungle survival instructor who used to use this method, and who kept the snakes alive attached to the stick so that they could be carried safely until time for a meal.

To prepare a snake for eating, gut and skin it before cooking over the camp fire. In general, reptile meat is best cooked by this method. The same cooking technique should be used for lizards who can be caught in the early morning with a small noose of fishing line attached to the end of a light wand.

Salamanders and newts should be avoided altogether as they are often poisonous; they are distinguishable from lizards by the fact that they have a skin rather than a scaley body. Some native American tribes feared salamanders claiming that their stare indicated the presence of an evil spirit.

Methods of Cooking Food

Cooking in the outdoors is essentially the same as cooking in the home—the only difference is that the resources are somewhat primitive. But I have never found this to be a problem. If anything it is an advantage as cooking techniques are reduced to simple logical processes. Given the ingredients, a campfire and a set of billies, most conventional meals can be cooked in the open; what you achieve is only really limited by your own imagination.

Remember that in survival situations you need fat for the calories it contains; you should therefore select cooking methods that do not waste this energy-rich commodity.

Baking: Baking is best suited to fixed camps or an expedition base camp where there is time and space to build an oven. I usually build an oven if I am backwoods camping for two days or more; it is one of the most morale-boosting fixtures of a camp. At meal time, when the smells of the forthcoming meal start to fill the air of the camp no call will be necessary to bring the expedition members to eat. If you have the resources with you for bread making organise a daily routine for the making of bread; in my experience people cannot get enough of camp-baked loaves. On one relatively short camp out I demonstrated bread baking for some venture scouts. Having spent most of the day building and setting up the oven there was only time to bake two loaves by sundown. I put the bread out so that all would have a chance to taste it, but in the time it took me to turn around one lone venture scout had downed half of one of the loaves. The lesson was plain. To start with make more than you anticipate needing. With long term or expedition camps the novelty will wear off after a couple of days and the demand should drop slightly. Aside from bread, cakes, (especially upsidedown cakes), biscuits, flapjacks and pies can all be baked in the camp oven.

The best way to make such an oven is to use a suitably sized metal box, or very large billy for the oven itself and to set this into clay or soil for insulation. If you have no such tin you can still build an oven using clay. To do this you must create an open fronted box construction using small twigs in the clay for reinforcement. For the oven floor try to incorporate a flat stone. Whether a simple clay oven or a box oven it must be built over a small trench where the fire will be placed to heat it. This trench should extend to the far back of the oven where a chimney can be built of clay. To do this, place a 5cm-diameter stick vertically against the back of the oven standing in the fire trench. Around this construct the chimney from clay. When it is dry enough to support itself remove the stick and start a small fire in the trench to dry the clay. Until the clay is completely dry your own oven will not function fully efficiently. A door is very important and must fit as snugly as possible, allowing easy inspection of the food. I usually use a piece of wood coated in clay, normally cut from a decaying tree stump. To hold this closed you can build a simple spring catch into the oven wall.

If you have not the time or resources for the above you can still bake but the results while good will not compare to oven baked food. The simplest way to bake is to place your bread mixture in the large lid of your billy set, and tilt this towards your fire, but not so steeply that the mixture can run out. Periodically rotate the lid so that the bread cooks evenly. As it cooks you should be able to increase the angle of the pan to the fire. I often use this technique on the trail. Using a household ready-mix cake mixture and lining the pan with some tinned pineapple, the result is a delicious pineapple upsidedown cake. This is excellent fare for sweet-toothed youngsters.

Another way to bake is to use your large billy as an oven. Place the lid on the ground and place some small pebbles inside it to prevent the cooking tray coming into direct contact with the metal of the lid. Place your bread mix in your smallest billy. Place this on top of the small stones and then place the large billy over the small billy. From the outside it should look as though the large billy is closed and standing upsidedown on the ground. For heat build a small fire all around the billy.

Boiling: This is a fundamental technique of outdoors cooking, especially for modern trail meals which cook with only the application of boiling water. If I am lightweight backpacking I try to do as much boiling as possible as it alleviates the problem of difficult washing up—a welcome saving of time and energy after a long day on the trail.

As was mentioned earlier for purifying water, when you do not have a container that can be heated over the fire rock boiling is a substitute. This technique can also be applied to boiling meat and making soups and stews. The secret is to add the ingredients a little at a time and cut them thin so that they cook more swiftly, particularly the meat.

Braising: With the meat from many types of small game, braising is the best way to both save juices and prevent it becoming tough. It is also an important process in the preparation of a stew (see below). To braise meat lightly brown it in the pan with a little fat (if you have some). If not there is usually enough in the meat itself. Having browned the meat add some water to the pan and simmer it slowly with a closed lid until cooked.

Broiling (grilling/barbecueing): This is the technique of cooking most popularly associated with backwoodsmanship. Meat is arranged so that it can be cooked directly over the heat from embers, this method is frequently used with many of the unusual foods mentioned above. But for joints of meat and such like it is of secondary importance in survival terms, as by this method most of the calorie-rich fat is lost. For speed and convenience as well as flavour though it is a fine cooking technique well suited to mobility. To be fully effective with large amounts of meat it is best to cut them into smaller pieces and cook kebab style. Choose green sticks of non poisonous hardwoods for any cooking utensils for broiling, I usually peel the bark off and dry the stick over the fire before use.

Another broiling technique is to use a hot stone as the cooking source. I often use this method to cook wild edible fungi as you can have more control of the process without the fungi scorching or disappearing into the ember bed.

Frying: This is my least favourite way of cooking in the backcountry; it produces a great deal of unnecessary cleaning which could be avoided by broiling. In a survival situation there are those who advocate this method as the food retains its high fat content. But my feeling on this matter is that while the food does retain a quantity of fat there is also a great deal wasted in the cooking; if retaining the fat is a primary concern you should use a technique that does not waste any fat at all such as steaming or stewing.

Most of the meat you will have to cook is light in fat content but there should still be enough to fry the meat with. If you do not find enough in the meat remove some from the skin. Any leftover fat in your pan should not be wasted though, this can be used to bait traps, make medicines, or seal and waterproof wood and hide. Native Americans did not wipe their greasy hands on a cloth but rubbed the fat into their arms and skin to protect them from the elements.

Pot Roasting: Obviously the most important factor for pot roasting is possessing a suitable pot for the task. A normal billy is not really suitable although one could be used at a pinch. Ideally you need a heavy walled container such as a dutch oven or an old iron saucepan. You will also need more fat than the meat itself possesses. Heat a little fat in the pan and place the meat in and cook it till it is well browned all over then drain off any excess fat. Place in with the meat any herbs and vegetables you wish to use for seasoning.

Replace the lid and cook slowly over the fire turning the meat two or three times during the process.

Roasting: Roasting is a similar process to baking except you are cooking meat. If you have built an oven there is no reason why you should not cook a roast meal. Use a pan to contain the meat which will collect any fat that comes off of the joint. During the cooking use these juices to baste the meat two or three times.

It is also possible to roast meat without an oven by suspending your meat to one side of your fire on a hanging cord which can be spun to achieve a spit roasting effect., Place a pan under the meat to collect fat and juices and baste in the same manner as for an oven. To reduce the cooking time place a reflector the opposite side of the fire to the meat. This technique is especially effective with waterfowl such as duck which can be excessively greasy when roasted in a pot or pan.

Steaming: I consider this to be the classic way to cook survival food, being reliable with little chance of burning the meal while saving all of the flavour and goodness of the food. If

The steam pit is a slow way of cooking which leaves your hands free for other activities; it also seals in all of the food's nutrients.

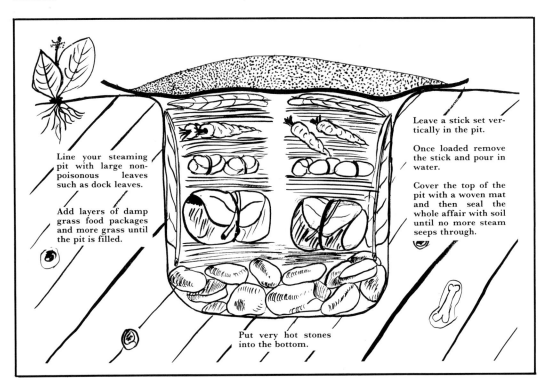

Line your steaming pit with large non-poisonous leaves such as dock leaves.

Add layers of damp grass food packages and more grass until the pit is filled.

Leave a stick set vertically in the pit.

Once loaded remove the stick and pour in water.

Cover the top of the pit with a woven mat and then seal the whole affair with soil until no more steam seeps through.

Put very hot stones into the bottom.

you are travelling, the easiest way to achieve this technique is to wrap your food in clean non-poisonous leaves. Wrap them in such a way as to make a neatly tied package, then cover the whole package in mud or clay, making certain that there is at least an inch of this all over. It will help enormously if you can mix the cladding to a sticky but firm consistency. With this done, none of the package should be visible. Bury the package in the embers of your fire. Fish will not take long to cook—45 minutes is usually right for an average sized river trout—but obviously the larger the fish the longer the time. Meat should be cooked three times longer on average that fish. The real beauty of steaming is that so long as the food is properly wrapped, you can leave it in the embers for some time without it spoiling. Be careful when you rake it out and open the package, as it will be full of scalding steam.

The more usual method for steam cooking is to use a steam pit. For this a pit is dug large enough to contain all of the food packages to be cooked and a fire is laid on top. The fire should be seeded with stones suitable for heating. When the fire has burned down to embers and fallen into the pit, line the pit with moist non-poisonous leaves—preferably large leaves such as burdock or dock. Then in the bottom of the pit place a layer of grass and then some more large leaves. Now place your food packages in the pit (same as for the above technique but without a mud or clay coating), starting with the meat and working up towards the top of the pit with those which take longest to cook nearest the bottom. Interlace each layer with a light covering of grass.

Once all of the packages are in, push a thumb-thick stick down through the middle of the pit to the layer of heated rocks. If you have laid the packages neatly in a square pattern with a central space this still will not break any packages. Pull the stick out and pour in water to create the steam. Now quickly cover over the pit with vegetation or preferably a mat (this makes opening the pit much easier) and seal the whole over with a layer of soil. This cooking process will take several hours. If I am cooking a couple of rabbits I allow a minimum of four hours. As with most backwoods cooking, with practise you develop an ability to judge cooking times. If in doubt leave the pit to cook until the soil

covering begins to cool.

To steam seafoods it is unnecessary to go to this length. Simply smother a well stoked fire with a large bundle of wet seaweed. Place the shellfish or fish on top, put another layer on top of this and leave until well cooked.

Stewing: The advantages of stewing wild foods have already been mentioned: the meat's nutritional value is saved, it is easily cooked, and less palatable forms of nutrition can be easily disguised. The secret to cooking a good stew is twofold. Firstly the meat should be lightly braised to seal in the flavour; browning on a stick over the fire is also suitable for this process. Secondly the other ingredients are added at the right time so that all of the ingredients are perfectly cooked. For example meat goes in first, roots perhaps (depending on the type) thirty minutes before taking the pan off of the fire, with fungi perhaps fifteen minutes and greens ten. These are the timings which I have used most frequently although again bush judgement counts for a lot here. Cook the whole stew slowly, simmering over a low heat. This is another advantage of this type of meal as it can be left for quite long periods just simmering while you go about other tasks.

Preserving Food

Food preservation techniques should not just be considered appropriate for long-term backcountry living. If you are trapping there are occasions when your trap line will produce more than you expected it to. This meat must not be wasted, especially when preservation is so easy.

Drying: Drying is the principle technique for producing what is known as jerky or biltong. The most common way to dry meat is to use the sun, but the dry heat of an oven at low heat or hanging the meat high over a low bed of embers is also effective, especially during bad weather.

To jerk meat it must be correctly prepared and butchered into long narrow thin strips. These are both easy to dry and rack. Commercially produced biltong is also seasoned with spices. The meat should be butchered under hygenic conditions; the greatest problem you face is from flies landing on the meat to lay their eggs. Once the meat surface is sufficiently dry the flies will lose interest so somehow you must keep them off until the meat has had time to cure a little. This is where a smudge fire comes into play;

this is not actually part of the drying process itself and should not be excessively smoky. A small smudge fire just potent enough to keep the flies off, will do the job perfectly well and will not taint the meat with wood tar. The native Americans who jerked meat and fish in large quantities would also locate their drying racks on high windy promontories where the breeze would keep flies off. One other technique I have seen used was meat lightly dusted with the pure white wood ash from a well-controlled fire. The ash supposedly acted both as an aid to drying and as a fly deterrent, although I am not convinced that this has any advantages over the more usual methods.

If you are using your oven to dry meat, the problem from flies is greatly reduced, although most backwoods ovens are not large enough to do more than a small amount of meat at a time. Keep the heat low and take your time; the aim is not to cook the meat but to drive off the moisture within it. Once dry it should be shrivelled and fibrously brittle. One pound of jerky is equal to four or five pounds of fresh meat so you can see its obvious advantage for a traveller.

As it is, jerky can be eaten raw or included in stews, or rehydrated and broiled. But that is not the end of the story. It can also be ground into a powder for the manufacture of pemmican (see below) or for use in stews. This is a useful technique for preparing less palatable meats and bony fish both of which should be split or quartered and dried more or less whole. Once dry, the meat is pounded to a powder along with the bones; this must be very thoroughly done. The result is a stew seasoning complete with the vitamins contained in the bone marrow. The most useful application of this technique is with small bony fish, which you might otherwise be tempted to waste.

Shellfish can be dried also, but firstly they must be thoroughly cooked. Then they can be strung on a thin sliver of wood or cordage and dried in the usual manner.

Once your meat is dried it must be carefully watched to make certain it is not attacked by insects. Damp weather is your greatest enemy. It is a good idea to provide your drying rack with a rain-proof roof and to locate it on well-drained ground; even so, in the damp there can be problems.

For drying plants and fungi see Chapter Six.

Smoking: This is essentially a way of flavouring and curing meat, although it is a stage which can be combined with drying. Particularly useful in damp regions, smoking helps to preserve the meat or fish. To smoke meat you will need to build a smoke house. The way that I prefer to go about this is to construct a rectangular structure, walled with large leaves to prevent smoke escaping. This structure is constructed to allow racks of meat to be placed inside it. Outside this is a small fire pit which interconnects with the smoke-house by means of an underground chimney. In this way the smoke has a chance to dry before reaching the meat. The meat does not risk cooking and the smoke house need not be opened to maintain the fire. The fire should be laid with dry aromatic wood such as alder; it is unnecessary to force the fire to become smokey; it will become smokey enough as it is. Once going well close off the fire pit so that the smoke must escape via the smoke house. Closing off the fire in this way will also slow the fire and make it more smokey.

As the meat dries it will become very hard. This can be prevented by pounding and working it occasionally although this is not essential. If you just want to flavour the meat so that you can eat it raw, remove it from the smoke house once it has dried so that it doesn't become too brittle. The type of wood you use for this task is essential, do not use poisonous woods and stay away from the resinous evergreens which will taint the meat with a resinous flavour.

Pemmican: Sometimes referred to as scout meat, wasna (pemmican) was the food of the Sioux scout who had to travel long distances cross country fast and unobserved in terrain where a fire would betray his presence to the enemy. Tasty and energy-rich, this highly concentrated food was compact and lightweight—factors which persuaded many of the early polar explorers to use it. Pemmican is just about the perfect survival food containing fat and protein in fact just about everything you need except vitamin C. It is also light weight and if stored correctly will keep indefinitely, in fact I am still using a batch I made five years ago, but that's no record. I have heard of a cache of Indian pemmican dug up by archaeologists that was perfectly edible even after the passing of nearly a century.

So how is this wonder food made? Well the

Using a fishing spear is easy but requires patience, especially as you tend to break the spear head until you have mastered the technique. In rocky riverbeds use the leister spear (inset top); this should not touch the river bed. In muddy or sandy rivers use a harpoon such as that shown and pin the fish to the riverbed.

Below: Various types of fishhook made and used by the author.

Once the skills are mastered, life becomes, if not easy, enjoyable. Note the properly constructed shelter with cot wall beds and fish cooking over the fire.

What fish you do not cook, dry and save for later.

Limpets and whelks served on a seaweed platter on the rocky foreshore. Even though you may be miles from civilisation good food presentation should not be lacking, it is an important factor in keeping your morale up.

Nothing smells better in camp than the aroma of newly baked bread.

Bread and cattail; a simple springtime repast.

Using a hand drill. Notice the coal forming in the notch and the bark slab used to hold the coal.

Making fire with a steel strike alight, flint and willow-herb down.

Carefully place the smoking coal in a nest of finely teased tinder.

Tinders left to right, top to bottom: clematis down, cattail down, thistle down, clematis bark, inner oak bark, cedar bark, honeysuckle bark, cherry bark, bird's nest, birch bark, dried grass, bird's nest.

Gently nurture the coal inside the the tinder by blowing; try to make the amount of smoke increase until ...

Using a fire plough.

The magic moment when you first succeed at fire lighting by friction.

... the bundle bursts into flame.

Group shelters.

The author living in the backcountry.

One-person shelter giving all-round protection.

A well-constructed shelter doorway.

Look for the rabbit's eye; be aware.

Arrowheads, scrapers, a saw of flint, a bone awl and two bone needles.

Rabbit tracks.

Flint axe in use.

Badger tracks.

Fox tracks.

Needles made of bone.

Spear heads.

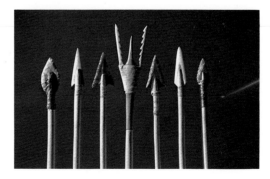

Above: making a rope from clematis bark.

Left: Weaving a Burden Basket

Adding in a few fibres of bark.

Above: A basket of cherry bark.

Left: Burning in a wooden bowl.

Using a crooked knife to gouge out a bowl.

Extracting clay from the ground.

Dried and crushed clay, with temper added, being mixed with water.

The extracted clay in its raw state.

Clay and temper combined and ready for use.

Finely powdered clay and temper.

Moulding a clay bowl in a wooden mould.

Burned and ground sandstone for use as temper.

Making a bowl by coiling clay.

Above: Scraping the dermis off the hide.

Left: Bow, buckskin bag and quiver.

Below: After brain tanning, staking the hide ensures softness.

A good woodsman is at home in the forest.

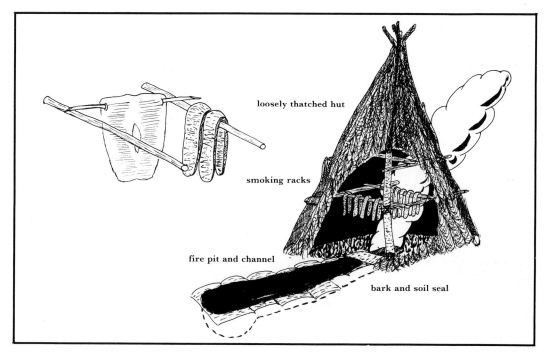

loosely thatched hut

smoking racks

fire pit and channel

bark and soil seal

If you have much meat or fish to preserve it is easier to make a large smoking house. A simple quadruped tipi is ideal for this purpose, the thatching need not be as thick as that of a shelter but should be weather proof so that it doubles as a food store house. Dig a shallow trench for four or five feet leading into the centre of the smoke house. Enclose this trench with bark sealed with earth, at the far end dig a small fire pit. In use a small smouldering fire is lit in the fire pit and covered over in the same way as the trench so that the smoke is forced down the trench into the smoke house, by which time it has cooled. Arrange the meat inside the smoke house on racks allowing plenty of room for the smoke to circulate around the meat. Halfway through the smoking process turn the meat over so that all sides are evenly treated.

first step is to jerk your meat and powder it. Now add to this an equal quantity of dried berries such as pitless wild cherries (the pits contain poison although this did not seem to bother the Native Americans who used them regardless), blueberries or any similar dried berry. To this mixture add melted fat, the general recipe is for a quantity of fat slightly less than the quantity of meat. I usually add more fat than this if possible as it prevents me nibbling the pemmican on the trail and makes it more useful as a stew ingredient and can be easily fried. As the fat cools, shape it into balls or better still sausage-shaped pieces. Once hard it can be wrapped up ready for use. Being so rich in fat it will keep indefinitely.

Cooling: Many people consider refrigeration to be a modern technique of food preservation, but of course this is not so. In the arctic, refrigeration was the principle way food was stored. In fact the problem there was more how to thaw the meat than how to cool it. Unless though you are in the arctic, refrigeration is for the most part impossible. Cooling however is another story, wherever

there is a cool running brook there is a means to cool food. On the trail, food packed in watertight containers can be anchored in a stream or brook to keep it cool.

Evaporation is another way of cooling foods although it is much slower. For this you will need to cover your food with a cloth or cotton T-shirt in such a way that the cloth is wet and can remain so by wicking up further moisture from a container. With this done, hang the cloth-covered food container in the shade were it will receive a draft of air. This draft will cause the moisture in the cloth to evaporate taking heat away from the food container. Given a chance to work this cooler is very effective.

Storing Food

One summer some years ago I saw a most amusing sight while lecturing at a scout site. A visiting party of young Dutch scouts had gone off on a hike and left their food boxes open with plenty of food strewn around. Of course the local wildlife, well versed in the potential delicacies to be found in unoccupied campsites, descended to the feast within

153

minutes of their departure—the jays and squirrels squabbling over who should have the most. Later in the day when they returned, the scouts immediately accused unknown persons of having raided their larders (despite the total absence of human sign), to the great amusement of the warden who had also witnessed the wildlife partying. You might say that we should have tidied up for them, but that is not the way of the woods; they learned a valuable lesson that day.

Food must be correctly stored whether you are travelling overnight or camping in one place for a week. In the backcountry there is only food not my food and your food. Once food is detected there are a host of creatures who will be trying to gain access to it. The first step to take in keeping it out of their reach is to wrap it securely in suitable containers, preferably that will keep down the scent of the food. Having so wrapped the food it can either be put away in a rucksack or suspended out of harms way up a tree. In bear country all food should be suspended high in the branches and well away from camp.

For longer term food storage or cacheing food for a return trip from the backwoods, your best option is to bury it. This is also the best way to store long-term supplies of food you have gathered. Choosing a well drained sheltered spot, perhaps under an overhang, dig a pit, trying where possible to keep the opening to this pit smaller than the pit itself. Now line the cache with plenty of dry grasses before placing the food in. With the food in place cover over with more dry-grass and mix some aromatic herbs to disguise the scent of the food. Finally, cover over the pit with soil and preferably some large rocks. Never underestimate the burrowing ability of a hungry mammal that can scent the food you have hidden. In some places you may be lucky enough to find small hollows in rock faces which can be sealed with a large rock to the same purpose. If you have been careful the food should be there when you need it.

*   *   *

NOTE: Many of the wild creatures described in this chapter are protected from hunting by law. It is only acceptable to gather them in real emergency situations.

Cordage, Basketry, Pottery and Glue

'Being not able to cut down trees, I burned them down, and
then burnt them off at proper lengths. This was our third
day's work after leaving our companions. The next day we
got our materials together, and completed our raft, and
floated with the stream again till we came to Wattock-
quitchey Falls, which are about fifty yards in length; here we
landed, and by a wreath made of hazel bushes, Capt. Ogden
held the raft, till I went to the bottom, prepared to swim in
and board it when it came down . . .'
(Major Robert Rogers, from his journals)

Despite all of our modern technology and materials we still depend upon rope and string containers and glues. Even in amongst the polypropelene, polythene and fast-acting adhesives the old backwoods products survive: baskets, earthware pottery, sisal string, manilla ropes and joiner's hide glue. In some of these cases better substitutes have yet to be discovered, but in all there is a heartfelt connection to our roots. The aroma of a squeaky old basket, the wholesome sight of home-cooked soup steaming in an earthenware bowl; these are the last remnants of our ancient past. What sailor can resist the appeal of a tall ship, her timbers responding to the changing swells and the slow subtle sounds of her canvas and tarred rigging filling with the wind? All of these emotions and more are brought to the surface in the backwoods where all of the materials for life must be fashioned from nature's bounty. For raw materials we will use the very fabric of the wilderness itself.

Cordage

Some form of cordage will certainly be required of every outdoors person at some time or other. In survival situations cordage becomes a necessity. But manufacturing cordage is a lengthy, time-consuming process— hence the lengths taken to avoid its use in the shelter-building chapter. However, if needed, cordage of almost any strength can be produced. Many people are of the opinion that really strong ropes cannot be made from fibres close to hand but they are wrong. Native people who are often referred to as primitive were able to manufacture cordage from grasses, other long-fibred plants and hair which were strong enough to capture elephants, to harpoon whales, to climb cliffs and build bridges across ravines. One of the greatest mysteries of the world, Stonehenge, must certainly have involved the use of very strong ropes in its construction. Cordage manufacture is a skill every outdoorsman should master; it is easy, requires the absolute minimum of equipment and is a skill which will be found perenially useful.

The most important aspect in the manufacture of any cordage is the type of fibre used. All fibres have their particular idiosyncrasies: some are greatly weakened when wet while others are made flexible when moist, overcoming a brittleness which would otherwise make their use totally impractical. Hide and sinew are covered in Chapter Thirteen although the rope-making techniques below are equally applicable to them. Plant fibres are most likely to be your first option for rope making, but if you are faced with fibres you are totally unfamiliar with, you will need to carry out some experiments to see whether the fibres are suitable or not:

1. Test different methods of extracting the fibres by light pounding. Split the stem and bend it back to break the pith for easy removal. Either peel away the fibres or use the whole stem. Repeat each of these tests with the fibres soaked in water.

2. Tie a simple knot in a single fibre and pull it tight. Check whether the fibre breaks or not. Do this with the fibres both wet and dry. Then repeat the experiment with a small bundle of loosely twisted fibres.

These tests are a very general guide, but when combined with the knowledge of how to prepare the different types of fibre listed below, you should be able to easily determine the best way to tackle unfamiliar fibres.

Fibres for cordage

Animal fibres: (see Chapter Thirteen for preparation techniques)

Buckskin

Hair

Rawhide

Sinew

Plant fibres: *Outer barks:* In most cases the outer bark is simply peeled away and used in long strips without any further preparation. Cherry bark is removed from logs in a spiral fashion. I find this easiest by scoring the strip you intend to remove then levering it off with the cambium attached which can be more easily removed later (only from dead trees or felled logs). An old poacher's trick is to select a willow wand strong enough to take a pheasant or rabbit and with a sharp knife to shave a long 6mm strip from the full length of the wand. This is achieved by using the knife

in the fashion of a draw knife with a smooth steady draw. This is then twisted slightly and becomes the snare itself. One year I was using a lot of willow wands for basketry and had the opportunity to collect a great number of these strips which I then soaked for several days, before laying into a two strand rope. While a little on the stiff side this rope was one of the strongest backwoods ropes I have ever made and only just over 1cm thick. Both clematis and bulrushes shed their outer bark naturally and need only be sorted into bundles of equal size for easy laying up.

Bulrushes *(Scirpus validus)*

Wild cherry *(Prunus emarginata)*

Wild cherry *(Prunus avium)*

Clematis *(Clematis vitalba)*

Willow *(Salix alba)*

Inner barks: Some of the finest cordage is produced from the inner bark of certain trees most notably the Western red cedar, basswood (and related lime trees), and elm trees. The process is somewhat labour intensive but the finished product is well worth the effort. The bark of a suitable tree is removed if possible in one long strip four or more feet long. To avoid killing the tree natives only removed one strip from each tree of about 30cm wide, but unless your need is dire or you are in remote heavily forested backcountry only dead or recently fallen trees should be considered a source of bark. Cedar trees can often be found in such a state at the margins of swamps and by careful pulling away extremely long strips of bark can be removed.

If the inner bark cannot be simply pulled away from the outer bark soak it until it is easy. You will find that fibres are most easily removed if stiff sections of bark or plant stems are broken so that the stiff woody pith or bark breaks, peeling away from the fibres enough to offer you a starting place. For most purposes the bark you have so secured can be easily turned to most of your needs although to produce the finest fibre it must undergo another process. For this you will need to boil the inner bark for some hours, preferably overnight. For this the Native American would often prepare a strong lye solution by boiling down concentrate of hard wood ashes. Using this to boil the bark in. Once the bark has been boiled it can be easily separated into finer fibres with a deft rubbing action between your hands, quickly learned with practise. Should you find any of the bark unco-operative pound it on a log with a wooden mallet. With the fibres separated you can lay up a rope using any of the techniques listed below.

Basswood *(Tilia spp):* Lime family

Buckeye *(Aesculus spp):* Horse chestnut family

Elm *(Ulmus spp)*

Hickory *(Carya spp)*

Oak *(Quercus spp)*

Osage orange *(Maclura pomifera)*

Western red cedar *(Thuja plicata)*

Willow *(Salix spp)*

Structural fibres: These fibres are generally more time consuming to gather than bark fibres although they are more commonly available. To separate the fibres gather the plants and leave them to dry, natives would gather the stems in the autumn when their life cycle was complete and they were dry. You will find that once stinging nettles are dry they have for the most part lost their sting. If you do not have time to dry the stems they can be soaked or boiled to loosen the fibres from the pith and outer bark though this is a much less effective preparation technique. Once the stems have dried they should be split and the pith removed by pounding and running bundles of stems around a post. With plants such as nettles it is far easier to prepare the fibres from a large quantity of stems. With the pith removed the fibres should be rubbed between your hands to further loosen and separate them. They can now be used for cordage manufacture.

Butterbur fibres should be simply stripped out of the plant's stem by snapping it near the base to reveal the fibres and then drawing them out. They are always better worked when allowed to dry and then resoaked.

Yucca and agave fibres can be crudely loosened by vigorous twisting of the leaf, although the better way to prepare them is to soak them in warm water and to pound out the fibres.

Agave *(Agave spp)*

Blackberry *(Rubus fruticosus)*

Butterbur *(Petasites hybridus)*

Dogbane *(Apocynum androsaemifolium)*

Indian hemp *(Apocynum cannabinum)*

Milkweed *(Asclepias spp)*

Stinging nettle *(Urtica dioica)*

Yucca *(Yucca spp)*

Roots: Those roots which a tree sends out horizontally just under the surface of the soil can be used for extremely strong binding material, particularly those of spruce trees. The thin rootlets should be dug up or searched for at the base of recently wind fallen trees. The thickest that is really practical for use are those which are the same diameter as the average pencil, while any thing thinner will be of use. The thinner roots can be used as they are. Wash off any soil that is adhering to them and remove the bark; this is most quickly done by heating the root quickly over a fire and then pulling it under the sole of a shoe held loosely to the ground. A more precise method however is to boil the root and then to pull it between a split stick. Old woodsmen used to use a metal version of the split stick for the same purpose.

The thicker roots should be treated likewise, but are best split into thirds before use. To split the root take a knife and split the root longitudinally in equal thirds, some roots will have a three armed mark in their centre; if so use this as your guide. Having made these cuts peel the three thirds out and grasp one in each hand and the third between your teeth. Now with an even pull on each third pull the root apart. If done correctly you should have three equal roots sections. If you had trouble, either the root was not boiled for long enough or the pull you exerted was uneven. These root sections make exceptional lacings and were used in the manufacture of birch bark canoes. If when you are carrying out some lacing the root seems to stiffen apply some hot water locally to soften it. Many more roots can be used those listed here.

Cotton wood *(Populus spp):* Poplar family

Hemlock *(Tsuga spp)*

Spruces *(Picea spp)*

Tamarack *(Larix spp):* Larch family

Western red cedar *(Thuja plicata)*

Withes: Withes are the least flexible of all the backwoods cordages. I first came across their use watching a hurdle maker gathering small sticks of hazel into bundles. Without any string to hand he would take a young hazel shoot and twist it until the wood loosened and split untidily along its length. The stem would tend to split easiest near the top so he would repeat the process every few inches starting from the base. Then cutting the flexible withe free he would use it to wrap the sticks, overlapping and tucking the ends where they met. After the first tuck he would hold one end under his boot and tug the other with his gnarled old hands. Another couple of tucks and it was tied and would not loosen. Two withe bindings per bundle and a withe handle between the two and the bundles could be fitted to a stick and carried hod fashion over his shoulder. Withes are quick and convenient for such uses and for binding shelters together. They can be made more flexible by heating with hot water. In the pioneer days of North America it was withes that were used to lash together log rafts. The greatest drawback is that they cannot be easily tied other than tucking the ends in a hoop. Sometimes the timber hitch can be tied if the withe is twisted as it is doubled back.

Ashes *(Fraxinus spp)*
Birches *(Betula spp)*
Hazel *(Corylus spp)*
Oak *(Quercus spp)*
Willow *(Salix spp)*

Rope Making Techniques

Rope making is an old and fascinating subject but here we are confined to the backwoods techniques which can be carried out alone, and without machinery. None-the-less the techniques are the same in principle to those used to fashion the giant hawsers of the dockyard. Fibres are taken and twisted together into a yarn; this yarn is combined with other yarns to form a strand and in turn strands to form a rope. The simpliest way to form a yarn is to take some fibres, tease them out into a line and then role this on your thigh with the flat of your hand, so that the fibres twist together and tighten on each other. If you are working with fine fibres like those of the stinging nettle, this is where you will need to start (many fibres are best soaked before working). You can continue working this way or transfer the yarn you have so far created to a spindle and spin up the rest of the fibres into a yarn. To do this tie the end of your yarn to the underside of the fly wheel and then bring it up around the edge of the wheel and attach it just above the wheel. Now spin the wheel keeping the yarn of fibres you are feeding into it held at an angle of about forty five degrees to the spindle the yarn will wrap itself around the spindle and the twist will be imparted to the fibre being fed onto the spindle. With each stop wind the yarn you have spun onto the spindle and feed some new fibres into the yarn. Of course it is essential to spin each time

in the same direction. Having produced yarns you are ready for serious rope making to begin. Long fibres need only to be rolled slightly on the thigh before the next step.

Thigh rolling: This is the easiest and quickest way to make lengths of two-ply cordage and has been traditionally employed by native peoples all over the world. Take two long fibres or yarns and tie them together (alternatively one long yarn can be doubled at its middle). Holding the knot in your right hand, roll the yarns the opposite way to the direction in which they were spun, using the palm of your hand on your thigh as shown. At the end of the action clamp the yarns to prevent the twist you have applied to them from unravelling and release the knotted end. If all is well this should twist up in the opposite direction to your rolling to form a two-ply strand. Now hold the strand where the yarns are separating—probably about fifteen centimetres from the knot—and repeat the process. With care you will be able to produce a tight length of cordage of any length. I often sit crossed legged for this process and hold the strand with the toes of my left foot, thereby freeing one hand to keep the yarns from tangling. If you are using long fibres simply add in another fibre. As you near the end of the ones you are already working, try to keep the cordage diameter even throughout the whole length.

Thigh rolling fibres into cordage.

Spinning: Two-ply cordage can also be spun by simply attaching two yarns to the spindle and reversing the direction of spin from that of the yarns. The spindle then twists the yarns together, but this technique leaves a lot to be desired since the strand is left quite loose and is not evenly twisted.

Hand-laying ropes: Twisting together

A spindle makes the task of spinning long lengths of fibres much easier.

yarns is referred to as 'laying up' and for thick fibres must be done by hand. While relatively slow and laborious, once your hands are trained to operate by feel, you will work quite quickly. This technique is the surest way to produce high quality cordage. You can use any long fibres in this process—even straw or grass—or better still use strands laid as by the previous methods. As a rough guide you are laying up a rope correctly if the fibres seem to tighten slightly and do not unwind from each other when released. You always twist in the opposite direction to a previous lay.

Start by tying two bundles of fibres or two already prepared strands together and holding them in your left hand. This hand should be held palm upwards with the knot held with your thumb so that the two strands pass either side of the index finger. If you are using unspun fibres you can use either of the following techniques—although most people find the first the easier to learn.

Right-hand lay: If you are usinf pre-spun fibres you must impart the twist to the strands in the opposite direction to that in which they have been spun. If you are uncertain of which direction this is, you are twisting in the correct direction when the fibres tighten up (and in the wrong direction if they open up and become loose). To use the right-hand lay method, the fibres should be tightening when twisted away from you; if they tighten only when twisted towards you, use the left-hand lay method described below.

Starting with the uppermost strand (that to the left of your index finger), impart a twist, away from your body, to this strand, by rolling it between the fingers of your right hand. When it is twisted to the point of almost kinking, clamp it between the thumb and second finger of your right hand to prevent it unravelling. Now draw it down to the position of the untwisted strand, between the index and second fingers of the left hand. As

you do this, use the free and extended right index finger to hook up the untwisted strand and transfer it across the left index finger to occupy the position vacated by the twisted strand. You can now let go of the twisted strand and repeat the process for the untwisted strand. Continue working in this way, twisting the strand to the left of your left index finger and exchanging it for the untwisted strand. After several repeats you should begin to see the rope appearing towards the palm of your left hand.

Left-hand lay: This must be used for fibres which tighten when twisted towards you, when held in the left hand. There are two ways to lay up these fibres: the easier is to use the above technique only working in the right hand. For this, start by holding the strands in your right hand (the fibres should now tighten when twisted away from you) and carry out the operations described above reading right where it says left and left where it says right.

Personally I find that I left-hand lay easier if I work the strands in my left hand in a slightly different manner, as this requires only the learning of a technique modification. Hold the strands as described for the right-hand lay, but this time impart the twist towards your body and to the lower strand, that which lies between the left index and second fingers. When this is twisted to the point of kinking, clamp it between the right thumb and index finger. Now draw it upwards across the left index finger at the same time using your extended right second finger to hook the untwisted strand down to lie between the left index and second fingers. Repeat the process to produce the cordage, in this case twisting towards you only the strand to the right of your left index finger and exchanging it for the untwisted strand.

The above descriptions may seem confusing, so it would well be worth spending some minutes with two shoe laces practising these techniques. To produce the best cordage, work at the tips of your fingers and keep the twist tight while you work. Most beginners tire after about a metre of cordage has been produced which shows as a deterioration in the evenness of the cord. But this problem disappears with practise.

Adding in: Eventually you will reach the end of the fibres or yarns you are working. To extend the cordage simply introduce some new fibres or yarns to the end of the old ones by laying them alongside and twisting them together. Once laid in they will be locked in place. To avoid uneven bulges where the joins occur, add them in gradually by staggering the ends of the yarns you are working, so that no two add in points lie directly opposite each other.

Braiding: Braiding or plaiting can also be used to produce strong cordage. For cordage, the best method to use is the round plait. This was frequently used in the production of horse hair ropes and snares. But the greatest value of plaits is that they generally produce a tape or flat length of cordage which is ideal for producing shoulder straps, belts and tump lines (straps attached to baskets for carrying, usually fitted across the shoulders and chest for men and to the forehead for women). The accompanying illustrations should be self explanatory. Fibres can be added in the same way as described above.

Modern Cordage for the Trail

One of my greatest annoyances is the quantity of nylon cord left behind by high-tech backpackers. Nylon cord is designed to be strong and hence it rots slowly and is a great hazard to wild life. If I am backpacking I will certainly carry a hank of nylon cord but I will never return with less than I set out with. In many parts of Europe it is possible to meet all of your cordage needs from the tangles left behind by less caring trekkers.

Wood Burning and Digging Out

Many modern people who are accustomed to swinging a metal axe have difficulty understanding how able early man was at felling large trees. In Poole harbour on the south coast of England, the remains of an ancient mesolithic dug-out canoe were discovered. No small vessel, this canoe was

Wooden bowls and utensils are durable and pleasing to use, at first they need only be functional items but as the days pass they can be refined. I carved the bowl on the left from a horse chestnut burl. The bowl on the right holds pemmican over five years old that is still edible!

hewn in one piece from a giant oak tree, the supporting ribs simply carved out of the wood itself. Speculated as being used for transporting trade goods this may have been the cargo vessel of its day.

The secret tool of these men was of course fire. Most woods can be hollowed with fire, the secret being to keep the fire small and slow burning and to work only with seasoned wood. Any areas that you do not wish to hollow should be protected with clay or mud. This same technique can of course be used to hollow bowls and cups. I have a noggin made from the burl of a tree some nine years ago, which has travelled with me to many parts of the world and though you may call me a romantic, I will swear that fresh clean spring water tastes better in no other container. The advantage in using a burl is that the grain of the vessel follows its outline, reducing any moisture loss from escaping along the grain. Take care with the burning, doing a little at a time so as not to split the grain, occasionally stopping to scrape out the charred wood.

Basketry

Basketry is one of the few backwoods crafts to have gained acceptance inside our bastions of concrete and steel, and has managed to survive in its perfect purest form. There is a magic in basket weaving; the fascinating interlocking weave of a basket speaks of the maker's understanding of the raw materials. No two baskets are ever exactly alike—as the Native American would say, each possesses its own medicine, and surely this is true. Take a simple household basket and stare into its mezmerising weave and there lies a story of growth and perfect harmony between maker and material. Weaving a basket is not an outdoors activity most students of bushcraft are interested in; it lacks the excitement and obvious value of the firelighting and shelter building. Yet to forage for the materials and then sit in the dappled light of a woodland glade to weave is one of the most absorbing and enjoyable experiences of woodcraft. When the basket is complete its weave will speak to you of the days of its making and the company of that time, every time you look at it or use it. Amongst the Pomo people of California it was traditional to give a beautifully worked feather-covered basket as a gift; such a gift spoke louder of friendship than any

words could, for bound up in its weave were many hours of the maker's life.

Basket weaving is of importance though to those who would be totally at home with nature for with this skill you can provide yourself food and cooking containers, water carriers and mats to work upon. The materials for basket weaving are available everywhere: any fibrous leaves grasses or similar vegetation can be used in some way for weaving. Where possible plant materials should be allowed to dry before weaving and then slightly soaked to make them flexible again. The following techniques will offer you ways to work each type of weaving material. The vertical fibres that form the sides of a basket are called warps while the horizontal fibres that weave around the warps are called wefts. In the following section I have confined the discussion to the simple basic techniques for survival use. For more detailed information on decorative basketry there are many excellent books available.

Basketry Techniques and Materials
Birch bark: This is one of the easiest materials to make into baskets although it is only available in sufficient quantities in the large birch forests of the north. Gather the outer bark in large wide sheets by levering it off the tree with care to avoid it splitting; you will find that it tends to curl up. While the experience of years has taught the northern red men to remove the bark without killing the tree you will find all of your needs satisfied by fallen trees. To make the bark more pliable for basketry, soak it or douse it with hot water, I also usually lay it out on some flat ground and weight it down with some heavy rocks to keep it flat. The white outside of the bark will form the inside of the finished basket so lay the bark white side up, cut out the design using a knife with a sawing action and fold it into the required shape with the further assistance of warm water.

These baskets are held together with simple lacing. For this prepare some spruce rootlets. Having decided where the lacings will be, bore the lace holes through the layers with a bone awl and then insert a match-sized peg to act as a temporary pinning. The boring of the lace holes is not easy. Take your time as it is all too easy to split the bark in line with its grain; it helps to bore the bark against a firm wooden support. With the container

Reeds, bracken or grasses can be woven into mats for beds, blankets, shelter doors or even roofing. While you can construct a loom for this purpose the weave is usually tighter if done by hand.

completely pinned, start to lace it together. If the basket is to be waterproof, apply pine pitch to the overlapping joints before pinning. I usually lace up the basket and then apply local heat with a fire brand to the pitch to encourage it to melt and seal the joint; the lace holes will have to be sealed last of all. For support to prevent the basket distorting, a rim must be formed using a thin sapling or split root, this is simply sewn on (see accompanying designs).

Plaiting: This is the simple under/over weave which is the fundamental technique of weaving. While there are many variations on this technique, the principle remains the same. It is an ideal technique for raw materials that come in the form of flat strips—such as some barks and long reedlike leaves.

Simple storage baskets can be made using this technique very easily. Plait a square or rectangular basket base leaving the warps and wefts protruding equally all round; these will be bent upwards to form the warps of the basket walls and another weft introduced to weave in and out of them around the basket sides. If extra material must be added to extend them, simply lay it along side the warp or weft it is to extend, and then work it into the weave.

More complicated forms of this technique can be used for effect passing the wefts over changing numbers of warps or plaiting at different angles; the possibilities are endless.

Twining: This is one of the most practical backwoods basketry techniques because of the ease with which it can be used with fibrous plants such as clematis and honeysuckle.

Starting with a set of warps, the weft is woven in pairs which are twisted around each other in between the warps. This technique can be used to produce blankets, sandals or burden baskets. The Paiute weavers could produce such tightly twined baskets that once filled with water and the fibres had swollen, they were waterproof—which led to waterbottles being woven with a typical bottle shape. The Apache also wove water bottles but they further proofed them by smearing the outside with pine pitch.

Coiling: Coiling is an easy technique to learn and produces strong rugged baskets. The principle is simple: a bundle of fibres such as grass stems are wrapped with another fibre such as bramble fibres, and coiled in a tight spiral being locked together by sewing to the previous coil as it is wrapped. An awl or large bone needle is a great advantage here. This is an excellent method of producing very large baskets of the 'Ali Baba' variety; they are ideal baskets for storing food in.

The accompanying illustrations show the basic ways these techniques are used to produce the most valuable forms of survival basketry. There is no end to the variety of baskets you can produce and no reason why the above techniques cannot be combined in one basket.

Pottery

Pottery is the backwoods equivalent to metal cooking containers and is well within the production capabilities of any fixed camp with a ready source of clay. In fact much of the world's most celebrated pottery was produced by primitive societies under the same conditions.

Gathering clay: Clay is difficult to mistake: it is a densely packed soil which has a slimy surface when wet and becomes plasticine like in texture when damp. I have always found the best naturally-occurring clay at stream beds and spring seepages where it can be easily spotted due to the water having washed away the obscuring detritus. If the stream or river bed has dried up, the clay may have dried out, although it should still be fairly easy to recognise. Dry clay forms hard lumps which crumble to a fine powder when crushed, and will exhibit the earlier characteristics when made wet.

Dry clay may well need to be picked from the ground with a digging stick or a pick improvised from an antler tine. Damp clay can usually be pulled straight from the stream bank. Once collected, store or carry the clay in some form of container such as a basket to avoid contaminating it with any more particles of debris and woodland litter than it already contains. Very damp clay occurs as slurry and will need to be collected in a waterproof container or large billy.

Preparing the clay: Occasionally you may be lucky enough to find a source of clay that is almost perfect in consistency and free from debris. If you are careful with your gathering, little more will need to be done to this clay save adding temper (below). But more often than not, the clay will need careful preparation. The easiest clay to deal with is dry clay. This should be dried and then pounded into a fine powder; in this process any leaf matter or other debris can be removed. The finest powdered clay has a similar feel to talcum powder. Once sifted of unwanted matter, it can be rehydrated to a slightly dry dough consistency, ready to have the temper added. Some people prefer to add the temper before the water as it can be mixed in more thoroughly, but this is not essential.

Wet clay on the other hand is more tricky to deal with, becoming more difficult the wetter it is. Clay that is just too moist but not runny, should be kneaded to remove unwanted matter and can then spread out to dry in the sun or on an absorbent material such as an old T-shirt or bark mat. Alternatively you can add quantities of dry powered clay; even temper can help to dry it out.

At its wettest, clay becomes liquid and is then referred to as slip, this can be very useful as will be mentioned later. However clay that occurs in this form takes more effort than is convenient to prepare, although once treated this can be some of the purest clay you will ever work. Place the liquid clay into a large container (preferably a metal billy or waterproof bark container). Now it is important that the liquid is well agitated by stirring; this will allow any particles to separate out and either float to the surface or sink to the bottom. Remove any matter that floats to the surface by scooping with your fingers and pour off the mixture into another container leaving any rubbish that has sunk to the bottom with the dregs. An added refinement here is to filter this mixture through a cattail leaf mat or loosely woven basket. Now let this sit until the clay particles have separated from the water and floated to the bottom. I usually leave this for at least a day. Should there be any more debris risen to the surface remove it before pouring off the water. With the water poured off you have a pure slip which can be saved for later use or dried for clay to work. To dry it, pour it out onto an absorbent mat and allow it to dry. If you have an oven it can be slowly dried as for jerking meat. If you are using a metal container this process can be speeded up by boiling the mixture to drive off more moisture in the form of steam.

Temper: Temper is an important ingredient in your clay mixture; it helps to prevent the clay from cracking as it dries, binding and reinforcing the clay. For temper you can use a variety of materials although each must be reduced to a fine powder if it is not already of that form: crushed sea shells, fine sand, crushed broken pots, fine stoneworking dust, cornmeal, can all be used. Plant fibres and hair can also be used. The amount of temper to add will vary from clay to clay and will be learned through experience, but as a rough-and-ready guide, between twenty to fifty per cent will do. My favourite temper are sandstone rocks that have been used in a sweat lodge; these are stones that have been heated to glowing in a fire and then rapidly cooled by dousing with water. Once dry they can be crumbled and ground down to a fine powder very easily.

Pot Construction Techniques
With the clay purified and temper added, you are ready to begin the construction of your pot. Start by kneading the clay thoroughly for a few minutes to work out any air pockets that may remain in it. If this is not done the air trapped inside the clay will expand when heated causing the pot to crack or shatter during the firing. With the clay well kneaded you can proceed to any of the following techniques.

Moulding: This is the simplest pottery technique: you simply take the clay and push and pinch it into the shape you are aiming to produce working slowly and carefully to avoid cracking. This technique can also be used in combination with a former or mould; a former is a suitably-shaped object that the clay can be formed around, such as a conical or oval boulder. Never leave the clay to dry

on the former as it shrinks during the drying and will crack. Instead, leave the clay for a few minutes until it is more manageable, and then remove it to dry, preferably elevated on a rack to allow air to circulate freely around it.

A mould is the opposite: a container or other pot that the clay can be used to line thereby taking on the correct shape; of course narrow-necked moulds cannot be used. If you wish to mould a narrow-necked pot you will need two moulds—one for the base and the other for the top. Moulded in halves, the moulded clay should be allowed to dry slightly so that it becomes more rigid and manageable, then the two halves can be joined and sealed together with water as for coiling (below). To prevent the mould or former sticking to the clay I wet the mould or former thoroughly with water and then cover it with temper. The moisture enables the temper to adhere evenly all over, which in its turn acts as a lubricant to prevent the clay from sticking.

Coiling: This is the most commonly used backwoods pottery technique which can be used to shape pots of many different shapes and sizes. The technique involves rolling out long snake-like pieces of clay and coiling them upwards in a spiral to the shape of pot you desire, in a very similar way to coiling a basket.

To begin with, it is usually best to form a base by moulding; for backcountry use a conical pot is more useful than a flat-bottomed pot. The conical base can be easily propped up between rocks or in a ground depression and when heated is a better shape for transmitting the heat to the contents. Let the base harden slightly while rolling out your coils. This is best done using a flat surface, but if you have no suitable work surface roll the clay vertically between your palm in a similar action to that used for hand drill firestarting. The coils should all be of the same diameter. To fit the coils to the pot, score the rim of the base where you intend to attach the coil and also the edge of the coil to be attached, then wet the surface with water or slip and bring the two together. I prefer to flatten the coils I use so as to form a higher thinner wall. The coil should be worked into the base and smoothed over but be careful not to trap unwanted air pockets. Continue adding coils in this fashion until the pot is of the size and

Even the crudest clay pot is a triumphant success for a survivor. With practice there is no limit to your creativity and skill.

shape you intend. Now while the clay is still malleable, smooth it all over or work a pattern into the surface. Rack the pot to dry.

Box or slab construction: This method was commonly used by native people particularly in South America where incredible pot designs were fashioned in this way, but is really only practical if you have a flat work surface available to you. The clay is rolled out into a flat slab in the same way as pastry is rolled out except that you move round the clay instead of turning the clay round. The clay slab should be evenly thick all over, about 6mm is a good thickness for most pots. From this slab the pot walls can be precisely cut out with a sharp thin blade. These pieces are then assembled by scoring along the joint and glueing with slip. An easy technique to start with is to form a square or rectangular box with a hole cut out for the top. This will make an excellent grain or flour storage pot. The only drawback with these pots is that they are far harder to fire than the more conventional curved designs.

Just as with basketry do not hesitate to combine these techniques to produce a particular design.

Tidying

When the pot has had some time to dry but is still damp to the point of feeling leathery, the final tidying up can be done. The aim here is to reduce the walls to an even thickness. If this is not done, the thicker parts of the wall will dry at a different rate to the thinner parts leading to cracking. There are two ways the walls can be thinned either by beating them

between a smooth stone and a wooden paddle or by scraping them back. The paddling method is well suited for coiled pots as it will compress the walls, bedding down any weaknesses between the coils. In fact any weak joints will separate in long cracks. While inconvenient it is better to discover these flaws now rather than after the firing. For the finest pots, paddle the walls and then scrape them as well, the walls can now be embellished with pattern or polished smooth. All of these processes will go towards reducing the chances of the pot cracking during the firing, and so time is well spent at this stage. Any scrapings that are produced can be recycled for clay. With the tidying complete, leave the pot to dry thoroughly—preferably in the shade where it will dry slowly and evenly. Pottery is not a craft that can be rushed; this drying process can take a week and one particularly damp British summer, my pots took a fortnight to dry.

Firing

Firing is really the simplest stage of pot production, but being the moment of truth it is fraught with anxiety. Even when you have spent hours carefully preparing all the preceding stages, the feeling of dread never goes away. So to help alleviate this tension follow the first law of firing: fire a batch of pots together, not just one pot.

There are no set rules to firing pots; this is one more of those times I have to say that you will learn by experience, but here are some tips. Pots will break during firing if they contain pockets of air, moisture, structural weaknesses or have walls of uneven thickness. They will also break if heated too rapidly, at too high a temperature, too long, too cool or too fast. There are many ways to arrange the firing, you can use your oven as a kiln, or construct a kiln, or bury the pots in sand with a fire on top, or just place them in a fire. But the best technique I have found is progressive firing. This allows the pots time for moisture and trapped gases to escape before the clay hardens. The greatest benefits of this method are that you can more or less see what is happening and it is the best method I know of firing pots in humid environments.

Progressive firing: The morning of the firing, place the pots to be fired around your campfire to drive off moisture (if I have a plastic bag available I place the pots in direct sunlight the day before the firing sealing them in the plastic bags just before sundown) and turn them occasionally to evenly distribute the heat. While this is happening, gather your firewood and prepare the kiln fire. This will need to be separate from your campfire. The temperature of the kiln fire will need to be gradually increased to really hot over a period of several hours without any cooling, so make certain you have gathered enough fuel. Placing the pots in a pile (neatly and evenly arranged), lace the pile with small dead hardwood sticks and build your fire in a circle around the pots about an arm span away, gradually moving it closer. Take your time here since this first stage should not be rushed. As you rake the fire closer, the pots will become hotter until the fuel in and amongst them begins to burn. At this point rake the fire around them and build the fire up to a frenzy. If you are well organised this should be done at a leisurely pace. Keep this fire going for at least an hour and then let it cool naturally until you can handle the pots, this may take all night or with really large firings, two nights. Never try to cool a pot with cold water.

To test those pots that have not cracked, flick their rim and listen for a crisp clear ring. If the ring is dull the pot is flawed although not necessarily useless; use it for food storage instead of cooking.

Pine Pitch and Resin Glues

Pine pitch or resin is exuded by some trees to close up cuts in their bark and prevent infections. Naturally sticky, it makes first-class waterproof glue. Gathering the pitch is a time-consuming business; you will need to find those trees that have been grazed and are oozing the pitch. To put it to its best use it must be purified and this can be done in one of two ways. The traditional method is to place the pitch in a muslin bag or bark container, and then to place this into a container of boiling water weighted so that it sinks. The heat of the water then melts the pitch which escapes from the container and rises to float on the surface where it can be scooped up. The other method shown to me by a flint-knapping friend involves placing the pitch into a flat container such as an old mess tin which has some holes drilled in it at one end. This is then heated so that the liquid pitch runs out of the holes, the tin being slightly tilted, into a collecting container. To use the pitch it should be heated and mixed with finely powdered charcoal. This makes it less brittle and helps to harden it. If you are really lucky you may find some beeswax which can be added to the resin for similar reasons. Other trees also produce pitch (such as the birch tree) and can be used in the same way.

Pine pitch is applied hot and hardens on cooling. As it hardens very quickly it is best to apply it to the general area to be glued first, and then to reheat it with the items to be fixed next to each other. As it cools, you can make the pitch surface smooth by running a wet finger down the still plastic glue. Once fixed, the glue is strong but tends to be brittle and becomes soft again near heat so mind those glued items near the campfire.

A word of warning: never look into a container of boiling pitch as it bubbles and spits violently. I once had a near miss when droplets of pitch solidified on my eye lashes. Unpleasant to remove, it would have been worse had it gone into the eye itself.

Stone and Bone Working

'He serves the stone and the stone shapes him: it has taught him to go slow, to pay attention; he has learned to be amazed. He will hold a proper stone for days, sitting patiently and smoking his pipe, waiting for the stone to reveal its form; his hands do the rest. He is no longer fooled that he is the maker; he allows the stone to use him. In return it shows him how to die: patiently, face full of sunlight, bathed in rain, dried in wind, slowly, slowly wearing away.'

(Old Man Carving Stone: *Journey of the Medicine Man* by Red Hawk)

Almost every skill of woodcraft requires the use of a cutting tool of some description. For the most part we take metal knives and axes for granted but there will be times when even the best prepared outdoorsman is without a cutting tool. It is at these times that the ability to produce a blade from stone will be very handy. At other times you may have a knife, but a stone tool specially designed to do the job in hand, is far better suited. I always use a stone scraper for arrow production and for hideworking. Stone tools do not have the same cutting action as steel and require a very different application; to use them to their best advantage requires a better understanding of the grain of the material being worked.

When I teach novices, I explain to them that in an ideal world they would not carry a knife until they were able to improvise an alternative cutting tool. Many of them doubt the effectiveness of stone tools but it was stone that played a large part in the forming of the world we know today. Man first started using stone tools several million years ago. If that span of time were to be represented as a year,

man started using stone tools on January the first and only stopped using them as the predominant tool on December the thirteenth at about 6 pm. From that time to December the thirty-first, man learned to work metals and developed the science and technology to take men to the moon and back. In Europe the use of stone tools survived well into the Bronze Age until bronze tools became accessible to all.

Before you embark upon learning to work stones, be warned that it is an addictive undertaking. I can think of no other woodcraft skill bar tracking, that is so totally absorbing. Every time you pick up a stone you will begin to see the possibilities it possesses; to start working it is to see the day pass as if reduced to the span of minutes. As your ability and skill progresses you will begin to create more beautiful and artistic artefacts. When this happens, to progress further you will need to meet other stone workers and compare and share techniques and discoveries.

A full description of stoneworking techni-

167

que is beyond the scope of this book so what follows is an introduction to stone working aimed at survival situations. The most important aspect of stone working is understanding the rock you are working with. In the backcountry there is little scope for choosing what is available to you, all you can do is experiment with the local materials to determine which best suits your needs and how best to work it.

Rock is man's most abundant resource material but occurs in many widely differing forms, each with its own unique physical properties—although in stone working terms each rock can be categorised by its predominent suitability to one of only a handful of stone working techniques. Assuming that you are faced with an unfamiliar rock type which you are uncertain how to work, the first step is to study it. Does it crumble easily? Can you grind it easily? Does it split like slate? Can you strike off a flake with a glancing blow and if so does it possess a mussel-shaped fracture? (see conchoidal fracture below)? It should not take long to determine the qualities of the rock. Before you begin to work try always to select a rock which is best suited to producing the tool or tools you intend.

Early man often went to great lengths to obtain the really best material for his tools, quarrying for flint at the cost of great labour, sometimes modifying the properties of the rock by heating. In those regions where good rock for tool making was not readily available, trade routes sprang up along which both raw material and finished tools were traded, sometimes across vast distances. So don't just settle for the first rock that you come across—unless it really does meet your needs.

Stone-Working Techniques

Abrading and grinding: The simplest yet one of the most superior of all stone-working techniques is abrading. As stone working goes this is a slow process that can be used even on the hardest rocks although it becomes less practical to do so. The method involves the rubbing of the workpiece against or with an abrasive rock such as sand stone. To speed the process up you can add sand and water. This is an excellent technique for sharpening stone blades particularly from materials like slate which can be sharpened to a very sharp edge

if thin enough. Flint axes were often abraded all over to give them a polish and more uniform shape, to ease hafting and strengthen their cutting edge. Using this technique requires patience and plenty of elbow grease. To achieve a high polish on the glassy rocks, abrasive stones of different coarseness were used, the final polish being achieved with bark and buckskin.

Pecking and crumbling: This technique is suitable for use with rocks which are dense but will not split easily or produce the mussel-shaped fracture necessary for knapping, although some of the coarser grained rocks which can be knapped can also be pecked. Pecking involves the repeated striking of the rock to gradually reduce the rock by crumbling off tiny particles. This process can be very slow indeed. To speed up the process use a quartzite stone to hammer with as this rock will present many tiny sharp faces to the work piece and cut more particles off more quickly. This technique was used mainly for cutting grooves in stones to enable them to be hafted easily for use as hammers or tomahawks. Because the best tomahawks and hammers are made from hard dense rocks which are slow to peck a groove into, I find that the best way to complete a work is a little at a time instead of sitting down to do the job in one working. A little and often done in those odd free moments by the campfire and the job is soon finished.

Incising engraving and splitting: Incising is the process of cutting or abrading a groove into the rock so that with the application of a blow or snapping force the rock can be broken in a precise manner. This technique was generally used with the really hard dense rocks such as nephrite. For survival situations these rocks are really too hard to work to be of practicable use. But for the native the very toughness of these rocks made them desirable for drill bits and chisel points as well as bladed weapons and cutting tools. In general they were worked by first incising and blocking out to a suitably shaped and sized work piece before being finished by abrading or pecking. In survival situations this technique may be of value in the preparation of more easily worked rocks such as the harder sandstones. For a saw you will need a thin slab of rock such as slate. This is worked back and forth like a saw with the addition of sand and water as extra abrasives.

With really thick pieces of rock it may be necessary to cut two grooves from opposite sides that almost meet in the middle. The desired section can then be struck off or broken off using an anvil stone.

Engraving is essentially a decorative technique whereby a sharp harder rock is used to carve small grooves out of the work piece. The best engraving tool for this purpose is a quartzite or flint burin, which has a suitably prepared point. If you are making primitive tools it is a shame if you only make them for function, around the campfire there is plenty of time to decorate and embellish the tools you have made.

Splitting is a technique which can be used with rocks that can be broken into more or less regular slabs. Slate is the obvious example although I once split a large piece of sandstone to produce a suitably thin flat base for an oven. The best guide to whether or not a rock can be easily split is the presence of visible fault lines. To split the rock improvise a wedge. This need not be thick. A long slender wedge is usually best, made from stone if possible perhaps by abrading. Place the wedge in the natural fault line and strike it a straight blow with a wooden baton. If all is correctly prepared the wedge should work its way into the rock widening the fault line. If the wedge disappears into the fault without your being able to split the rock, carefully repeat the process with a slightly larger wedge. The real key to success is patience, if you move up to a much larger wedge the rock may snap on the weak side rather than splitting. Really long slabs should be split from both ends to avoid this problem.

Drilling: Rock can be drilled for making net sinkers, spindle fly wheels and hammer hafting. Even glassy rocks such as flint can be drilled given the time. At the simplest a rock drill is simply a wooden drill rotated between the hands or by means of a bow or pump drill. The cutting is achieved by the abrasive action of sand and water at the drill base. But this can be improved by the use of a stone drill bit (see below). In almost all cases drilling rock is a slow laborious process, most holes being drilled from opposing sides to meet in the middle, creating a characteristically hourglass-shaped hole.

Knapping: Knapping is the technique used to work glassy rocks or rocks that break like glass with a mussel-shaped fracture. This is called the 'CONCHOIDAL' fracture which is common to many rocks. Because the rock fractures in this way you can predict how the rock will break when struck in a particular fashion. The technique then involves the removal of flakes from a core by means of pressure or blows applied at a predetermined angle. This technique of stone working is the most complicated having many variations designed to meet the wide range of circumstances met when working the stone. Yet for all its complexity it is the most versatile and quickly used of all the techniques. With practise and the correct materials you should be able to produce an axe in roughly one hour or less and an arrow head in between twenty to thirty minutes depending on how refined you decide to make them. (Of course real craftsmen may take longer over particularly beautiful pieces of work.

The first step to flint knapping is obtaining suitable stone to work. Some of the rocks which can be used such as obsidian which is a volcanic glass are more or less problem free whereas flint is often full of problematic fossils and fractures. This is particularly true of the surface flints most easily available to you. These are exposed to the elements and can develop hairline fractures due to the freezing and thawing action of winter frosts. These hairline fractures will act as effective barriers to the shockwaves from your blows causing the stone to break in an unpredictable manner. Such fractures can be very difficult to detect until you actually start work, although a good field guide used by most European flint knappers is the tap test. A good flint when given a light tap with a hammer stone (see below) will ring out with a clear clean note, whereas a fractured flint will give a sharp or dull note. With practise you can become quite proficient at guaging precisely how good or bad a piece of flint is by this means. If you find a flawed flint, it is often possible to strike the stone along the flaw to produce one or even two clear ringing pieces.

Having selected the stone you are going to work you will need to prepare the tools required for the preliminary knapping. The most useful tools you will need are a couple of 'hard hammers' these are rounded stones ideally of quartzite that will not shatter when used against the flint. They should be as heavy as can be easily managed. For most of your needs you will get by with one hammer

Quartering a flint nodule with a hard hammer.

To produce the finest blades abrade the edge with a rough stone.

Removing a blade with a soft hammer, the soft antler billet allows more control of the work piece.

Indirect percussion allows control and economic use of flint nodules.

about the size of a large apple and the other the size of a lemon. With these tools you should be able to prepare the flint for every basic survival need. For finer work you may prefer to use a 'soft hammer'; these are usually made from the densest heaviest antler available to you. Also of importance at this stage is an abrading stone. This should be of a coarse sandstone or similar rock.

Direct percussion: The real art of flint knapping is the ability to take a raw piece of stone and shape it into a form suitable for the production of specialised tools. (Within the world of craft flint knapping there is a growing trend to band-saw a piece of stone into a parallel sided slab perfect for knapping into beautiful long, thin leaf-shaped blades, but to purists this is defeating the real art of knapping.) Most flint as it is found naturally is covered in a layer of white chalk-like material referred to as cortex. The first stage in flint working is to remove this cortex which acts as a shock absorber to your blows. To

start you must expose the grey or black flint. Look for a projecting lump or nodule and strike this an angular blow with the larger hard hammer. To hold the flint, most knappers prefer to rest it on the knee with a skin or bark pad for comfort and protection. If the blow was delivered at the correct angle the lump should have sheared off cleanly exposing what is described as a platform. Now using this platform as your striking point aim your blows to direct the shock waves across the stone to remove the cortex. At its simplest any of the flakes which you remove in this process should be sharp enough for most cutting jobs.

To progress towards an axe continue in the manner you started, trying always to produce an almond-shaped core. Aim your blows to remove flakes along the ridges left by two or more previous flakes, thinning as much as possible early on. The greatest difficulty you will face is in the correct preparation of the striking platform. This must be strong enough to receive the full weight of your blow thus transmitting it to the flint as intended. If the platform is too weak it will break off causing difficulties; if it is too strong either nothing will happen when you strike it or the piece will break too deeply or worse than either, you will impart fractures to the workpiece which will interfere with later operations. The diagram will show the very basics of direct percussion. As the work becomes thinner switch over to using a soft hammer and pay extra careful attention to the platform preparation.

This technique is basically all that is required to produce an axe or adze for survival purposes. The flakes you have removed in the process are all razor sharp and usually many can be turned into first class arrowheads by pressure flaking (see below).

Indirect percussion: While axes and adzes are very useful, ninety-nine per cent of your survival tools can be produced more economically from the flakes produced. This was a fact our ancestors realised devising techniques to produce suitably shaped flakes or 'blades' for easy manufacture into other tools. While the skilled flint worker can strike these off by precisely placed direct blows with a hard or soft hammer, you will find it easier to begin with, to use indirect percussion (plus it serves to introduce another valuable technique).

For indirect percussion you will need another tool, an antler punch. Preferably this should be of a straight piece of antler and shaped with a blunt point. For blade production the core needs to be prepared in a slightly different manner. Instead of producing an almond shape your aim is to truncate it so that you are working more or less a cylinder. From a flat striking platform, you will be able to punch off blades. As always, abrade the edge to strengthen the striking platform and then place the punch on the edge and strike it with a hammer or wooden billet as shown. Be careful here as the full energy of the blow is released in the parting of the blade which comes off with a great deal of force. Now simply work around the core striking off blades as needed. If the blade does not break off cleanly you have not prepared the platform correctly or not followed the blow through. Replace it in the step that is left on the core and strike it directly vertically with a firm blow of your soft hammer. With

luck this blow will dislodge the step and complete the intended blade. If the step is not removed in this way invert the core and strike off a blade to connect with the step from the other side.

Pressure flaking: The blades produced can now be knapped into arrow heads, scrapers, burins drills and small razor-like blades for spearpoints. But for this yet another technique must be learned, that of pressure flaking. Here again some special tools will be needed: a pressure flaker manufactured from an antler tine and a small hand pad of thick buckskin rawhide or similar leather. Pressure flaking is a miniature version of what you were doing in direct percussion except that you are not striking off flakes but pushing them off with pressure concentrated at the point of the antler tine. Do not underestimate just how much force is required in this process, you will find that most of your body strength comes to bear. Platform preparation is just as critical for this operation as for any of the others. Hold the blade or flake in your left palm (assuming that you are right handed) which is protected by the leather pad, I usually roll the top of the pad several times to effect a vice-like grip. Now with the antler tine held in your right hand, apply pressure to the edge of the flake to remove a tiny flake. If you are carrying this operation out correctly, you should hear and feel this flake pop off cleanly without crumbling. Work around the flake in this way, gradually creating the shape that you want. The angle at which you apply the pressure will determine the angle of edge you eventually achieve.

Pressure flaking with an antler flaking allows the fine working needed to produce arrowheads.

171

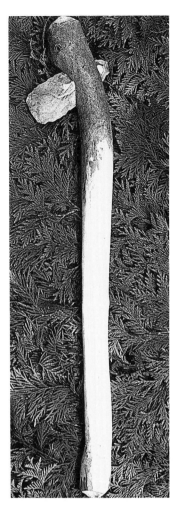

Left to right: a flint axe, a flint adze and a flint dagger. Hafted by carefully carving sockets for the blades and hafting with rawhide cordage these tools are very serviceable. The dagger blade is hafted with rawhide and pine resin.

Below: a simple hand axe can be made in five minutes. This will perform at least ninety per cent of the jobs you might otherwise use a knife for.

The design of tool you eventually produce will depend upon your needs, the materials available to you, and your level of skill, but even a simple broken cobble will give you a sharp cutting or scraping edge suitable for most of your backwoods manufacturing needs. Even if you don't have any antler available to you there is no problem. One of the finest flint knappers I have met works almost exclusively with a hard hammer producing the finest blades.

Bone and Antler

While stone produced the razor edge for the native craftsman, it was brittle, making it unsuitable for many tasks that today can be accomplished by metals. It was bone and antler that bridged the gap between wood and stone. Being hard, they are capable of taking a sharp edge yet flexible to a degree of resilience enabling them to be used successfully for projectile points and hook barbs. It was also from these materials that the first needles were fashioned, revolutionalising the fit of man's clothing particularly in the cold northern climates where the art of backwoods tailoring was perfected.

The great advantage of these materials was that they could be easily carved into a variety of tools and very often were already of a very adaptable shape. This is a fact that was brought home to me recently when I was paying a visit behind the scenes of the British Museum. Descending into the bowels of one of the museum's store houses, I was led by the head of the department to the dark corridors between giant moving vaults where humidity and temperature could be precisely controlled. Turning a large wheel, two of the vaults parted like a scene from the Old Testament, revealing a dimly-lit passage walled by carefully-labelled trays. The head removed one of the trays and brought it very carefully to a giantish table presumably made that way to avoid unfortunate knocks. The tray was long and thin with a hinging lid. 'I think you'll appreciate this' she said, lifting the lid. As the lid folded back the flicker of the fluorescent lights fell on the polystyrene lining, and then precisely fitted into this was simply the most beautiful example of backwoods carving that I have ever seen: a short atlatl carved from antler in the shape of a mammoth, one of the targets it would have been used against. The design had obviously been inspired by the experience of the maker, and despite the centuries since it was carved the life and animation of the carving was as fresh as ever it had been. The carving was cleverly incorporated into the tool so that the tail became the hook for connection with the spear and the body of the carving acted as a weight. There was that familiar empathy between the carving and the antler, common to many native carvings. The figure seemed to be flowing from the work piece as if the craftsman had seen its presence in the antler and merely set it free. It seemed strange that in this unlikely treasure house, two twentieth-century people were marvelling over a work of art that was probably a talking point among the Magdellanian party of its maker, hunting in France fourteen or more thousand years before. It had obviously been a prized possession which was shown by the fact that a break had been carefully repaired. I left that Aladdin's cave with the feeling that a craftsman had reached out from the past and touched me, setting a standard we can all aspire to. This is the magic of advanced woodcraft as your skills develop you join a fraternity of craftmen and women that spans the centuries.

Bone

Bone is not only available as a by-product of your hunting efforts it is also a product of the hunting of other predators. Bone can also frequently be found by streams where unfortunate creatures have been trapped in boggy ground. Add to this the bones of those animals who have simply moved on to other hunting grounds having lived out their allotted time and there is a great deal of bone to be easily found in the outdoors. If you have started to think native and travel off trail you will undoubtedly have come across many skeletons and kill sites. So long as the bone has not become powdery or very brittle, all of these sources will provide you with ideal bone for tool making. Bone is nearer to stone than wood in its properties; it is for the most part more brittle than antler but will take a sharper edge if carefully abraded. I prefer to use bone for arrow points, knives and awls which are all quite robustly fashioned tools. While bone can be fashioned into good needles I find that they are more prone to breaking than needles made from antler. Bone makes first-class gouge blades because of its natural semi-circular cross section. Shoulder blades can be easily fashioned into hide scrapers; femur's (thigh bones) are generally the best to use for knives, arrow heads and chisel/gouge blades; shin bones are straight and perfectly suited to making points barbs and awls.

Antler

While antler can be collected by hunting, this is not necessary since most deer species drop their antlers each spring. A sorry time for the stag, his crown gone, he holds his head low with a shattered pride and skulks away to start the process of growing another set in time for the rut. If you have been using antler hammers for stoneworking, you will have realised that what at first feels brittle and quite fragile, is in fact a very strong material indeed. In fact antlers were used as crow-bar-style picks by early flint miners to lever flint nodules out of solid chalk!

Antler truly lies halfway between wood and metal it is flexible and strong and will also take a sharp edge. Because of its flexibility antler is in effect stronger than bone and wins out every time in the manufacture of spear points needles and arrow heads. But probably its greatest advantage is that it occurs in large pieces, and in more useful shapes than bone. Each deer species also possesses antler of unique qualities some are dense and hard almost solid antler, such as reindeer while others are more or less full of the coral like marrow such as red deer. Each has its advantages the less solid varieties are easier to carve into projectile points and needles while the solid varieties make excellent handles hammers and wedges.

If I have a choice between making tools suitably shaped antler and suitably shaped bone, antler wins every time simply because of its resilience—particularly for harpoon barbs and fish hooks where some flexibility is a strong advantage. For arrow heads I prefer flint which is razor sharp and hard. Although more brittle I can make two or three good stone points in the time that it takes to make one good bone or antler point—even when using metal tools to work the bone.

For the most part the techniques used for working bone and antler are very similar, but because of the differing nature of the two materials it is better to consider them separately.

Working Bone

Bone is the least forgiving material to work and a mistake often results in the ruining of a workpiece and a return to the start. While it can be softened by soaking I prefer to work it dry, constantly reminding myself that it is a brittle material easily shattered and fractured. Fresh 'green' bone is much less brittle and more waxy and can sometimes be worked like antler.

Smashing: This is a technique more or less unique to bone working simply because it is almost impossible to smash most antlers. Smashing is the crude and inefficient way to section a bone into fragments suitable for

carving into gorge hooks and barbs. The advantage of this technique is that in emergency conditions you can produce a number of useful pieces of bone with the absolute minimum of effort. Find a rock or boulder suitable for use as an anvil and smash the bone with a heavy blow from a large hammer stone.

Sawing: Sawing is a far better way to tackle a bone. It allows you the ultimate control in the way you section the bone, enabling the most efficient use of the raw material. As a saw you can use a flint blade with a pressure-flaked serrated edge; this is often better than more modern saws, but is a slow process. However it is one where you can use the bone's brittle nature to your advantage by only sawing half way through the bone or deep enough to sufficiently weaken it, so that it will break along the cut when struck lightly with a hammer stone.

Scoring: A similar technique to that described above is scoring, and it is one ideally suited to those cuts which are too long for comfortable sawing. Using a stone or prepared engraver, score a deep groove to enable the bone to be accurately splintered. This is how both bone and antler needles are blanked out. It is not a quick technique but if carefully done is both accurate and efficient.

Wedge splitting: Best used in combination with scoring, this technique involves splitting off splinters by driving a chisel-shaped wedge into the bone. I only use this technique where I have previously cut a deep groove, as it is difficult to predict just how the bone will break without it.

Scraping: Once you have blanked out the more or less suitably sized and shaped work piece, this is the quickest way to work it down to the tool you are aiming to produce. Any sharp flake or blade can be used—simply draw it across the bone at ninety degrees to the work surface to scrape off fine shavings.

Abrading: This is the archetypal bone working technique. Bone needs to always be worked slowly and carefully to avoid any unfortunate breakages. Abrading is the slowest and most certain way to work down a piece of bone. Again it is best to start with a suitable blank, then using a sandstone block, sand out the shape you are aiming for. This is also the method used to put the sharpest edge on bone blades.

Drilling: Drilling out around a predetermined shape is an easy way to blank out complicated shapes. I describe this as backwoods fret work and require only a stone drill the same as that used for notching arrows. Make certain that the pilot hole is deep enough otherwise the drill will skate all over the hard bone surface.

Working Antler

Burning: Antler is notoriously difficult to cut, and even with modern saw blades it is not easy. In the backwoods it requires quite drastic handling techniques, none more so than burning. For this you will need a glowing fire brand or small pile of embers. The fire brand (a glowing stick from your fire) is best as you can more easily apply the heat to precisely where it is required. Assuming you want to remove one of the tines, place the glowing end of the brand against the tine base where it meets the main stem. Now blow on the brand to increase its heat and there by scorch the antler. It is worth mentioning at this point that the smell produced is quite repugnant. As the antler begins to scorch move the brand around the tine so that you are beginning to weaken it all around. Eventually you will find that a sharp blow to the ground or several sharp blows from a heavy stone hammer at the tine base, will snap the tine free. If you have been able to produce a stone adze or chisel, the process can be speeded up by cutting away the charred antler and repeating the process until sufficiently weakened.

Sawing: Antler can be sawed through although being a more waxy material than bone, the process is much slower. I usually reserve sawing for already formed blanks and prepared pieces of antler that are thin enough to make it a viable option.

Incising: This can be carried out in the same way as for bone. However the incised grooves must be much deeper to overcome the flexibility of the antler. Deep-cut grooves can be more easily broken by wedge splitting.

Abrading and scraping: Both of these techniques can be used in the same way as for bone working although of the two, scraping is the most effective.

Carving: This is an option available for bone working but far less effective than when applied to antler. Soak the antler for a day or two beforehand to soften it. It can then be easily carved using a sharp flake of stone or

prepared engraving tool.

Antler has a core of very tough marrow, which can be incorporated in the tool you are making without causing any problems. It is in fact much stronger than its delicate form would suggest and largely responsible for the difficulty with which antler can be smashed. In short it is much easier to incorporate this in your design than try and carve it away from the solid part of the antler.

Bone and Antler Tools

Wherever possible, try to utilise the natural shape of the bone or antler in your design. Both of these materials are strongest when strain is put on them in the directions it would occur naturally. Both can also be hardened by very gentle fire hardening although this is hardly necessary and can result in unwanted brittleness. Both can also be somewhat shaped by heating with hot water or steam and then bending into the desirable shape and allowing to cool in this shape. In the arctic where wood is in short supply, bone and antler were frequently jointed together to form long lengths; the joints being formed by drilling holes and then stitching the pieces together with wet rawhide (see Chapter Thirteen) which would shrink slightly on drying and become virtually rigid, locking them together.

Shells and Teeth

Teeth: Incisor teeth, particularly of beavers and other rodents were frequently hafted to handles for use as gouges and carving tools although they were mainly used in the carving of embellishing decorations. However, I once made an atlatl with the canine tooth from a fox skull found on a hike, and used it as the peg against which the tail end of the spear presses. Stay alert to the possibilities of these materials.

Shell: Shell is a very common and surprisingly useful material of the seashore; it can be worked more or less in the same way as slate although I have occasionally found shells that can be crudely pressure flaked. On several occasions I have used shell knives to cut up fish and saw in the groove of a bowdrill fireset, to say nothing of making arrow heads from shell. Most people totally overlook this extremely useful material.

The most useful shells are those of the bivalves, particularly the larger mussel shells, clam and scallop shells. The latter especially are useful because of their saw-like wavy shell edge. The way I usually go about working shell is to simply snap or crumble it to a rough shape. For this use a small pointed pebble and a larger anvil stone. Once you have formed the rough outline of the tool, abrade in the fine details with a coarse abrading stone. To obtain a really sharp edge it is best to use finer abraders, but do not over-thin as the edge of the shell is always very brittle. If you spend time beachcombing you are almost certain to turn up one or two really thick-walled shells. These might even be strong enough to be formed into chisel or adze blades.

Bivalve shells have also been used for making spoons and ladles, the mussel shell in particular is perfectly shaped for the job. All that needs be done is to haft the shell onto a handle of driftwood. It can help here to drill a couple of holes near the edge of the shell to help attach the handle. Larger bivalves can also be used for transporting fire by placing a glowing coal inside the two cases with some finely teased tinder such as cedar bark to keep the coal smouldering. This can then be loosely wrapped and carried to wherever the next fire is needed. In cold weather this method makes a first-class hand warmer.

In General

The tools described in this chapter are greatly underrated by most outdoors folk raised in an age of metal. The sad part of the way we use metal knives and axes is that we have lost sight of the real advantage of such tools. It is not that they are quicker—for time is a relative thing for the backwoodsman. Whether a job takes him a day or a month is for the most part irrelevant. After all, as one old forester said to me: 'I've a whole lifetime to fill . . .' So perhaps the advantage of the tools is that they make the work easier. Yet early man seemed to have no difficulty producing works of art which better any I have seen produced by modern backwoods craftsmen working with metal. In fact in some instances the primitive tools are better suited to a task than modern tools . . .

No, the real advantage of metal tools is that more economic use can be made of resources. With a sharp axe or knife I can coppice saplings with absolute certainty so that they are not killed but grow back to offer me more resources. I can then take the sapling which I cut and split it with far more precision than ever I could with primitive tools. Only recently I split a three-inch ash sapling into two quarter and four eighth segments, enabling me to make from one sapling two bows and a pair of snow shoes. This is where metal wins out. When carefully used, it enables us to make the full use of the materials at our disposal. If only everyone who carries an axe or knife in the outdoors were to realise this, we would see far fewer unnecessarily scarred trees on the trail. A knife is a tool—not a macho symbol of manhood. In an ideal world no one would carry a metal knife until they had first learned to improvise a similar tool from the wilderness. This is the best way to appreciate the true value of such a tool.

Hideworking

'The owner of a neighbouring tent had killed a large elk, the
skin of which the women were then busily employed in
dressing. They had stretched it out, by means of leather
straps, on the ground near the tent, and the women were
scraping off the particles of flesh and fat with a very
well-contrived instrument. It is made of bone, sharpened at
one end, and furnished with little teeth like a saw, and, at
the other end, a strap, which is fastened round the wrist. The
skin is scraped with this instrument till it is perfectly clean.'

(Prince Maximilian zu Wied 1933)

Rawhide and buckskin. The very words
conjure romantic visions of the pioneers and
Indians of the American western frontiers,
and rightly so, for while western clothing
predominated in the established cities and
settlements, those folk who ventured into the
mountains and the wild unsettled interior
relied heavily upon the native garb. Not only
were skin clothes cheaper and more readily
available in the bush, they were more hard
wearing and better suited to the environment,
providing protection from thorns and
abrasive rock and allowing a unique freedom
of movement and quietness in close cover.

The only western cloth to be readily
accepted in the bush was the wool blanket,
which provided warmth even in wet weather.
Blankets became one of the major trade items.
Lighter than heavy fur robes, they could be
easily fashioned into leggings, mocassin liners
and most popular of all, long hooded coats
called 'capotes'. So popular were these wool
blankets that they were completely absorbed
into the culture of the native peoples. Even
today the phrase, 'To pick up the blanket,'
refers to a native who has returned to the
traditional ways of his people. So let us pick
up the blanket and learn the way to make
clothing of hides as our ancestors once did.

Backwoodsmen the world over revel in
controversial fireside debate about bushcraft
techniques; and no topic is more certain to
spark a heated discussion than hideworking. I
have heard many good woodsmen staunchly
advocating the merits of their favourite
tanning agent which may range from battery
acid to the egg white from a duck's egg mixed
with cornmeal and powdered oak bark. The
possibilities seem endless, for in truth there
are as many ways to tan a hide as there are
ways to skin an animal, and probably more. I
have decided to confine myself to the simplest
native processes which can be carried out in
the backcountry. Because these techniques
are fundamental in their nature, there is no
reason why they cannot be applied to almost
any hide.

Obtaining Hides

Any talk of using animal skins is apt to raise

177

vehement opposition to animal's 'exploitation' for clothing—particularly for luxury items which have in many cases led to the virtual hunting to extinction of brother creatures. Make no mistake I would always prefer to see the skin worn by its natural owner, but at the same time I do not believe in wasting any life. Every year many deer are culled under controlled conditions to maintain the natural balance which has been upset by destruction of habitat and removal of predators. While the meat and antlers of these animals have a use, the skins have virtually no commercial value and are simply thrown away as waste.

Very often the estate manager responsible for the seasonal culls will be very helpful in providing you with the occasional skin to work, he also would rather see the skin put to a constructive use. Be aware that as an experienced countryman, he will have much to teach those with open ears about deer, for his life revolves around them; his wealth of deer lore is unmatchable.

Of course in real backcountry survival situations where you are hunting for food, skins will be a natural by-product of your food gathering. As always, it is the woodsman's respect for nature that dictates that nothing be wasted and the skin be put to full use.

Hide Working

I am firmly convinced that hideworking is one of the most valuable woodcraft techniques to learn; it teaches patience and unstinting effort. Once you have completely tanned a hide to buckskin you will always think twice about discarding even the smallest scrap of leather as waste, remembering the long strenuous labour involved in its preparation. As I sit here I have around me various articles of clothing, tools and pouches made of or incorporating buckskin or rawhide. Each contains memories of people, places and days spent in cool breeze or sunshine as I worked my own energies into the hide, so that the end product is a symbiosis of the deer's growth and my labours.

Whatever the end process, the most important first step in hide working is the skinning. Here you must take absolute care to avoid cutting or scoring the hide with a careless slip of a knife. As mentioned earlier, I only use a cutting tool to open the hide, preferring to use my hands and fist to separate

Defleshing a hide is a laborious and unpleasant task. On your own it is best carried out over a log.

the skin with plenty of elbow grease. Try to leave as much fat as possible on the flesh rather than on the skin. This may require the judicious use of a blade to sever connective tissues. If you intend to make a long length of cordage you may consider removing the neck skin as a tube which can then be cut round in a long spiral of the desired width.

With the skin removed you must decide whether you intend to leave the fur on or not. For most purposes you will need to remove the hair, but if you decide that a fur is needed for winter insulation follow the procedure for hide preparation with the fur on.

Fleshing: This is where the hide working really begins in earnest, and there is no stage in the process which is more important. The fresh hide referred to as a 'green hide' in the U.S. or as a hide, 'in the blue' in the U.K. is taken and carefully scraped to remove all traces of fat or flesh which are adhering to its

178

Unpleasant work such as defleshing is always easier when there are two of you.

Once defleshed the hide should be dehaired. Several days' soaking in a weak lye solution and lots of elbow grease are the order of the day.

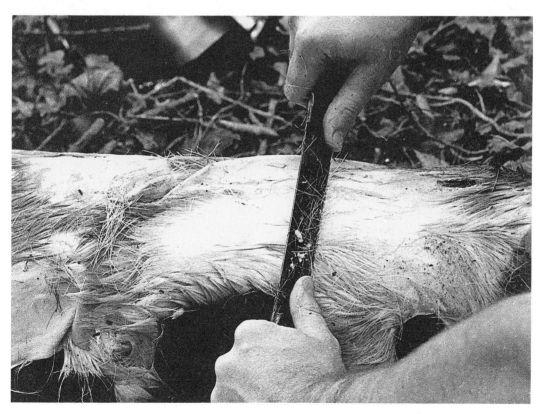

flesh side. This process is long and laborious. I find that the best way to achieve this is to wrap the hide over a small smooth log so that the skin can be pulled taut and secure, allowing you to push off the flesh with a scraping tool such as the back of an old file or a deer's leg bone split off down one side to provide a scraping edge. I leave the hair on for this part of the process as it acts as a buffer between the log and the skin thus preventing tears from occurring. This is a particularly unpleasant operation and a useful piece of additional equipment is a clothes peg to prevent the smell reaching your nostrils! Without any doubt at all, de-fleshing is the smelliest most disgusting and obnoxious activity in the field of woodcraft.

If you are unable to work the hide immediately, soak the hide until you are able to flesh it. This makes the whole process even more disgusting. Do not leave the hide soaking for more than a couple of days before you de-flesh it though. I was once unable to work some hides for five or six days by which time they smelled mighty high, having begun to decay. From the hides I developed an infection in a small cut on one of my fingers. This infection caused the finger to balloon to alarming proportions and drained me of my energy, despite the advanced medication of the twentieth century; in the backcountry such an infection could well have had far more serious implications. Despite the poor state of the hides things turned out fine.

With the flesh removed the hide can be dried on a rack for storing or returned to soak to loosen the hairs. If you have not completely de-fleshed the hide as it dries you will see translucent areas where the fat has penetrated the skin. These will cause problematical stiff regions for softening the buckskin.

When soaking a hide either for fat or hair removal, it helps enormously to use a lye solution. This can be achieved in one of two ways—either by boiling down a concentrated lye solution from hard wood ashes, and then adding this to your soaking solution, or more easily by wrapping the hard wood ashes into the hide before soaking. This is the best method to use if you are soaking the hide by weighting it down in a stream.

De-hairing: Most deer hides will require two to four days of soaking before the hair will begin to slip off easily. Once the hair does slip freely, return the skin to the fleshing log, and using the scraping tool push off the hair, being careful to avoid breaking the hairs if they will not pull out. Even the best soaked hides will provide areas where the hair is hardest to remove. These occur along the top of the neck and around the legs, particularly the underbelly side. At these places you will have to resort to pulling these hairs out in small clumps manually. This is a slow and tiring process, though far less unpleasant than the de-fleshing. The hair you remove should of course be dried and saved for uses such as forming insulative liners for winter mocassins.

With both de-fleshing and de-hairing, it is good practise to work the hide over a period of several days, returning it to soak each day so that the labour is more evenly distributed; like running long distance it is far better to pace yourself.

Racking or pegging: To dry the hide it should be stretched out tightly. This can be done either by pegging it out on some dry sun-drenched ground, or better still by racking it up in a frame with lacing cut from around the edge of the hide. Pegging out is a technique useful in areas where materials for racking are scarce or for use with extra large hides. It was a technique commonly employed by the plains nations for drying buffalo skins. The pegs need to be strong and securely hammered into the ground as the skin will shrink as it dries. Cut the holes for the pegs about two centimetres from the edge of the skin and parallel to the edge. The pegs should be placed about a spread hand's breadth apart, and the skin should be evenly tensioned throughout. If possible raise the skin on the pegs so that it is about five centimetres off the ground at the edges. This will allow a draught of air to pass under it, speeding up the drying process.

Racking is my preferred way to deal with a hide. Its advantage is that the hide can be suspended out of the way of animals and in shade, or under the rain-proof lee of an arbor. Also, because the hide is held upright, the work becomes less of a back strain. The rack can either be formed with one or two growing saplings as the uprights, or by lashing together a free-standing rigid frame. I have used both and come to the conclusion that there is little to choose between the two. The frame incorporating living saplings is the more rigid of the two and enables more pressure to be applied to the skin as you work it on the rack—while the free-standing rack is mobile and can be placed at any convenient angle or positioned in or out of shade, but is much more prone to lose its shape and contort unless very securely lashed. If you are brain tanning with the fur on though, the free-standing frame has the definite advantage of being able to be tilted to the horizontal when applying the brains solution.

The rack should be larger than the hide by several hand spans so that allowance is made for the skin which will stretch when tensioned in the frame. Cut the lace holes in the hide the same way as described for pegging out, and lace the skin to the frame. If you are using lacing produced from the skin, a length produced from cutting around the complete edge of the hide three times should suffice. Make this strip a centimetre wide and cut it before making the lace holes. The simplest way to lace the skin to the frame is to tie one end to the frame and then to pass the lace through a lace hole and around the frame and so on until the hole is laced up. It can then be tensioned by simply adjusting the tension of the laces. If you are producing buckskin however, you will need to remove the skin from the rack at least once, which may lead you to favour either tying individual laces to each lace hole, or as I do, lace the hide around its edge and then using individual laces tied to the frame tie the edge lacing into the frame. Both of these latter techniques require considerably more cordage.

Once the skin is racked you can leave it to dry, although it is a good idea to check to see that you have not missed any areas of fat or hair. In general a periodic scraping during the drying period does seem to help produce a well softened hide. When the hide is fully dry you will find it has stiffened and shrunk, tightening the laces. It should be a creamy colour, although the colour may range from dark brown to a translucent buff colour. This is rawhide, one of the finest backwoods materials and so long as it is kept dry and insect free will store indefinitely (see uses of rawhide below).

Rawhide is the halfway house to buckskin, which is convenient as you can store skins as rawhide ready for turning into buckskin at some later date. You should find that the epidermis or scarf skin, the thin outer layer of skin on the hair side has been removed in the de-hairing process. If not remove this by scraping and peeling it off the dry racked rawhide. This will ensure that the buckskin has its usual suede-like finish on both sides.

Making Buckskin

It is said that the best hide for making buckskin is the summer skin of a wild doe. Legend has it that this skin is lighter and stronger than others. I cannot confirm this with any certainty for the strongest hides I have ever worked belonged to bucks at rutt—as well my aching fingers testified for many days after. But there may be some truth in this old nugget of woodlore for summer skins have less fat on them and are therefore easier to de-flesh which, it is possible, means that more effort can be spent of producing fine soft buckskin. Whatever the answer, the secret to making really fine buckskin is starting with really well cleaned rawhide. Rawhide is a useful material and comes in many forms. In Iceland the Sagas were transcribed onto parchment which was, in reality rawhide from sheep skins scraped really thin. I once experimented making some parchment from a carefully prepared yearling roe deer skin; it was so fine that it could even be torn like paper. The transformation of rawhide into buckskin is a change in many ways as miraculous as changing paper into chamois leather.

Soaking and stretching: Before you can proceed to making buckskin the hide must be re-soaked and softened by stretching and general manipulation. Unless you are leaving the hair on the hide this is best done off the rack. Do not be tempted to rush on to the next stage. The better soaked the hide the more efficiently the brains solution will penetrate the skin. Remember that every minute or hour spent manipulating and softening a hide counts towards the finished product.

Braining: For the tanning agent you will need either the brains of the animal that provided the skin or a similarly-sized brain. This should be simmered in a pan with just enough water to cover it. If you cannot find a brain of the right size, bulk can be made up with a finely chopped up liver. Mash this mixture until it is liquid. It will produce a sweet smelling creamy mixture. This should now be worked well into the skin side of the hide which will change consistency becoming similar to wet pasta. To test whether or not it is thoroughly soaked with the brains, try blowing through the hide. If your breath passes through easily the process is complete. Alternatively cup some of the liquid in a fold of the skin and squeeze it. If the liquid passes easily through, it is ready. Repeat this process several times in different areas of the hide—particularly the thicker neck and shoulder regions. Once thoroughly soaked, you can proceed to the next step although I usually leave the skin in a container with water and the brains mixture to soak overnight. Wring the hide out thoroughly—the traditional way being to twist the hide tightly around a standing sapling. Re-soak the hide in water and wring it out again. Now re-rack the hide.

Scraping and staking: As the hide begins to dry, scrape it to an even thickness using a knife or stone scraper held at ninety degrees. The most important area to concentrate on is the neck. The very finest buckskin is of a uniform thickness throughout; this is very important if you are making clothing. For mocassins it is a good idea to leave the skin as thick as possible, where the soles will be cut out. Be very careful not to cut or score the hide. If there are any holes or cuts in the hide now is the moment to sew them up preferably with sinew.

Staking is the process of stretching and pulling the hide during drying to soften the skin so that it does not dry stiff. For this you will need a wooden graining stick. This should be about three feet long and have a wide flat or round point which must be carved and sanded smooth. A traditional tool for this job is the handle end of a canoe paddle. I actually prefer a slightly shorter graining stick of about eighteen inches; it encourages me to use more arm strength and less body weight which helps me to feel just what is happening inside the skin, so reducing the chances of wearing a hole in the skin. With this stick push the hide firmly all over as it dries. Do not let the skin dry too fast or your stretching will be in vain. This is a long slow task but absolutely necessary. If the weather is fine and you are working in the dappled shade of a forest this is a most satisfying woodcraft chore. Continue staking until the hide is completely dry. You now have a beautiful white suede-like leather with a detectable toughness, but you are not quite finished.

Smoking: Smoking is the last essential stage in producing buckskin. It is responsible for the colour of the finished leather and most importantly of all seems to strengthen the hide and protect it from stiffening after a soaking. To smoke the hide, light a small fire having nearby some dry wood chips—preferably from a hard non-resinous wood such as oak or ash. While the fire is burning to embers, sew up the hide into a long cone with the hair side inward. Once this is done put out the flames and add the wood chips so that they smoulder to produce smoke but no flames. Now suspend the hide over the smouldering fire so that the smoke is trapped inside it. If you are smoking more than one hide a more elaborate arrangement would be that described earlier for a smoke house. Make absolutely certain that the wood does not catch fire. The longer you smoke the skin the darker colour it will take on, from cream to a yellow or beige colour. Check the hide periodically to see how the colouration is progressing. Once it has reached the stage you desire, take it down and leave it wrapped up to cure for a few hours. With the advantage of the modern age I usually roll it up with plenty of smoke still in it and then put it into a smoke-filled plastic bag and leave it over-night. Some people prefer to smoke the hide on both sides. If so repeat the process with the flesh side innermost to the cone.

Buffing: The very finest buckskin has a soft nap to its surface. This is produced by buffing the hide either with a coarse abrasive stone or by running it backwards and forwards around a post. Either way, the aim is to brush up a suede-like surface. You can always tell brain-tanned buckskin from commercially-produced equivalents by blowing through it. With traditional buckskin your breath passes easily through it, while with commercial buckskin you almost burst a blood vessel trying.

Preparing Hides with the Hair Left On

Not all hides lend themselves well to tanning with the hair on: deer species for instance tend to have hairs that continually shed or break off—most notably the stiffer winter hairs—which is inconvenient. There is little that can be done to alleviate this problem. However hides with softer hairs such as foxes, coyotes, buffalo, bears and rabbits to mention a few, do not shed hairs. Some of the smaller species, especially the mustelidids such as weasel and mink, have a rank odour, and the only way to alleviate this problem in the backcountry is to soak the hide in a lye solution. But the preparation must begin always before the fur begins to slip.

The method of preparation is essentially the same as for other hides except that de-fleshing should be carried out very carefully working mainly from tail to head. Once the hide is dry (including the fur) it should be possible to gauge whether or not the hair is going to stay on or not. If it looks as though it is going to shed at every opportunity, return it to the soak and de-hair it. Those furs which promise to retain a healthy show of hair can now be brain tanned. Do not remove the fur from the rack but instead tilt the rack to the horizontal; this is where the free-standing rack is a boon. Soak the hide and apply the brains mixture, working it well in. Now leave the hide to soak up the brains mixture. I find that when using this method it helps to prepare the brains solution to a more viscous consistency so that it adheres to the hide surface evenly and doesn't run into a well in the centre. When the hide has had the chance to absorb the mixture for several hours (or overnight) rinse off the solution and leave to drain for some minutes before beginning the staking process. Most of the hides you will tan by this method are likely to be small mammals which will demand more care and less force at this stage. Smoking is carried out essentially from the flesh side and will require longer than usual although if you wish you can also smoke the fur side.

There are many other ways to tan hides which you may wish to experiment with, but the above is the basic backwood's technique. I should point out however that the way you work the hides must be in sympathy with the hide, that is to say you should adapt the technique to the hide's particular needs. I very rarely work a hide in exactly the same way twice because each hide has its own characteristics depending upon species, season, and the animal's physical condition.

* * *

Rawhide

Without a doubt rawhide is the most useful form a hide can be worked to. When damp it becomes soft and pliable but dries hard and stiff shrinking some in the process. Its major use is in the making of rawhide lacings and bindings. These are produced by cutting a piece of rawhide in a spiral fashion (in most cases the rawhide will need to be softened in water before it can be easily cut). These rawhide laces can be used as they are without any further treatment, or by having fat or oil worked into them. Untreated, the laces can be used for lashings. Applied wet they will dry shrinking in the process and if correctly applied, binding tight. With oil worked into them they are called whangs; the oil keeps them flexible preventing them from hardening. Both of these forms are extremely hard wearing and make excellent cordage for the bow drill firelighter. I have a rawhide cord on the bowdrill set I use for demonstrations which is made of tough neck rawhide stretched while wet and laid up into a two-strand cord. It has been used regularly now for three winters and still shows no sign of wearing out; even the best modern fibre cordage for the task—outboard motor pull cord—never lasted a season let alone three. I use the same technique to manufacture bow strings from rawhide, using a section of hide of a very uniform thickness cut into a long strip about 5mm wide. This is twisted to make it more or less round in cross section before being folded in half and laid up into a two-strand cord with the fold left to form an eye in one end for a noose. This string is best greased to help prevent it loosening in damp weather, although in rain there is little that can be done to prevent this.

Because of its toughness rawhide was also used for the soles of moccasins used in dry rocky regions. In some cases such as the Navaho moccasin, the rawhide sole was pre-shaped around a wooden former. Water containers were also made from clean rawhide which was gathered into a bottle shape around a filling of sand. When dry the sand was emptied out at the neck and a hollow piece of wood was bound tightly into it and a wooden bung fitted to this.

Rawhide can also be used to cook in. Either it is used to line a pit, or it is suspended under a four-pole tripod-style frame where once water is added, it takes on a cauldron shape. This arrangement can then be used for rock boiling. In real emergencies rangers, mountain men and Indians have all been known to have cooked and eaten their rawhide clothing, usually in the form of a stew or a soup.

Rawhide was also the native's choice of material for manufacturing shields; none were better made than those of the plains tribes. Using the skin from the hump or chest of a buffalo because of its exceptional thickness, the shield was formed by steaming and shrinking the hide till it was much thicker—sometimes more than a centimetre thick. At this stage it was also shaped either concave or convex. A good shield would deflect an arrow and some it is claimed could even deflect a musket ball, although as much store was placed in the designs and decorations which were the product of a warrior's personal vision, and imbued the shield with supernatural abilities to protect its carrier.

Because of its ability to shrink and tighten when dry, rawhide is the natural choice for the manufacture of drum skins. Applied wet to a hoop or hollowed log, and laced tight, the drum heads shrink on to give a fine tone which varies according to the humidity, as though it has a mind of its own.

Parfleche containers, drums and other rawhide objects were frequently painted using natural pigments from various plants, berries, clays, rocks and charcoal. The rawhide should be painted while still damp so that the colours are literally rubbed into the hide instead of just sitting on the surface. The traditional brush for this job was formed from the marrow part of a bone or antler which would absorb the paint while giving enough rigidity to allow it to be worked well in.

Buckskin

Buckskin is a very different material to rawhide; it is soft and better able to resist the wet weather which reduces rawhide to its raw and smelly state. Because of this, buckskin is the traditional choice for clothing, robes and pouches. The most important aspect to recognise when working with buckskin is that it will stretch with use according to which part of the hide it was cut from. In general, a buckskin hide prefers to stretch across its width rather than its length. To minimise problems with uneven stretching, always try to use the skin in a similar way to that in which it originally fitted the animal.

Moccasins are the classic use for buckskin; a travelling warrior or scout would carry two pairs. They are light and no modern equivalent is as quiet when stalking. When they become damp however, they soften, hence the reason for carrying several pairs. Winter moccasins were fashioned from heavily smoked hides which were more resistant to moisture. On the plains these were obtained from the blackened top hides of an old tepee cover. If you are confronted with very damp ground it may be better to travel barefoot and keep the mocs dry. This is not as alarming as it may sound for if you have been wearing real moccasins for any length of time your feet will be well seasoned. The term tenderfoot was no fanciful backwoods joke; newcomers to moccasins had quite literally tender feet. The moccasin's greatest advantage for stalking is that you can feel EVERY twig or stone, so that you soon learn to place your feet more carefully rather than relying upon the protection of a strong shoe. When a buckskin moccasin dries it tends to stiffen slightly; if the skin has been properly smoked the moc can be easily worked supple again before use, although most were simply softened by walking in them.

Buckskin shirts and jackets are the classic mountain-man garments, but in truth do not deserve the priority they receive. Leggings to protect from thorns and scrub are far more essential. For the most part native peoples seem to have been better adapted to their environment, wearing only their skin in conditions that would to you or I require several layers of insulation. When the early explorers first ventured to Tierra del Fuego they were astonished at how the natives went about virtually naked in snow. But this is not all that remarkable. I know several Dartmoor farmers who will happily roam the moor in an open-necked cotton shirt, corduroy trousers and an old overcoat even in the coldest weather when hikers and backpackers are reaching for duvets and fibre pile. It seems to be a matter of acclimatisation. Several years ago I took to sleeping with all the windows open and a minimum of insulation to try and acclimatise myself better to cold. At first this was a hardship but as the weeks faded into months it became the norm. Eventually I was able to sleep quite comfortably without a sleeping bag or insulating shelter so long as I had a correctly constructed bed or sleeping mat and a loose covering of leaves or a cagoule (more for cosiness than warmth). But after working in an overheated building for a few weeks I was back to square one. I cannot claim that my test was scientifically conclu-

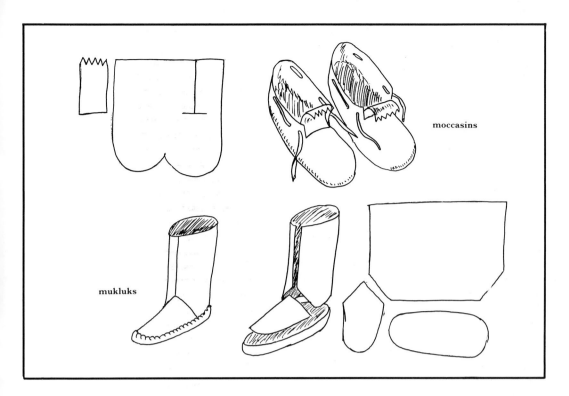

Buckskin is a fine, comfortable and very tough material which makes good clothing. Pattern for making simple moccasins and mukluks.

sive but I am convinced that acclimatisation is possible, especially when coupled with the correct mental approach. It seems to be the case now that I can acclimatise more quickly than previously, although you cannot beat the comfort of warm clothing.

In cold climates the clothing you fashion will need to be far better tailored than would otherwise be the case. The best example of this are the stylish anoraks skilfully stitched together by the arctic communities, which show an innate understanding of how best to use the qualities of the buckskin. If you are contemplating fashioning any winter clothing for the outdoors, whether of buckskin or modern materials, it would be well to visit your local anthropological museum to see how the arctic tailors went about it. It's a pity that more attention is not paid to their skill and knowledge by modern clothing designers who seem to place fashion above practicality in their 'creations'. The arctic folk managed to combine both!

The simplest shirt that you can make is that commonly used by the plains tribes of North America, which makes simple and effective use of the hide's natural shape. This can be either carefully sewn up or more easily laced together.

Making Clothing from Skin

Whatever the garment you are intending to make, do not rush the construction. Because the clothing is made from skins does not mean that you can use any less skill than if you were using modern materials. Take especial care with the fitting; it helps if you can think three dimensionally. Probably the hardest item to make is a moccasin. Depending upon the design, many of the native designs can only be fashioned from brain-tanned buckskin which is exceptionally soft and flexible. As a teenager my first attempt at making a moccasin ended disastrously with a crudely-shaped moccasin that would easily have fitted my foot even if it had been in a plaster cast. Fitting is essential, as is carefully working through each stage and remembering to allow for the skin stretching with use. New moccasins were often worn initially wet and walked in until dry. In this way they took on the shape of the wearer's foot. The great thing about buckskin is that it will take on the shape of the limb or wearer, thereby giving exceptional comfort. Never make jackets or leggings too tight; for comfort they should be quite baggy.

Sinew

Good, strong and fine cordage as has been mentioned earlier, is difficult to come by in the backcountry. Strongest of all the natural fibres available to you are the tendon sinews of the game you are hunting and trapping. These can be found either side of the spine and along side the bones of the limbs. If you pinch the back of your ankle just above your heel you will find the tendons in your own legs. Aborigines remove the sinews from game by breaking the joint of the foot and severing the skin around it so that it hangs loose. Then using the foot as a handle, they pull the sinews out with a strong sharp tug; it helps if the leg has been severed above the knee. I usually carefully remove the sinews by cutting them free before I butcher the game, clean all of the flesh off them and then hang them up to dry. Once dry they can be prepared for use. Using a boulder as an anvil, and a hefty wooden

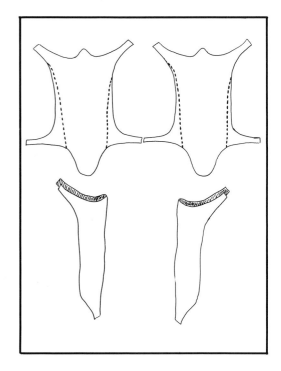

How to make buckskin leggings from two deer skins.

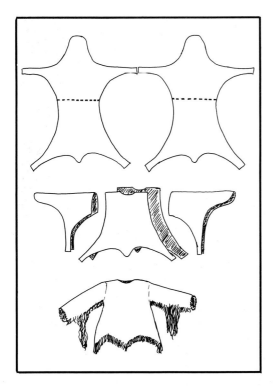

How to make a buckskin shirt from two deer hides.

mallet, pound the dried fibres. Some say that the sinew should be scraped off the outer covering before pounding, but this is unnecessary as the outer sheath is separated in the pounding. As the sinew flattens it will begin to break into fine fibres which can then be pulled apart. This shredding should be continued until you have fibres of the size you require.

For strong cordage the sinew fibres should be laid together in the same way as plant fibres. For sewing, the fibres can be used as they are with a bone needle or awl; few Native Americans travelled without a bundle of sinew and an awl for clothing repairs. Before using sinew it can be softened in the mouth or in water. Used for lashing on arrow heads, no elaborate knots are required; the sinew lashing is started with a simple half hitch and the ends tucked in. This dries securely because the sinew contains its own natural glue.

Sinew was also used for backing bows, by gluing it on to the bow back in strips with hide glue. Taking several weeks to dry, the sinew gradually tightens and shrinks, pulling the bow into a reflexed shape. These bows are stronger and have a greater cast, size for size, than other primitive bows.

In most situations of long-term bush living, hide and sinew are vitally important resources. Even the internal organs can be used for cordage and containers. Intestines can be cleaned of their contents and washed to be either stretched and dried for strong cordage or used as a container for pemmican rather like a sausage. The bladder can be used as a pouch for tinder or other small items. The stomach lining can be used for a cooking pot (as described for the skin) or as a water carrier. The list is almost endless. In fact the plains tribes who hunted the vast herds of bison secured nearly all of their everyday needs from this one animal alone, including their tepee covers. It's hardly any wonder that they had such a great reverence for living things.

Horn and Hoof

Horn is a less common material for the survivor to come across. It can be used pretty much in the same way as bone or antler, and because of its convenient shape and size can be fashioned into cups and containers. Some of the nomadic tribes used a horn to carry fire. To do this a horn was lined with fibrous bark, teased as for a tinder bundle, and a coal was added with a wooden plug fitted to the open end. With little air for combustion, the coal would smoulder slowly, allowing the horn to be carried in much the same way as a powder horn slung over a shoulder on a cord.

Dew claws were sometimes used to fashion into arrow heads or rattles, though the main use for hoofs and dew claws is in the manufacture of hide glue, a smelly and time consuming process. Hide scrapings, odd ends of hide, hoofs, claws and bone scrapings, should be cut up or better still crushed with a heavy stone and then boiled down in water. This process can take several days depending upon the quantity of glue you are intending to produce. The best way is simpiy to suspend the kettle over your fire whenever it is in use and allow the mixture to boil down over

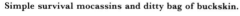

Simple survival mocassins and ditty bag of buckskin.

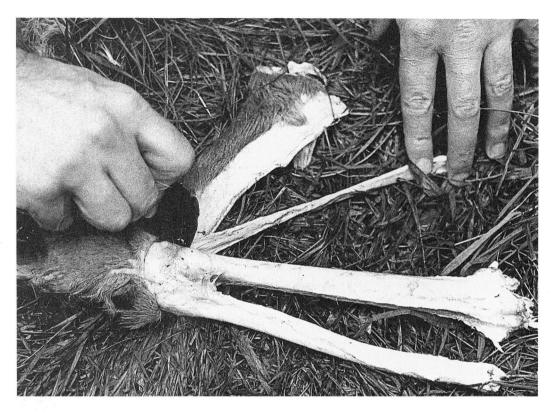

Removing sinews from a deer's foot. Never waste any part of the animal you have hunted.

Fully prepared sinew left, pounded sinews middle, dried fresh sinew right.

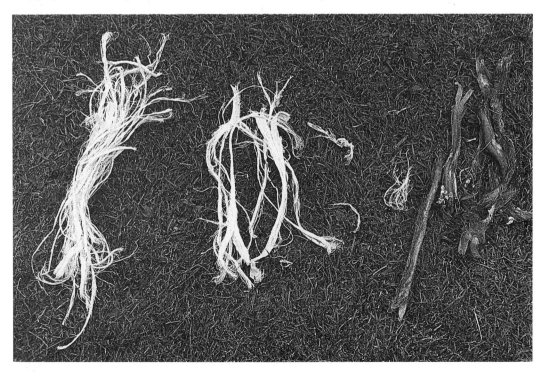

Pound sinews against a hard anvil until the individual fibres begin to separate.

Shred the sinews by pulling apart or with a bone-comb- like shredding tool.

several days to a glutinous mass. It will almost certainly need filtering before it reaches this state. For a filter use a bundle of grass. In this state it can be either diluted slightly with warm water for use or dried for future use. Every arrow quiver should contain a glue stick for minor fletching repairs. This is simply a small hard wood stick onto which hide glue is built up into a small mass. Whenever a flight needs re-fixing this stick can be moistened with luke warm water and used as a crude glue brush. Hide glue is not waterproof but is very strong. If you have the materials and time it is well worth the effort of making as a little will go a long way.

Hitting the Trail

'The old Lakota was wise. He knew that man's heart away from nature becomes hard; he knew that lack of respect for growing, living things soon led to lack of respect for humans too. So he kept his youth close to its softening influence.

(From *Land of The Spotted Eagle* by Chief Luther Standing Bear (Sioux)

Any foray into the wild parts of the world will require navigational ability. Using a map and compass is one of the first skills you should learn, but I have left the teaching of this to the excellent books already written on the subject which are listed in the bibliography. You will probably find as I have, that the confidence you gain from the above skills enables you to relax with your navigation in wild country giving you time to rely more on understanding the lie of the land, the directions in which mountain ranges stretch and which way rivers flow, than upon following an unswerving course from your map. This does not mean you need not navigate, but simply that you have lost the fear of becoming lost. The old Indian reply when asked 'Have you ever been lost?' is 'No, but I was once a might confused for three or four days.' When you truly begin to think like this I reckon you are coming close to mastering the art of woodcraft.

A good woodsman should be able to navigate to pin-point accuracy if he is given a detailed survey map and compass. Assuming that you are already familiar with the workings of a compass, there are a few advanced techniques which will enhance your

navigational ability, particularly in forests where the trails are unsurveyed. Even in the densest forests where there are no recorded or official tracks there are trails, made by the local animal population or natives. Rather than trying to cut a direct trail on a compass bearing it is far easier to follow the trail which most nearly leads in the direction you wish to travel. Then, by counting paces and taking the bearing from corner to corner, you will be able to plot the course of the trail you are following onto your map. At trail junctions, again take the path that seems to lead in the right direction. If you are able to take a resection at any time, do so to re-zero your plotted course. In this way you will produce a detailed map of the local trails and should you need to, will be able to retrace your steps with ease. With your pace counting take the average stride of several members; counting this will help to reduce errors occurring because of varying stride lengths. You should experiment with how many paces it takes your party to travel 100 metres on the flat, travelling uphill and travelling downhill when you have suitable terrain.

Using this plotting technique, you may find that your trail skirts your objective but never actually reaches it. In this case you may have to cut a trail or better still simply ease through the undergrowth on a direct bearing. For the sake of accuracy it is best to use two peeled saplings as surveying poles to enable you to maintain a direct course.

When faced with lakes and marshy ground it is usually easier to box around them using a paced-out right-angle box, although some lakes and rivers can be negotiated by building a boat or raft.

Navigating without Map or Compass

Today, even though for the most part we are spoiled with the availability of highly-detailed survey maps, there remain remote parts of the world where even if they have been surveyed, detailed maps are next to impossible to obtain. In these situations you may at best hope to use a tourist map, or a hastily sketched map from information gleaned from locals. Either way, this sort of travel can be far more interesting and challenging than when your course is waymarked or plotted. While you may travel further than expected, you will make up for this in the sense of achievement and remoteness. One of the commonest observations that I make on the trail is that many people are 'compass crazy' spending more time looking at their map than at the land they are passing through, hills becoming points of bearing rather than the new horizon that perhaps prompted the journey. If you are on foot and do not mind walking, for the most part your map can remain in your rucksack needed only in poor visibility, bad weather or where there may be cliffs and other obstacles to negotiate.

Before you travel you should have read the map to gain a general overview of the terrain through which you are travelling, and decide which way you are going to walk or ride, which directions the valleys run, where the local waterholes are, which way the local rivers run, which high peaks can be used as reference points, what shape the hills are, what type of vegetation you expect to encounter and so on. You should build up a three-dimensional mental map. This should always be the first step to any navigating, but you would be surprised at just how often people do not do this, preferring instead to follow a course like a paper trail. If you are

travelling as a party this overview should be explained to all the members, so that each can enjoy the journey. All too often parties in the hills follow the leader blindly without any idea where they are going or how long it will take. Try to adopt the habit of picturing the way the valleys relate to each other and which way the obvious lines of communication lead; usually you will find they follow geographical features such as rivers or hills. Try this in your own home territory; even in urban areas you will find that the same skills can be applied.

In those situations where you are without a map or compass, your navigational abilities will be greatly increased if you have even the vaguest idea of the local topography. If not, you have one of two options to follow. Either you can follow a geographical feature in the hope that it will eventually lead to civilisation (rivers are a particularly reliable guide if followed down stream, although in high country you must always be aware of the danger of cliffs and waterfalls) or you can choose the compass direction which is most likeky to lead to civilisation and follow it rigidly. When you are tired you will find that you are biased to walk more to the left or the right—particularly if injured or carrying a load—and for this reason you must check your bearings every few hours to prevent yourself walking around in circles. If the visibility is poor, you may have to check these bearings more frequently. The danger of these circumstances should never be underestimated; there are still areas remote enough to keep you lost just long enough to kill you through starvation or exposure. It maybe that you have to decide whether to keep going or stop every day long enough to trap or catch food; my rule here is that you should keep your belly full as it will keep your morale intact.

The first emergency navigational technique of use (and the method most often 'overlooked'), is to use high ground to scout ahead, or even to climb a tree to look out over dense forestry. In most situations you can see far more of the terrain than you would imagine possible, particularly at night when the lights of a distant town or settlement will show clearly. By lining these up with two straight sticks set into the ground you will be able to relocate the settlement in daylight and take a bearing or plot a course using the topographical information you can see.

Smoke can also be a useful guide to civilisation, although there is always the risk that what you are seeing is a backcountry forest fire.

The Sun

It is highly likely that at some time you will need to gain your bearings relative to north or simply to set a direct course in a cardinal direction. Without a doubt, the most practical way to do this (without the aid of a compass) is to use the sun. Because it is easier to find west and east it is easier to think in terms of sunset and sunrise than north and south. The sun rises in the east and sets in the west whether you are in the northern or southern hemisphere.

To gain a guide to the cardinal directions from the sun place a straight stick upright in the ground on a level patch of earth. Where the end of the shadow falls from this stick place a small stone. Now you must wait for the sun's position to alter. As it does so the shadow will move. When several inches are between the first shadow marker and the new position of the shadow end mark where the end of the shadow now falls with a twig. You have now created an east-west line, the twig being the east marker and the stone the west marker. Now, by scratching or marking out with sticks a straight line joining these markers, north and south can be found at ninety degrees to this line. This method will work on all but the most cloudy days. A quick guide to the direction of north or south can be gained from the knowledge that at midday the sun is south of you when you are standing in the northern hemisphere, or north of you if you are standing in the southern hemisphere. There are of course variations according to season but for our purposes this is enough information to get us out of difficulty. If you have a watch this can also be used as a means of finding north, assuming you have corrected its time to G.M.T. (Greenwich Mean Time). See diagram.

Of course the sun can be of much more use in navigation terms than just the methods described above. The more you know about this the better. But before moving on to other heavenly compasses, a useful guide for the woodsman who would know how long he has before sunset is the finger guide. As the sun nears the horizon hold your hand at arms length so that the fingers are parallel to and touching the horizon, each finger that fits between the sun and the horizon represents around fifteen to twenty minutes.

The Stars

The tracks of departed warriors hunting in the 'happy hunting ground' are another reliable point to take bearings from, requiring only the most basic of astronomical know-how and a clear sky. In the northern hemisphere, the best guide is polaris, the north star. This can be found by using 'the big dipper' and 'cassiopea' as pointers (see diagram). Polaris is never more than one degree from the North Celestial pole.

In the southern hemisphere there is no convenient star at or near the South Celestial pole that can be seen by eye; the area is so devoid of stars that it has been nicknamed 'the coal sack'. But its approximate position can be calculated by using the Southern Cross (see diagram).

The belt of Orion gives an indication of your east-west line.

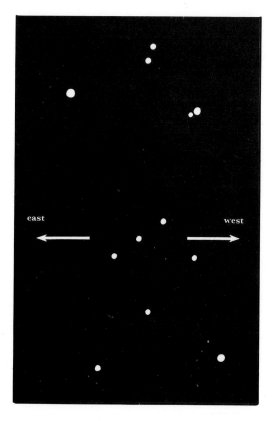

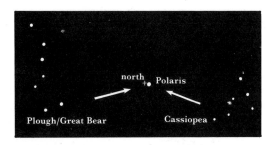

Finding the north celestial pole. For navigation purposes Polaris, the north star can be your direction pointer.

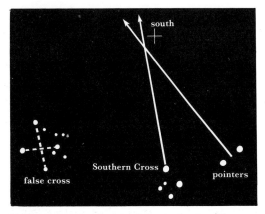

Finding the south celestial pole by the Southern Cross.

A crescent moon can also be used as a rough and ready guide to direction. By joining the crescent points with an imaginary line stretching to the horizon, this will indicate roughly south in the northern hemisphere and roughly north in the southern hemisphere.

Other Indicators of Direction

There will of course be times when the skies are clouded over and the above methods are not practical. In these situations navigating even in the most rudimentary of ways is extremely difficult. There are some natural signs which may help you find your way but none are infallible, so they should never be regarded as sufficient indication alone. Always look for several different indicators to check out your theory. The best indicator that I have found to be of use is an isolated tree in open but sheltered ground. The detritus at the base of the tree is more often than not driest on the side away from the commonly prevailing bad weather. Of course this assumes that you already know what the prevailing weather is. The same is usually true for large isolated boulders or tors. Trees

which are isolated or the windward sides of woods are usually wind swept by the prevailing local wind. But this is far less reliable, as the local winds may be very local in nature, channelled perhaps by valleys or a steep-sided mountain pass. One of the most underrated methods of determining direction is the strength and number of branches a tree has on its sunward side. The sunward side usually has more branches and mostly horizontal whereas the opposite side has fewer and they tend to be more vertical. During winter, when deciduous trees are all but bare, this can sometimes even be discerned in a forest. But here make certain that the trees or tree are on level ground where they are exposed to the sunlight for the full length of the day without a shadow falling upon them, from for instance a mountain.

Although at a pinch these techniques will work they have little to recommend them over the following techniques.

Navigating the Native Way

The following are simple skills which can be used whenever and wherever you are navigating either with or without a map. They are little used today, yet were once the skills which enabled man to safely explore the trackless wilderness and find their way home in safety long after their ordinary tracks had been wiped from the ground by the elements. If you are lost and bush navigating without reliable indicators to direction, these techniques will keep you from becoming further lost, by which I mean you will be able to find your way back to your last fixed location.

First and foremost pick a noticeable landmark to travel to, in the direction you wish to travel. Consider whether or not this will still be visible when you have travelled some way towards it. Try to find another reference point with which to double check this first point. As you travel keep a careful eye on your reference markers. If the primary marker seems to be disappearing from view, choose another marker between you and it on the same line. (A native scout who intended to remain concealed would 'aim off' from his bearing reference.)

Secondly and most neglected of all by modern navigators, look over your shoulder and view the terrain you have just traversed. It will look very different; you never know when you may need to return the same way.

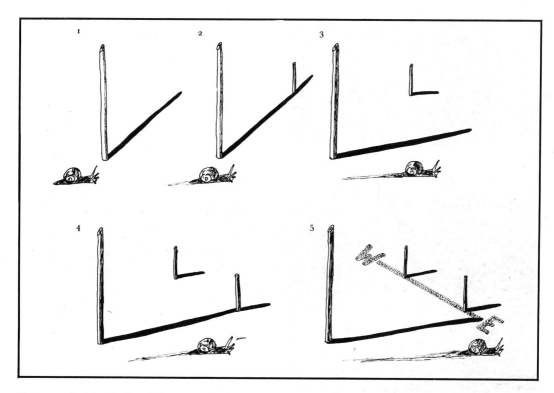

Finding north with a shadow stick. 1 set up the shadow stick. 2 set a marker stick at the end of the shadow. 3 wait for the sun to move causing the shadow to move. 4 mark the end of the new shadow with a second marker stick. 5 draw a line joining the two marker sticks; this is your west-east line so the north-south line can be constructed at ninety degrees to this line.

Thirdly and again a neglected technique, mark your trail. A native with a keen eye for changes in natural patterns would spot the subtlest of trail markers such as piled up stones or broken twigs and bent grasses. I make use of this technique very often, especially in areas of dense undergrowth. Try to decide upon a consistent place for your markers: on the right of a trail or always at the foot of a tree for instance. If you are practised at this it will be enough to leave an indicator at trailheads and junctions. As you mark your trail try to give descriptive names to the landmarks you pass such as the forked tree, or the elbow oak, to help fix these landmarks in your memory.

Trail blazing is a more permanent method of marking trails whereby the bark of a tree is slashed off in a prearranged code. These are still made in some parts of the world by foresters, park rangers, and trappers, though I prefer the less damaging trail signs. While I have included some of the more common trail signs and blazes here, you will undoubtedly evolve your own code. These blazes are a very

much more useful navigational tool than many modern outdoors folk realise. Every year in the vast forests of the world, a few hikers will become hopelessly lost, panic and then run into even more confusion. In most cases they become lost only a few metres from their campsite. Especially in thick woodland it is easy to become turned around. In these situations it is best to mark where you first realised you became lost and then to trail mark along an exploratory route back to camp. In this way you can always find your way back to the first place you were lost and then try an alternative escape route. This is more often than not a far quicker way to find your way back than to guess and get it wrong. I have used this successfully on several occasions never having taken more than a half hour at most to find landmarks I was familiar with.

The panic of which I speak is a very powerful one fuelled by the survival instinct. Once I was asked by some walkers in the New Forest where their car park was because they were lost. So preoccupied were they that they

Trail blazes. **Pine cone direction marker.** **Bent twig trail marker.**

were completely oblivious to their surroundings, and indeed had difficulty believing me when I told them that they were only about 100 metres away. You only have to walk a few feet off trail to become turned around by mischievous elves so practise the above skills.

Rescue

If you find yourself in the situation of needing rescue as any of us can, no matter how experienced or skilled, it is vitally important that you know the correct rescue signals.

Any rescue signal works by creating an obvious contrast with the normal conditions; the type of signal you use falls into one of two categories: passive or active.

Passive signals: These are signals which in themselves cannot reach out and attract the attention of a rescuer, but if noticed or looked for, give indication to your location and predicament. These signals include cleared spaces in dense vegetation, arrows and S.O.S. symbols marked on the ground. When making any such marker try to build it in relief so that it casts a shadow to reinforce and emphasise its outline. Letters or symbols must be as large as possible. Brightly coloured clothing is also a passive signal as is a parachute laid out on the ground. Think in terms of contrasting shapes, movements, colours, sounds and smells.

Active Signals: These are the most valuable as they enable you to attract the attention of potential rescuers. If you use the international emergency code, your need for help should be plainly understood. These signals include the use of fires for smoke or flame; three fires set in a triangle shape are the correct code. A mirror for signalling is first class as it can be seen at great distances, as is a torch at night. All of these signals pinpoint your exact whereabouts. Also active and much used in mountains is the whistle; six blasts with a minute gap between each set of six are the recognised rescue sign.

If you are entering regions where you know that you may need to signal for help, apart from the whistle you should always carry flares or smoke canisters. For helicopter rescues, smoke canisters are by far the best signal as they pin-point your position as well as indicating the wind direction. In fact long after the smoke canister ceases producing smoke, a large arrow of red smoke drifts away pointing at where you are. These should only be used when you are certain the smoke will be seen. Flares are much less reliable although they have saved many lives. They have a double signal: firstly they make an audible bang and secondly they show a bright light in the sky. On expeditions always carry stocks of flares which are fresh and not older than the expiry date.

Signalling for help: The following are the agreed international emergency signals, used to signal for rescue!

Six blasts on a whistle or horn in quick succession with a gap of a minute between each set of blasts. Or the same pattern of flashes with a torch.

S.O.S.: Three short, three long, three short blasts of sound or flashes of light.

Red flares or smoke.

Three fires positioned to form the points of a triangle.

A rescue party may answer your signal with a pattern of three flashes or blasts interspersed with a minute or by using a white flare. This means message understood. In bad visibility keep signalling to guide your rescuers to you.

Hazards on The Trail

I have left these subjects to last because they are really much less of a problem than the dramatic stories which surround them suggest. In each case if you are heading into regions where they are known to be a problem seek advice from the locals, although beware of scaremongering and old wives tales.

Snakes: For the most part snakes will only be seen slithering away from you. If you spot one further along the trail they can be encouraged to quit your path by lobbing a stone or stick in their vicinity (there is no need to throw this directly at them). The greatest danger comes from those activities where you are searching around rocks and poking into crevices. If you have to lift rocks in snake country do so in such a way that the rock is always between you and any angry snake you may disturb underneath it.

Personally I walk quietly in the hope of observing snakes in the wild. It is always a rare and special treat to see them although a somewhat unnerving one too, as frequently you can be within striking distance before you see through their camouflage by which time they know you are there. Remember then that a snake strikes towards movement so stillness is better than flight. But if you are in any way worried by snakes make some noise or otherwise announce your presence as you travel to give them ample opportunity to escape.

Remember though that where you have seen one snake others are sure to be found so perhaps resort to using a stick to test thick undergrowth before entering, and wear sensible footwear.

Snakebite: Unlikely as it may be, should you be bitten by a snake the chances are greatly in your favour that you will survive. Not all snakes that bite are venomous, and those that are equipped with venom, do not always poison when they bite. In practical terms there are basically two types of venomous snakes: those that possess hemotoxic venom and those with neurotoxic venom. Each of these venoms works in a different way. Hemotoxins are digesting venoms that attack the body's red blood cells and destroy protein. They cause severe pain and swelling, often to horrific proportions. The tissue damage in these cases is often so severe as to cause the amputation of the limb. The only positive nature of a hemotoxin is that you are certain that you have been envenomated because of the pain. Neurotoxins on the other hand cause little pain and local reaction. As is suggested in their name they attack the nervous system. While immediate signs of envenomation are minimal—nausea, vomiting, abnormal sweating and headache—can lead to a severe fall in the patient's blood pressure, loss of muscular control and eventual respiratory failure and heart stoppage. It is important to keep the air passage way clear to prevent the patient gagging on his own tongue.

The field treatment for snake bites is a subject of great controversy, but the following is the treatment which seems to have the greatest support from those who deal regularly with the problem.

1. In all cases it is important to calm the patient and encourage them to remain still. Only water can be given.

2. Because venom is transported via the lymphatic system the affected limb should be completely bandaged, (in the same way you would bandage a sprained ankle) firmly but not tightly.

3. To further reduce the transport of venom through the lymphatic system the limb should be totally immobilised by splinting. The lymph system achieves its motive force from muscle contractions, a completely stilled limb can completely reduce this motion.

4. The patient should be evacuated to hospital, preferably treated as a stretcher case. Should their blood pressure drop so severely as to cause collapse, the legs should

be raised. If respiratory failure occurs, effective resuscitation should be carried out.

Additionally, it will greatly aid treatment if the species of snake responsible is identified, even a sketchy description is better than none at all. Fortunately there are few situations today when you are likely to be outside the range of medical assistance, but if you are, then and only then, might you consider an attempt to remove the venom by suction. Some tests indicate that a significant proportion of the venom can be extracted by suction within the first five minutes of the bite. Suction should not be carried out by mouth as a mouth sore or cavity will act in the same way as the fang puncture. Syringe-style suction devices available commercially are the best solution here, and should be carried when travelling well away from communication in snake country. Cutting the wound to ease the venom extraction is also controversial as it increases the risk of infection and may allow the venom more easy and widespread access to the lymphatic system. If cuts must be made for use with a suction device they should be no more than a couple of millimetres deep. These actions should ONLY BE USED WHEN NORMAL MEDICAL ASSISTANCE IS UNAVAILABLE, and then only within the first five to ten minutes after being bitten.

Bears: Bears are dangerous but now are much reduced in numbers finding refuge in only a few areas of wilderness, mostly in America and Canada. The most dangerous is undoubtedly the grizzly bear. But the 'Bear Problem' so often a talking point among novice outdoorsmen, is not what it seems. It is more a case of the 'Human Problem'. When you set foot in bear country you are the intruder and menace, not the bear, it is his territory.

There are many different methods recommended for dealing with bears almost as many in fact as for dealing with snake bite. But the general rule is simple; never argue with a bear! If he is in camp and likes the smell of your food, be the diplomat and consider his dining a sign of his appreciation of your culinary skills.

The following advice was given to me by a U.S. park ranger who works in bear country, so I pass it on. If you are confronted with an angry black bear it is usually enough to run away; this bear will normally recognise that you are fleeing and pose no threat, and then lose interest. But if on the other hand you are confronted by an angry grizzly, oh brother you're in trouble! The best policy is to move very slowly and carefully away; any fast gestures may be construed as a threat. Try to move down wind to avoid your scent carrying to the bear. If you are being charged you probably won't have time to climb a tree, but if you can, do so. In the worst circumstances (you fall into the claws of a grizzly) play dead with one hand protecting your throat and the other your genitals. Experience has shown that apart from a few nips and bites you will probably survive, but if you fight back the bear feels threatened and you will more than likely be killed.

The best policy with bears is to let them know that you are around when travelling so they have time to move away. In some regions, hikers are encouraged to wear bells on their rucksacks to give the bears due warning and to avoid attracting them to your campsite by fastidious hygiene in camp. Meals should always be prepared and eaten away from camp; food should be stored away from where you sleep and hoisted high into the trees. Watch for any sign of bears and avoid pitching your tent on streamside trails. There is also some evidence that bears can be attracted to female menstrual odours.

Some folk reckon the best way to deal with a bear is a 44 magnum revolver, if so the following advice gleaned from an expert backwoodsman should be followed. 'Be sure to file off the front sight of your magnum before entering bear country.' Why? 'It's less painful that way when the bear shoves it up your ...!'

In general with the above hazards remember that you share the wilderness with them and should give them the respect they demand, this way you should have few problems. I have yet to meet any experienced backwoodsman who does not relish with a sense of humble thanks, the opportunity to watch these much maligned creatures living out a truly wild life. Perhaps even in some sense they envy them.

Poison ivy (*Rhus radicans*): Poison ivy can occur as a shrub stem, a creeping vine or trailing vine. It usually has a reddish tinge to the stem. Contact with any part of this plant can result in dermatitis, especially contact with sweaty skin. Watch for this plant in creeper form on your firewood, as the smoke from incomplete combustion of this plant can also cause problems if inhaled. The rash from poison ivy has tell-tale white blisters. If you are aware that you have come into contact with this plant the effects can be reduced or avoided even by washing with soap and water soon after. If you become infected the medical advice is to burst the blisters and apply an alkaline solution. The juice from jewel weed has been used as a bush remedy for poison ivy rash as has a strong tannin solution.

Poison oak *(R. toxicodendron):* Similar to poison ivy, it only occurs as a shrub, but causes the same problems and is treated in the same way.

Lumpraiser and the no-see-ums: So far we have looked at the dramatic trailside hazards with fabled fierce reputations, yet none are as great a nuisance to your enjoyment as the biting insects. Apart from the risk from malaria, the mosquito is a common and unwelcome visitor to any camp. To avoid these insects at the height of their season, camp on dry ground away from marshy, water-logged ground or bodies of water. A breezy ridge is the best protection from flying insects; a smudge fire is the alternative for still conditions, the smoke acting as a repellent. In areas where they are extremely numerous such as rain forest and muskeg you may need to use face veils and mosquito nets, in which case douse these in chemical repellent as a further foil to these persistent bloodsuckers.

Whereas the mosquito prefers to attack solo, inflicting one or more large lumps as the result of its blood extraction, the midge prefers to attack en mass peppering you with many tiny bites. Particularly around the face. In Scotland the midges can be so bad as to be almost unbearable, they are also or at least seem to be more difficult to repel than mosquitoes, although the same camping routine applies; stay on breezy ridges and use smudge fires away from water.

The other most noteworthy insect is the horse fly; it bites with the ferociousness of a miniature bulldog. Large, ugly and obvious, these flies will attack solo or in pairs and despite being so noticeable manage to sneak past even the best defences. The only defence against these is a tidy and clean campsite situated on a breezy ridge, equipped with a smudge fire for when the breezes are still.

Light airy clothing covering all skin areas is of course the obvious way to prevent insects biting; smudging your hair and clothes with smoke is also a useful deterrent as it reduces your body scent.

Ticks are probably the most unpleasant of all biting creatures. These are very tough little creatures that sit on the undersides of leaves waiting to leap off onto the backs of deer or hikers. Once on your clothing they search for exposed skin and begin to insert their mouthparts, so that they can engorge blood. While this may seem horrific and painful, the problem is that it often goes completely unnoticed, particularly with the smallest ticks which are often no larger than a pin head. If you spot one tick, there are bound to be others; fortunately they take several hours to become properly attached, during which time they can be easily flicked off. Work with a partner to inspect each other at halts for meals or before turning in for the night.

If you do find that one has become properly attached, smear it with vaseline, axle grease or fat to block up its breathing apparatus forcing it to let go. Do not try to remove them with a lighted cigarette, alchohol or iodine or by squeezing them. Squeezing them only forces their internal fluids into you, increasing your risk of infection. Especially in some regions of the world, ticks carry Scrub Typhus (Rocky Mountain Spotted Fever).

There are of course many other nasty, biting, stinging creatures which you might encounter depending upon where you are and what season you are there. But the above are those which you are most likely to encounter. While their presence is annoying and sometimes painful, it is only in exceptional circumstances that they are the first thing you will remember of a journey. People and places, great scenery, majestic wildlife and wildness far outweigh their nuisance value.

Making Tracks

So we reach the end of our short journey. If you have practised all of the skills covered in the preceding pages you should be well on the way to seeing the world through native eyes and gaining the understanding that comes from such a vision. All you need now is practise and some adventures. I wish you well on your travels and hope that you find similar enjoyment to that which I have experienced. If you follow Nature's rules and give respect where it is due you will come to no harm. Walk with caution rather than with fear and know yourself.

Remember that even if we have difficulty recognising it, the truth is that for our well-being, we still interact with the same natural forces as our aboriginal cousins. For life we need fresh air, clean water, healthy food, space to spread our shoulders and wild places to refresh our spirit and renew our closeness to the earth.

Bibliography

A Field Guide to Mammal Tracking in North America by James Halfpenny (Johnson Books)
ISBN 0 933472 98 6

Animal Tracks and Signs by Preben Bang and Preben Dahlstrom (Collins)
ISBN 0 00 219633 6.

New Generation Guide to Fungi of Britain and Europe by Stefan Buczacki (Collins)
ISBN 0 00 219448 1.

Pocket Guide to the Sea Shore by John Barrett and C. M. Yonge (Collins)
ISBN 0 00 219321 3.

A Field Guide to Animal Tracks by Claus Murie (Peterson)
ISBN 0 395 17978 6.

A Field Guide to Edible Wild Plants of Eastern and Central North America by Lee Allen Peterson (Peterson)
ISBN 0 395 20445 3.

Mushrooms and Other Fungi of Great Britain and Europe by Roger Philips (Pan Books)
ISBN 0 330 26441 9.

Trees in Britain, Europe and North America by Roger Philips (Pan Books)
ISBN 0 330 25480 4.

Wild Flowers of Britain by Roger Philips (Pan Books)
ISBN 0 330 25183

The Wild Flowers of the British Isles by Ian Garrard and David Streeter (Macmillan)
ISBN 0 333 32679 2.

Poisonous Plants in Britain and their Effects on Animals and Man (HMSO)
ISBN 0 11 242529 1.

Journey of The Medicine Man, Poems by Sun Hawk
ISBN 0 935304 63 0.

Two Little Savages by Ernest Thompson Seton
ISBN 0 486 20985 7.

Index

203